The Saga
of the Völsungs

Also by GEORGE K. ANDERSON:

The Legend of the Wandering Jew
The Literature of the Anglo-Saxons (1949; 1962)
English Literature from the Beginnings to 1485 (1950; 1962)
Schoolboy with Satchel (1979)
and many others.

The Saga of
the Völsungs

Together with Excerpts
from the *Nornageststháttr*
and Three Chapters from the *Prose Edda*

Translated and annotated by
George K. Anderson

Newark
University of Delaware Press
London and Toronto: Associated University Presses

© 1982 by Associated University Presses, Inc.

Associated University Presses, Inc.
4 Cornwall Drive
East Brunswick, N.J. 08816

Associated University Presses Ltd
69 Fleet Street
London EC4Y 1EU, England

Associated University Presses
Toronto M5E 1A7, Canada

Library of Congress Cataloging in Publication Data

The Saga of the Völsungs, together with excerpts from the
Nornageststháttr and three chapters from the Prose Edda.

Bibliography: p.
Includes index.
I. Volsunga saga. English. II. Norna-Gests saga. English.
III. Edda Snorra Sturlusonar. English.
PT7287.V7E52   839'.63   81-14833
ISBN 0-87413-172-3   AACR2

Printed in the United States of America

To the memory of
WILLIAM H. SCHOFIELD
*who first taught me Old Norse
sixty years ago*

Contents

Foreword   9
Genealogical Table   11
Notes on the Pronunciation of Old Norse Words   13
Specimen of Old Norse, with English Translation   15

PART ONE: The *Völsungasaga*
    Introduction   21
    The Saga of the Völsungs   55
    Explanatory Notes, the *Völsungasaga* 138

PART TWO: Excerpts from the *Skaldskaparmál*, the *Norna-*
    geststháttr, and the Southern Branch of the
    Saga—the *Nibelungenlied* and the *Thidrekssaga*
    From the *Skaldskaparmál*   159
      Notes on Excerpt from the *Skaldskaparmál*   168
    From the *Nornageststháttr*   171
      Notes to the *Nornageststháttr*   188
    The Southern Branch of the Saga: A Brief Consideration
      of the *Nibelungenlied* and the *Thidrekssaga* 192
    Two Views of the *Nibelungenlied*   207
    Synopsis of the *Thidrekssaga*   211

Glossary of Minor Characters   223
Bibliography   228
Index   257

Foreword

When Professor George Anderson died on January 2, 1980, he had just sent the final draft of this book to the publisher. It was one of several projects that filled his productive years of "retirement." During that period, after I had assumed his teaching duties, Professor Anderson and I frequently got together to discuss mutual interests in Old English, Norse, and Celtic studies, including this work on the Völsungs. As one who had enjoyed watching the book take shape, I was glad, when asked, to see it through the press. The problems that remained were mechanical rather than substantive, and it would be tedious to enumerate them here. A few words are necessary, however, on the subject of transliteration (see "Notes on the Pronunciation of Old Norse Words," below). Germanic thorn (þ) is transliterated as *th*, and edh (ð) is transliterated as *d*, except in titles of scholarly works, manuscript readings, or Norse words to be explained. Vowel quality has been indicated in many Norse names, most often when these appear in the notes, less frequently when the name appears in the translation. Names of important characters usually appear without diacritics, especially where Anglicized forms are established in general literary usage (e.g., *Gudrun*, not *Gudrún*). My goal has been to accommodate the mixed audience of scholars, students, and general readers for which the book was designed.

GEOFFREY RUSSOM

Brown University

Genealogical Table

THE VÖLSUNGS

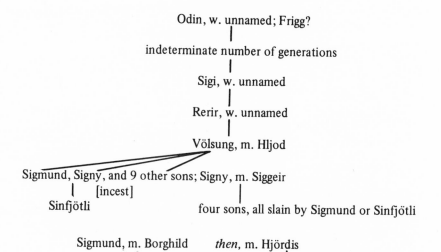

Odin, w. unnamed; Frigg?

|

indeterminate number of generations

|

Sigi, w. unnamed

|

Rerir, w. unnamed

|

Völsung, m. Hljod

Sigmund, Signy, and 9 other sons; Signy, m. Siggeir

| [incest]

Sinfjötli   four sons, all slain by Sigmund or Sinfjötli

Sigmund, m. Borghild   *then*, m. Hjördis

SIGURD, m. Gudrun

Eyjolf, Hamund; Helgi, m. Sigrun

Sigmund; Svanhild, m. Jörmunrek

THE GJUKINGS (Burgundians)

Gjuki, w. unnamed; *then* m. Grimhild

|

Gutthorm   Gunnar, Högni, Gudrun

Gunnar, m. Brynhild; Högni, m. Glaumvor; Gudrun, m. SIGURD, m. Atli, m. Jonak

Solar, Snaewar, (H)Niflung Sigmund, Svanhild

Eitil and Erp

Hamdir, Sörli, and Erp

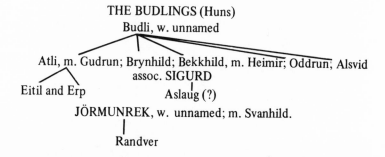

THE BUDLINGS (Huns)
Budli, w. unnamed

Atli, m. Gudrun; Brynhild; Bekkhild, m. Heimir; Oddrun; Alsvid

assoc. SIGURD

Eitil and Erp   Aslaug (?)

JÖRMUNREK, w. unnamed; m. Svanhild.

|

Randver

Notes on the Pronunciation of Old Norse Words

In this translation not many Old Norse words are to be found, except in proper names, but a few elementary observations are in order.

VOWELS: The general quality of the vowels is Continental European, as in German, Italian, or Spanish. One must make sharp distinction between short and long vowels; the latter are indicated by an acute accent (ʹ). The accent falls on the first syllable of all words except verbs, in which the root syllable is accented.

a	English *con*	á	English *father*
e	English *set*	é	English *late*
i	English *sit*	í	English *sea*
o	French *repos*	ó	English *soak*
u	English *full*	ú	English *droop*
œ	French *deux*	æ	English *that*
y	French *tu*	ý	French *pur*
au	English *how*	ö	English *on*; formerly spelled ǫ
ei	English *they*	öʹ	English *dawn*; formerly spelled ǫ́

CONSONANTS:

b	English *b*
c	not used
d	English *d*, but dental rather than alveolar
f	English *f*, but between vowels, *v*, and before nasals, *m*, as *jafn*, sometimes spelled *jamn*
g	English "hard" *g*, as in *got*, *given*; sometimes, between vowels, the *g* in German *sagen*; before *s* or *t* = k (*eggs* = ekks)
h	English *here*; but note slight difference in *hv-* or *hr*, as "hvart"; "hring"
j	Consonantal *i(y)* as *York, yarn*; omitted before beginning of word, as in *ar* ("year"), *ungr* ("young"), and preserved as *y* in Iceland
k	English *kith* and *kin*
l	English *let*

13

m	English *met*
n	English *need*
p	English *put*; but before t =*f* (English *loft*)
q	not used
r	English *rat*; but as the usual end of masculine nouns, not syllabic. *Dagr* (''day'') is considered monosyllabic.
s	English *house*; always voiceless, even between vowels
t	English *take*, *lest*
v	English *have*
w	Became *v* in preliterary period
x	not used
z	English *ts*
þ	The *th* sound in English *thin* and *thick*; came to be used only initially
ð	The *th* sound in English *there* and *them*

Specimen of Old Norse, with English Translation

Þá mælti Völsungr konungr: "Þat munu allar þjóðir at orðum gera, at ek mælta eitt orð óborinn, ok strengda ek þess heit, at ek skylda hvárki flýja eld né járn fyrir hræzlu sakir, ok svá hefi ek enn gert hér til, ok hví munda ek eigi efna þat á gamals aldri? Ok eigi skulu meyjar því bregða sonum mínum í leikum, at þeir hræðiz bana sinn, því at eitt sinn skal hverr deyja, en engi má undan komaz at deyja um sinn. Er þat mitt ráð, at vér flýjum hvergi, ok gerum af várri hendi sem hreystiligast. Ek hefi bariz hundrað sinnum, ok hefi ek haft stundum meira lið, en stundum minna; ok hefi ek jafnan sigr haft, ok eigi skal þat spyrjaz, at ek flýja, né friðar biðja."

Then said King Völsung: "All men can say in their own words that I gave my word, as an unborn child, and made this vow, that I would flee from neither fire nor iron because of fear, and so I have done even until now. And why should I not do the same also in my old age? And maidens shall not throw at my sons in mockery that they were afraid to die, because each one of us must die once, and no man can avoid death in his time. It is my counsel that we flee not at all, but do with our hands as bravely as we can. I have endured a hundred battles, and I have had sometimes a greater troop and sometimes a lesser one, but I have always had victory, and it shall never be said that I would flee or sue for peace."

—Chapter 5 of the Saga

*The Saga
of the Völsungs*

PART ONE

The *Völsungasaga*

Introduction

I

The unique parchment manuscript containing the *Völsungasaga*, henceforth called the Saga, was given to King Frederick III of Norway and Denmark in 1656 by Bishop Brynjólfur Sveinsson of Skalholt, Iceland.[1] It was accepted at the Royal Library in Copenhagen and was then mislaid on the wrong floor of the Library. Not until 1821 did it receive its proper place and formal registration in the Library, where it is at present. As manuscripts of such age go, it is today in relatively good condition, and is known officially in the "New" collection as Ms *Ny kgl. Saml.* 1824 b4°, referred to henceforth as Codex. During the period in which it was "mislaid," however, it must have been known to some, for a total of twelve paper manuscripts were found in Copenhagen alone, to be dated mostly from the late seventeenth century (with two or three from before 1800). Three more have turned up in Sweden, all from just before or after 1700, three from Iceland of about the same date, and three in Britain (two in the British Museum and one in the Bodleian at Oxford). There are twenty-one paper manuscripts in all. Before 1821 there had also been a printed edition: the first, *editio princeps*, by E. J. Björner at Stockholm in 1737,[2] which contained translations into Swedish and Latin. Another, by Van den Hagen in 1831, is negligible.

Codex contains in actuality two sagas. The first, long unnamed because its heading was missing, became the "so-called" *Völsungasaga*; the second became identified as the *Saga of Ragnar Lodbrók*, which purported to be a continuation of the Saga that

21

could show the relationship of the Saga to the kings of Denmark, thus linking the Danish royal line with the mighty Völsungs and Gjukings. Indeed, an early translation of the Saga into German[3] went so far as to say that the Saga was only the general introduction to the *Saga of Ragnar Lodbrók*, but, considering the fact that our Saga is almost as long as the *Saga of Ragnar Lodbrók*, this statement is absurd, and the whole theory has been discounted, for reasons that will appear later.

Following Björner and Van den Hagen, there comes the first important edition of the Saga, that by C. C. Rafn in *Fornaldar Sögur Nordlands* (Copenhagen, 1829), which considers not only the Saga but also that most valuable supplementary piece, the *Nornageststháttr* (see below). In 1865, however, came what we should consider the first "modern" edition, that by Sophus Bugge, which constitutes volume 8 of *Det Norske Oldskriftselskab*. Bugge was inclined to ignore the various paper MSS, which is a pity, for they are sometimes most useful when the parchment Codex is illegible. Yet his edition is still fundamental, having served as the basis for three or four important subsequent editions. These are by Ernst Wilken (Paderborn, 1877; 1895; 1912), Ranisch (Berlin, 1891; 1908), and Hannaä (Copenhagen, 1907). The most recent has been a synoptic edition and translation by Robert Finch (London, 1965), with a good translation, insufficient annotation, and no glossary. Of these various editions, I recommend Wilken's, especially the first two printings, for in his 1912 edition he has cut out almost all introductory material and relegated his glossary to a separate volume. Moreover, he has made some changes in readings that I believe are insufficiently explained. However, he includes the original texts of the *Prose Edda* and the *Nornageststháttr*.

It has been just over a century now since the first edition of Wilken's work, and during the first half of that century there has been a great deal of controversy about (1) the relation of the Saga to that of *Ragnar Lodbrók*; (2) the relation of the Saga to the poems of the *Older* (or *Poetic*) *Edda*; (3) the question of sources, whether immediate or indirect; (4) the inconsistencies involved in the portrayal of Brynhild; and (5) the virtually insoluble questions pertaining to the antecedents of the Saga.

The Eddic poems concerned, involving as they do nearly two-thirds of the *Poetic Edda*, have been put through the scholars' analytical mill, but with still inconclusive results (particularly as the different question of Celtic influences has begun to grow in importance). Moreover, while virtually everyone has conceded that the author of the Saga—hereafter called the Author—knew these Eddic poems, there remain always the questions: How well did he know them, and Were there others now lost? To the first question, the answer is easy: he knew them well, but some better than others. The second question is most difficult to answer, save by a qualified affirmative. The fact is that in the Codex Regius MS of the *Poetic Edda* (Regius 2365), there is a whole quarto of the manuscript missing. There has been general agreement that in this gap there was at least one longer poem about Sigurd (a *Sigurdarkvida in meira* to match the existing *Sigurdarkvida in skamma*). This longer poem accounts for the so-called *Meiri* theory, about which more in a moment. The gap, however, is large enough to include a few more short pieces, some of which may be gnomic or didactic poems of general worldly wisdom, which leads to a *Forna* or ''ancient'' theory. Chapters 20 to 28 of the Saga seem certainly to contain much material of the Meiri poetry; chapter 21, on the other hand, seems to be pointed toward the Forna (''ancient lore'') storehouse. Both these theories concerning the missing material have their supporters and are probably valid. In any event, nearly ten chapters of the Saga derive from unknown material, and there has been great disagreement about this perhaps most famous lacuna in medieval literature.

One of the last detailed analyses of the relation between the Eddic poems and the Saga is a vocabulary study by Per Wieselgren in 1934, which shows that the Author relied most heavily upon three Eddic poems, the *Sigrdrifumál* (''Ballad of the Victory-Bringer''), the *Fáfnismál*, (''Ballad of Fáfnir''), and the *Gudrúnarkvida II* (''Second Saying of Gudrun''), in that order, which is only natural, since the Author quotes directly sixteen stanzas from the *Sigrdrifumál* and includes from the *Fáfnismál* the long, rather ridiculous paratheological dialogue between Sigurd and the dying dragon. Wieselgren's study, however, merely confirms what we already know—that the Author was well acquainted with the Eddic poems, but does not merely render them into prose. Moreover, Wieselgren is the first to concede that the whole matter of sources is highly complicated, with so many possible factors that the whole matter seems insoluble.[4]

My own suggestion would be that the Author followed the Eddic poems and even used their language freely on certain occasions, but at other times he did not. He filled in the gap caused by the break in the *Sigrdrifumál* with material from a lost poem or poems (the *Meiri* theory), with a chapter (21, Olsen 22) of practical advice and homely wisdom (the *Forna* theory), and inserted almost verbatim a section of another Saga, the *Thidrekssaga* (see below), which constitutes chapter 22 (Olsen 23) of our Saga. For the remaining chapters up to chapter 30 (Olsen 32), the Author may be obligated to the *Meiri* theory or to an earlier prose saga on the same subject, for it is by no means certain that the Saga as we have it was the first full-length work to treat the story. As for the events that follow Sigurd's family difficulties and death (chapters 33 through 38), he follows rather closely the two Eddic poems *Atlamál* and *Atlakvida*, both of which carry the qualifying adjective *groenlenzku*, or Greenlandish, which is now regarded with suspicion if not downright distrust, for whether or not they are really Greenlandish is an open question.[5] The final sad chapters 41 and 42 (Olsen 43 and 44) rely heavily on the two Eddic poems usually placed last in the collection, *Gudrúnarhvöt* ("Gudrun's Urging On") and *Hamdismál* ("Ballad of Hamdir").

Even with these reliances, however, there are several little divagations, indicating the Author's faulty memory of the Eddic poems. They are not serious, but in my opinion significant. Thus in chapter 37 (Olsen 39) Gunnar is cast into a snakepit, where he charms to sleep all of the serpents save one by playing a harp with his toes (his hands having been bound), and that is the way the Author puts it, whereas the *Atlamál*, stanza 62, describes the toes in a bold kenning as "sole-twigs," or *ilkvistar*. This, of course, may be but another example of the Author's studious avoidance of kennings, the short metaphorical compound phrases characteristic of Germanic poetry. Yet his changes are not all from the poetic to the prosaic, as I shall attempt to show. In that same poem, Gudrun sees a block of wood (stanza 73), which she uses as a chopping block to cut the throats of her two sons by Atli. In the Saga the boys are merely playing with a block of wood. In short, the Author knows his sources well enough, but often imperfectly; perhaps it is enough to say that he remembers what he chooses to remember.

Now, considering the relative dates of these Eddic poems (950 to 1150 or even 1200) and the Saga (probably composed in the later thirteenth century, with Codex at least a century later, or near 1400), such slips of memory are easy enough to explain. It must be remembered also that the Author has blended the two Eddic poems *Atlamál* and *Atlakvida* in skillful fashion, and omissions or alterations may be deliberate. I am inclined to believe, however, that it is impossible to maintain that the Author had the Eddic poems before him all the time. Besides—and this seems to me highly important—we can be sure that there were other forms of narrative, perhaps another saga or sagas, certainly other tales, stories within stories (*thaettir*), and prose pieces, in or out of an Eddic context, which the Author knew but which we have lost. Some idea of the nature and direction of the various controversies will be gleaned from a perusal of my comments in the bibliography.

II

Whatever approach one cares to take, one will have to assume that the Author composed the Saga as we have it as much as a century before Codex. That would mean around 1270-75, well after the close of the skaldic era, yet pretty much in the heart of the age of saga writing. The Saga is usually classed as a Heroic Saga (*Heldensage*), and shares with the *Thidrekssaga* the honor of being the most important member of this class. Yet it clearly deals with ancient matters, as does the *Fornaldarsaga*, and in its occasionally tense domestic scenes it has something in common with the Family saga. Moreover, the chivalric idealization of Sigurd, the knightly protagonist, and the presence of such words as *kurteis*, *ást*, and *ágaetr* for ''courteous'' (in the chivalric sense), ''courtly love,'' and ''excellent,'' respectively, reminds us of the *Riddarsögur* or Knightly Sagas much favored by King

Haakon IV, or *inn gamli* ("the Old"), but I believe that too much can be made of this point, except that it argues for a date not much after 1270 for the composition of the Saga. Codex should then be dated 1375-1400.

At any rate, the Saga, as we have it here in Codex (always bearing in mind the possibility of an earlier lost version or versions) can obviously be divided into five parts, any one of which would be material for a saga in its own right. These five parts would be (1) the background of Sigurd, with cursory accounts of his ancestors back to Odin, and a considerable story of his father, Sigmund (whom I regard as the protagonist of an originally separate saga), his aunt, Signy, and his half-brother, Sinfjötli, including also the story within the story, or *tháttr*, of Helgi Hundingsbane; then (2) the youth and upbringing of Sigurd, his revenge on Lyngvi, slayer of his father, which culminates in the killing of the dragon Fafnir, the forestalling of his foster father Regin's treachery by his killing of Regin as well, the acquisition of Fafnir's treasure (the Accursed Treasure), along with his meeting with Brynhild on Hindarfell; next (3) the account of Sigurd's relations with the Gjukings, ending with his murder by one of his brothers-in-law. The story then shifts to (4) the subsequent life of his widow, Gudrun; her marriage to Atli; the killing of her brothers, Högni and Gunnar, who had fallen heir to Sigurd's treasure, which Atli coveted; and Gudrun's revenge on Atli. Finally, the story concludes with (5) Gudrun's marriage to Jonak, which involves her with Jörmunrek and his marriage to her daughter, Svanhild; Svanhild is put to death by Jörmunrek, and the attempt at revenge on Jörmunrek by her two half-brothers, Hamdir and Sorli, proves abortive, for they are killed and the Gjuking line comes to an end. All five of these parts are in effect subsagas, each having the required combination of introduction, involvement, climactic revenge or failure thereof, resolution, and conclusion.

To put all this in other words, for each of these five subsagas we are at liberty to assume short pieces of prose or verse, the *rímur* or *thaettir* already mentioned. Some of these may once have been committed to writing, of which there is some slight evidence, but most, I fear, have been lost irretrievably, for I doubt that any considerable part of those not yet salvaged will ever be recovered. In recent years, therefore, much of the controversy that began as far back as Bugge's edition of 1865 and raged until after the First World War or even a little later—something over a half-century—has said about all it has to say.

None the less, when we survey the battlefield we discover that some of the older theories have held their ground. Thus almost from the beginning there has been postulated an earlier *Völsungasaga*, or possibly two. In other words, Codex is not the earliest telling of the story, for it cannot have been written during the Author's lifetime. Besides, in Codex we come upon certain scraps of verse that cannot be referred to any surviving Eddic poem. These are most likely scraps of a version in verse (covering the story in part or in whole), although they are so scanty that it is often impossible to determine their metrical form. Other passages in verse, however, are from an Eddic poem that can easily be recognized, or they may be from the hypothetical *Meiri* and hence are unrecognized. The first eight chapters are a problem. No source has survived except for a slipshod ballad known as *Rímur frá Völsungi hinum óborna* ("Rhymes about Völsung the unborn"; i.e., not born in the usual way, for he was cut from his mother's body), incomplete, late and very cursory in its relevant parts. It is not a source, but rather an analogue. Therefore, failing proof, I consider it a reasonable assumption that there was a lost *Sigmundarsaga* or perhaps a shorter *Sigmundarkvida*—perhaps more than one, because in my opinion Sigmund is a not inconsiderable Germanic hero preceding Sigurd, very likely a hero of maritime persuasion, as I shall try to show in a moment.

Finally, there is still another source to be considered, one that has been constantly played down—the imagination and story-telling gift of the Author himself. For even if the Saga as we have it today in Codex may not be precisely the same as that composed by another author a century or so earlier—and, of course, we cannot prove that it is not—there is a little doubt that it is substantially the same, and the Author should be given due credit for what has survived. He has taken a mass of narrative elements and put this mass into an orderly tale, whatever one may think of his style.

III

We should now try to look for a historical *terminus a quo* for the Saga, because it has relations to the folktale, and a tale of this category, including myth, tends to arise out of actual occurrences befalling actual people. Here the obvious point of departure is the fourth century in Western Europe. This century represents a reasonably early stage of the so-called Heroic Age of the Germanic peoples. This term was first given wide currency in the successful book of that name by H. Munro Chadwick (*The Heroic Age* [Cambridge, 1912]).[6] The book is an old book now, yet even so it is more "recent" than about three-fourths of the subsequent literature concerning the Saga. Chadwick's analysis there was both subsumed and then expanded in the later work that he wrote with his wife, Nora Kershaw Chadwick, *The Growth of Literature* (Cambridge, 1932–45).[7]

In recent years there has been a tendency to deride the term *Heroic Age*, on the ground that there are no such things as heroes any more—therefore there never were—and that more attention should be given to the social and cultural history of the fourth century than to its "bloody tyrants." I prefer to ignore these objectors, leaving them nameless, but I must insist that while there may be no heroes today, there assuredly were many in the fourth century and later. Whoever takes such a limited view of history certainly knows nothing of the century in queston, but it would probably be wiser to think of the entire span from before the birth of Christ to about 1000 as the Mythopoeic Age of the Germanic and Celtic peoples. This is a period in the childhood of nations when ordinary mortals, because of leadership and personality and other idealized attributes, become magnified into legendary heroes of fictive nature (whether deservedly or not), even perhaps magnified to be gods (euhemerism), and the gods themselves can descend to be mortal heroes, while fairy tales, *märchen*, and etiological tales abound. Every nation has had them at this particular stage of its ethnic development, when he who best represents the ideal of that nation in terms of strength and powers of offense and defense and victorious achievement becomes an object of veneration and even worship. Now, because everyone knows what is meant by the expression, I shall continue to speak of the Heroic Age, by which I mean any time during the first thousand years of the Christian era and even a bit before and later.

In considering the Western European epic heroes alone, I note that two Celtic gods related to nature-worship, Cuchulain and Gawain, have also become epic protagonists, eventually dying. Others, however, are historical figures: Charlemagne, Roland, Attila, El Cid, Hygelac, possibly even Arthur. They are all mortal, nevertheless. Others, like Beowulf and Lancelot, appear to be purely fictional. The historical Hygelac may coexist in the same epic poem with Beowulf—the historical uncle with a fictional nephew. Underneath all this, however, there runs the hard vein of history, and it is only our own abysmal ignorance of certain areas in the past that prevents us from working out some system of cause and effect.

In speaking of this fourth century, one basic historical fact that we know about (among the multitude of things we do not know) is the invasion of Eastern and then Western Europe by the Huns, a Turco-Mongol nation that, whatever the pressures behind them, debouched across the Volga River into Western Europe about the year 350, then ravaged their way through central and southern Europe, the Balkans, and the Carpathian area, overwhelming the Gothic (Germanic) and Gallic (Celtic) peoples whom they encountered, and even threatening Rome, where the Western Empire was approaching the last stages of decrepitude.

For about a century the Huns carried all before them but never actually took Rome, no doubt because of fiscal prearrangements made between the Empire and the Hunnish leaders. An Ostrogothic king named Ermanric (Hermanric, Eormanric) was among their earlier victims. His empire then embraced most of central Europe, yet when he saw himself threatened by these terrible Orientals, he is reported to have committed suicide in despair at the hopelessness of his situation—this according to the nearly contemporary historian Ammianus Marcellinus of the fourth century.[8] Yet a chronicler who followed, the sixth-century historian of the Goths, Jordanes, has a more colorful account. According to him, Ermanric once had a woman named Sunilda executed by ordering her to be trodden to death by horses for the alleged treason of her husband, who was apparently not available at the time. Her two brothers, Sarus and Hamnius, in an attempt to avenge her, severely wounded Ermanric. From the valetudinarian condition arising from his wounds, Ermanric died soon thereafter at the overripe age of 110.[9] In less than two centuries, therefore, a legend-making process had begun, and Ermanric takes his place as the protagonist of a story-cycle, if not precisely the "hero," for he is known as a greedy, ruthless tyrant who did his people no good and who possessed an enormous treasure. He seems to have been one of the very first historical characters with whom we are acquainted in Germanic legendry, and hence it is no surprise to see him in the Saga as Jörmunrek; his victim, Svanhild; the would-be avengers who wound him severely, Sörli and Hamdir.

The next great victory of the Huns, as far as the Saga is concerned, was over the Burgundians, a Gothic nation, in 436 or 437. (Dates are particularly hard to fix with accuracy at this point, for the early chroniclers are reluctant to tell us. Nor is the precise site of the battle known.) The Burgundians were badly beaten and lost their king, Gundahari (Gundicarius), who is generally taken to be the Gunnar of the Saga. It seems, however, that the report that the Burgundians were extirpated is something of an exaggeration. They continue to be heard from until the year 513 or 514, at which time they were merged with the rising Frankish empire. About the year 500 their King Gundobad had drawn up the *Lex Burgundionum*, or Burgundian Law-Code, in which appear the names not only of Gundicarius but also of Gibica, Gondomar, and Gislhari.[10] It is now generally agreed that the family of the Gjukings in the Saga (representing the Burgundians) derived its name from Gibica, but no evidence of the survival of the other two names in the Saga is at all convincing, although they appear in the southern or German versions. There is no doubt, however, about Attila, most famous of the Hunnish leaders,[11] eventually defeated by a Gothic-Roman army under the Gothic-Roman Aetius at the Battle of the Catalaunian Fields (451), probably near Châlons. Attila survived the battle but died in 453 of a stroke, reputedly on his wedding night with Hildico

(Ildico), supposedly a diminutive for Hilde, but attempts to identify her with Brynhild or Gudrun or Grimhild of the Saga have been at best desperate enterprises. Attila, however, survives in legend as Atli (German Etzel), who in the Saga is brother to Brynhild and in general an unsympathetic character, foreshadowed by his swarthy complexion. We are to regard him, in any event, as representing the Huns, just as the Gjukings represented the Burgundians, and the conflict between these two factions in chapters 30 to 35 of the Saga is a political allegory as well as the representation of a domestic feud.

Not long ago Gudmund Schuette[12] called attention to the presence in history of a King Sigismund of the Burgundians, whose second wife expressed dissatisfaction with her stepson, whom servants of the king proceeded to strangle, to the great dismay of Sigismund. An old man, not otherwise identified, observed that Sigismund should be grieving for himself rather than for his son.[13] This, Schuette suggested, is a historical parallel to the death of Sinfjötli in chapter 10 of the Saga. More compelling, I believe, is the case of King Gundram of the Franks, whose second wife became extremely jealous of her stepson and gave him poison. After that she was dismissed and "did not live very long."[14] Both incidents are recorded in Gregory of Tours's *Historia Francorum*. I suggest that in folk memory these two incidents got mixed and influenced the development of the Saga. Again, Gregory tells of a princess and queen named Brunihildis, daughter of King Athanagild of the Visigoths, who was a very fair and gracious maiden but became a grim and overbearing older woman who played at power politics and paid for it with her life. She was married to King Sigibert of Metz, who was assassinated in bed by his sister-in-law Fredegund in 575. Later Brunihildis was married to King Maravech, who treated her abominably. She was in and out of prison and was finally executed for "regicide," much in the manner of Sunilda, in either 613 or 614.[15] It is further recorded that on at least one occasion she donned armor and fought as a man, in the manner of Brynhild or Gudrun in the Saga. Attempts have been made, despite her name, to make her the prototype of Grimhild or of Kriemhild in the southern branch. With this I myself am inclined to agree, though I believe that both Brynhild and Sigurd, as they appear in the Saga, belong together as the fairy princess and fairy prince of the *märchen*. They are both fictional and in a sense mythological in their origins.

These historical characters just mentioned, apart from Sigurd, Brynhild, and possibly Sigmund, give us at least hints and names, and although none of them can be called precisely a "hero"—some of them, indeed, quite the contrary—they were living in an age of legend-making, when there was very little written literature, and mythopoeia prevailed. There can be no argument, however, about the two great events in Europe between 350+ and 450+, the defeat of the Burgundians in 437 and the rout of the Huns in 451. It is well to bear in mind also that a national defeat can linger in folk memory as well as a national victory.

To the names already cited should be added that of Theodoric (Thidrek, Thydrick, Dietrich, Dirck, etc.), king of the Ostrogoths, who died in 526. He does not appear in our Saga, but another, the *Thidrekssaga*, makes him the protagonist, and he remains an important figure in the southern branch of the story, as the outlines of the *Nibelungenlied* and the *Thidrekssaga* below will show. We cannot be sure about Högni (Hagen in the southern form), although I see no special reason why we should not identify him with Hagen of Troyes,[16] a Frankish count of contemporary insignificance who, however, grew mightily in legend. In fact, Hagen and Kriemhild tend to dominate the *Nibelungenlied* after the comparatively early death of Siegfried. I wonder, however, if we need to find historical prototypes for *every* character in the story. Some allowance must surely be made for the fictional process.

IV

The first reference to our Saga to survive in written literature comes in the Old English epic poem, *Beowulf* (ca.725+ –ca.750+), a southern Scandinavian story told in Old English, very likely the composition (oral, of course) of an Anglo-Saxon cleric of Norse antecedents living in central or southern

England, well versed in the traditions of the accepted professional Old English bard, or *scop*, and speaking English. The manuscript in which it was written down (Cotton Vitellius A XV) is close to 1000 in date. The relevant passage, which I shall examine in a moment, was long regarded by German scholars as *dunkel*—obscure, cryptic. I see none of these qualities in it. The situation is clear enough. King Hrothgar of the Danes has been plagued for twelve years by a night-monster, Grendel, who visits his hall each night and devours thirty of his warriors. The news comes to Beowulf, a leader of the Geats, whose father, Ecgtheow, was once befriended by Hrothgar. As a recompense Beowulf goes to help Hrothgar in the latter's hall, Heorot, and when the night-monster Grendel appears, Beowulf mortally wounds him. (This, the so-called Bear's Son folk-motif, is one of the most widespread of folkloristic themes.) The Geats (O. N. Gautar[17]) follow Grendel's tracks to a mysterious mere, at the bottom of which is his abode. Satisfied that he has been disposed of, they begin their return journey to Hrothgar's hall, Heorot. They celebrate by racing their horses in sport, entertained meanwhile by the *scop*, who recounts the feat of Beowulf and sings his praise.

In more ancient times, no doubt, any hero performing an epic feat would himself celebrate it on the spot. Thus when Samson in Judges 15:16 slew a thousand Philistines with the jawbone of an ass—a truly epic feat indeed—he rejoiced on the spot: ''With the jawbone of an ass, heaps upon heaps, with the jawbone of an ass, have I slain a thousand men.'' In the course of time, some thousands of years later, we find that there are professionals to help the hero celebrate. In Old English times they were called *scops*; in Old Norse, *skalds*; in Old Irish there was a graduated hierarchy of *senchas, fili, ollamhs*, the last group, the *ollamhs*, requiring a vigorous twelve-year period of training and a repertory of at least three hundred and fifty stories.[18] If, as many believe, the Old English poem *Widsith* is a poem of application by a *scop* in quest of a patron, the applicant professes a knowledge of nearly one hundred and fifty kings and tribes. The *scop*'s method of composition, whatever his ethnic background, was entirely oral. The process can still be found today, as Parry and Lord have demonstrated.[19]

Put in more technical terms, in the passage from *Beowulf* to be quoted below, we witness the beginning of epic composition. The bard (*scop*) tells of Beowulf's feat of the night before—what Chadwick has most aptly called the ''occasional bardic lay''; that is, composition by a professional bard of a lay that met the standards of style, meter, and imagery required by tradition of that bard, to celebrate a particular *occasion*—an epic feat, some dire event, a victory or a defeat, a birth or a death. Of course the *scop* differs from the *skald* in his techniques, as the *ollamh* or *fili* does from both, and in varying degree. We can then trace the oral development; the connecting of more than one occasional lay with the same protagonist constitutes a heroic epic. Inevitably there will come Stage 3, a popularization of the material for the common people, not the ruling class. After this third stage comes a final stage (4) in which the material can go in more than one direction. In the Norse and Celtic, this later fashion of narrative dictates the prose saga; in the English and German, under French influence, the trend is toward the metrical and then the prose romance. In the long run, of course, the extended prose narrative begins to take over, not only in the saga but also in something like Malory's *Morte Darthur*, which is based on several long metrical romances and prose versions.

Except for Stage 3, this process is mainly from an aristocratic source. I think we should also remember that the tradition of the professional bard lingered in the tradition of educated men and women who were not of their company. Like Chaucer's Squire, they too could ''endite.'' One is reminded of an Icelander like Grettir Asmundarson, who could, after some notable feat, toss off a stanza or two of verse as well as any *skald*.

To return for a moment to the passage from *Beowulf*. Having celebrated Beowulf's feat (ll. 871–72), the *scop* goes on to tell—speak, recite, chant with harp?—of other heroes and other times. The entire passage is so revealing that I take the liberty of quoting it in its entirety, calling particular attention to italicized words and phrases.[20]

Then the warriors	and many a young man too
Took their journey	returning in joy,
Riding their horses	from the mere as heroes

On their white steeds.   *There was told the glorious deed*
Of Beowulf; many a one   often said that south nor north
By the two seas no other man,   on the spacious earth
Under the expanse of sky,   was better among shield-bearers,
Worthier of a kingdom.   Nor did they in any way
Reproach gracious Hrothgar,   for he was a good king!   875

　　At times those battle-brave   let leap ahead
　　Their light-colored horses,   let them go racing,
　　Where earth-paths seemed fair,   known for their excellence.

At times a thane of the king,   a man laden   880

With many a story of glorious deeds,
Mindful of heroic lays,   one who remembered
A countless number   of other stories,
Framed a new story   founded upon fact.
This man began   skillfully to recount   885

The adventure of Beowulf   and to utter well
An appropriate tale   and to vary it with words.
He told nearly all   that he had once heard
Of the mighty unknown   deeds of Sigemund—
The struggle of the Waelsing   and his far journeys,   890

His feuds and crimes,   of which the children of men
Knew but little;   only Fitela with him,
Nephew with uncle,   when one would say
Aught of his adventures,   *for they were boon companions* 895

In every fight.   Their swords had slain
A mighty host   of monster-broods.
To Sigemund himself   after his death-day
No little glory when he,   the brave in battle
Had killed the dragon,   the hoard-guardian.
Beneath the gray rock,   there alone did Sigemund   900

Son of an atheling,   venture on a deed courageous,
Nor this time   was Fitela with him.
Yet it was granted him   his sword pierced the wonder-worm,
That it stuck in the wall,   that lordly iron.
The dragon died the death.   Then the champion   905

Dared so bravely   to enjoy the ring-hoard
At his own discretion;   he loaded the sea-ship,
Bearing there   into the bosom of the boat

That bright treasure,   did that son of Waels.
The heat within   melted the serpent.   910

That man was of wanderers   most widely known
Among the tribes of men,   a defender of warriors
By deeds of courage;   he prospered thus of yore.

If we keep in mind the approximate date of this passage as between 725 and 750, there are several points worthy of note:

1. Sigmund (note the Old English form *Sigemund*) was the most widely known of wandering heroes (l. 911), and was a Völsung (ll. 890 and 909)—more properly a son of Waels, for the Norse *Völsung*, as applied to an individual, must be incorrect, because the patronymic suffix *-ung* should not be applied as a given name to an individual.[21] In l. 909 the Beowulf Poet has got it right.

2. The teller of the story, the *scop*, a man who remembers a great many old stories (ll. 880–82), has a very large repertory that he can deliver according to the rules of his art, using repetition and synonyms and formulas and the required alliterative form (ll. 880–87)

3. The presence of these formulas, repetitive phrases, and the like, has been long familiar (although apparently rediscovered in 1953)[22]; it is implied in *varying it with words* (l. 887), which also points toward the distinctive style of the *scop*. As for stories, he knew *a countless number* (l. 884). This last fact lends sense to the statement in *Widsith* that the poet knew kings and tribes from everywhere far beyond the limits of his own lifetime. Finally, it should be noted that the composition is entirely oral. The *scop* does not read from either notes or a script.

Now let us turn our attention to Sigmund, as the Norse called him. There is no earthly need to identify him with Sigismund of the Burgundians. His name, with the very common first element *Sig-* ("victory") and the equally common second element *-mund* ("power over"), does not help us one way or another. And, as I have observed, the analogy between Sigismund and his slain son, as told by Gregory of Tours, is not quite so close as that between Gundram and his slain son, also told by Gregory.

In this passage from *Beowulf*, the "monsters" or "monster-broods" (l. 896) are called in Old English *eotenas*, which I think is correctly made cognate with the O.N. *jötunn*, meaning "giant." But in *Beowulf* this word appears four times and is always applicable to "sea-monster," once to the depredating Grendel himself (l. 761). This suggests that Sigmund may well have been originally a sea hero, especially since he loads the dragon's treasure into his "sea-ship" (l. 907). But in our Saga he makes only a normal sea voyage in chapter 5 with his father Völsung, although his ship is mentioned in the Eddic poem *Gudrúnarkvida II*, stanza 16. The matter does not admit any more evidence, and is perhaps a minor consideration. More important for us is the lavish praise bestowed upon Sigmund as a hero (ll. 911–12), which sounds comparable to the eulogy of Sigurd in the Saga.

One other little point obtrudes itself. Fitela (of course the Sinfjötli of the Saga) is called the nephew of Sigmund (l. 893). The Old English *nefa* is, of course, Modern English *nephew*. In rare instances it can mean "cousin" or even "grandson," but I see no reason for such interpretations here. Often this uncle-nephew relationship is expressed as "sister's son," which, in the ancient world of Germanic matriarchy, seems to have been at one time a closer relationship than "brother's son." Now, it is true that Sinfjötli is Sigmund's "sister's son," but it has been an incestuous relationship, as we learn from chapter 7 of the Saga. Perhaps the Beowulf Poet as a cleric might object to this union and so suppress the fact; there is no way of telling. Perhaps, for that matter, he knew nothing of the incest, for this detail may be a later Norse addition. There is little doubt, however, that as late as the tenth century, when there was composed an elegy on the death of King Eirik of Northumbria—the *Eiriksmál* (954)—the two great heroes who are preparing Valhalla for the arrival of their newest guest, Eirik, the two most famous occupants of Valhalla save Odin himself, are these same two, Sigmund and Sinfjötli. Nearly two centuries after the probable composition of *Beowulf*, there is still no mention of Sigurd.

It appears likely, then, whether or not he derived his name

from the Burgundian King Sigismund, that Sigmund had his origins on Germanic soil. Meanwhile, on the evidence of the *Beowulf* passage alone, there is every indication that Sigmund was the protagonist of a saga of his own, the *Sigmundarsaga*, which the Author must have followed for the first eight chapters of the Saga.

V

Meanwhile, what of Sigurd (Siegfried, Sigfrit, Seyfrit, etc.)? The older idea, still commonly held, is that he was a mythical, fictional character originating on Frankish-Burgundian soil, whose fame gradually drifted northward and eastward. A persistent school of critics, however, although rejecting as his prototype Sigibert, King of Metz and first husband (d. 575) of the redoubtable Brunihildis, have insisted that Sigurd has a historical origin. Led by the tireless Vigfusson,[23] these critics have kept preaching that Sigurd was a real person with a real beginning, even though no one by that name has been properly identified, and even though the first element of his name is extremely common. About fifteen years ago Otto Höfler[24] first suggested that the name Siegfried was *symbolic* of the Chersoni leader Hermann, or Arminius, who defeated the Roman legions under Varus in the year 9 at the great Battle of the Teutoburger Forest in Westphalia, supporting his thesis with some plausible circumstantial evidence. Indeed, in my opinion the evidence is a little too plausible, and the theory seems strained and somewhat made to order to fit a Procrustean bed. And in his latest publication (1978) Höfler even goes as far as to identify the Accursed Treasure of the Nibelungs with an archaeological find made more than a century ago in the general vicinity of the Teutoburger Wald, considering it to be the private treasure of the Roman general Varus, transmuted by time and romance from mostly silver to immeasurable gold. Why, one may ask, should a Roman general be carrying along a vast private treasure into the confines of darkest Germania? Was he trying to bribe the natives? His soldiers were being paid in coin of the Empire.

There has always been some objection to "Arminius" as a non-Roman name. Yet with all due concessions to folk-memory—and there have been some remarkable instances—from the year 9 to about 1000, virtually a thousand years, is a long, long stretch. I cannot frankly accept Höfler's theories, but I must respect them. In retrospect it all seems a little forced. In the Saga, Sigurd is a manly ideal, a fairy prince, and fairy princes have been around a great deal longer than Hermann or Arminius. Like Sigmund, if Sigurd ever was a historical character, he has long since been translated into folklore. But as *Symbolik* he looms large.

As to the joining of Sigmund and Sigurd as father and son, since it has not yet happened by 954 in the *Eiríksmál*, we can still do no more than guess that the union took place not before 1000—in other words, the eleventh century.

VI

Granted that Sigmund and Sigurd both had a Franco-Burgundian origin, how did their stories reach Scandinavia? We may assume that they moved on the Continent, north and east from ''Frankland'' into Denmark, as Nornagest did, thence into the Scandinavian peninsula. British chroniclers of about this same time (sixth to eighth centuries), such as Gildas, know little about the Norse, although they have plenty to say about the Angles and Saxons and Jutes. Once in the Scandinavian peninsula, the Norse suddenly exploded westward and southward in the eighth century, colliding with the Celts in the Orkneys, the Shetlands, the Hebrides, the north of Britain (Gaels), and Ireland (Gaels). They crossed the Atlantic to Iceland, to Greenland, to Finland (probably Labrador and Newfoundland). Blend of destructiveness and commercial activity as this so-called Norse Scourge tended to be, it brought the Vikings into contact with a literary tradition that was more advanced than their own by two or three centuries, for the Irish had accepted Christianity as early as the fifth century, and the Welsh narrative literature had advanced to the epic poem, as exemplified in *Y Goddodin* by Aneirin (ca. 600), and even to the prose saga. In every aspect of literature, it can be maintained, the Celtic got there first.

This makes for enormous problems. The earliest known Norse *skald*, the half-legendary Bragi Boddason *inn gamli* (''the old'')[25] flourished about 850; the Icelanders can boast of Úlfr inn Óargi

("Ulf the Fierce"), who appears to have been roughly contemporary with Bragi. The skaldic tradition blossomed during the reign of Harald Fairhair (860–933). This tradition, however, soon began to decline in Norway but continued to thrive in Iceland, especially during the eleventh century. One can only make surmises about the nature of oral composition in Scandinavia before 800. From what is known of oral epic composition elsewhere, one can still postulate the occasional bardic lay, even perhaps the combination of more than one lay. A hypothesis this must remain, however.

Similarly, one can see resemblances in the metrical structures of the various poems. Thus alliteration locking the hemistichs (half-lines) is a feature of Old English, Old Saxon, and Old High German, and of the formal *fornyrdislag* of Old Norse. But we can find it in the pre-Padraican verse of Ireland as well as in the epic verse of Wales. Yet strophic structure is a prime characteristic of Old Norse poetry, as it is in Old Welsh and post-Padraican Irish, although it is a comparative rarity in Old English. This whole matter needs further extensive comparative study.

All in all, if we discount that which has been lost forever, I am prepared to suggest that the Celtic literature that the Old Norse met in their explosive expansion had a primary influence on the Norse. This is not to say that there is a Celto-Germanic relationship comparable to the Graeco-Roman. The Norse rune and the Gaelic ogham do not make for a common written literature, but in oral traditions there can certainly be much interplay. In his excellent study of some twenty years ago, *Kelten und Germanen* (Berlin-Munich, 1960), Jan de Vries discusses the resemblances and differences between the two races as to language, literature, religion, and general culture, and finds almost as many resemblances as differences. What should be of special interest to us is that in considering the story of Sigurd he cites these parallels:

1. Sigurd's testing of the sharpness of his sword Gram by a wolf's hair and a strand of wool is found in an incident of Cuchulain's career.

2. The horny hide that Siegfried attains by bathing in

dragon's blood is matched in the Irish *Tain Bo Cuailgne*, when the hero, Ferdiad, acquired a similar keratosis in the same way.

3. There is a fatal physical vulnerability (the epic flaw) revealed to Siegfried's enemies by his wife (almost a universal Indo-European theme).

4. Sigurd learns the language of birds by tasting dragon's blood, as does Finn by cooking and eating a magic salmon.

5. The "flickering flame" or. *vafrloga* surrounding the abode of Brynhild in the Saga is matched in one of the voyages of Maeldun, where an entire island is discovered to be surrounded by flames.

To these should be added the many "Celtic" motifs recognized long before de Vries: the sword in the stone or tree trunk, to be pulled out only by a chosen warrior; the curative weasel, as in Marie de France's *Eliduc*, assisted in the Saga by Odin in the guise of a raven, as in chapter 9 of the Saga; the mysterious old man in a boat (Odin) who carries off the body of Sinfjötli in chapter 10 of the Saga; finally, the incestuous relationship between Sigmund and his sister, Signy, to produce Sinfjötli, and the incestuous union of King Arthur and his half-sister Belisande to produce the villainous Modred. One could use a great deal more of this kind of comparative study, for the resemblances are too many to be passed over. Nor are they only in the literary materials. In prosody, some of the Old Irish genealogical poems have the same kind of interlocking alliteration as the Germanic poetry, and can be scanned in almost Sieversian manner. The great stumbling-block, of course, is the comparative paucity of Old Irish sagas, not so much in oral tradition as on the printed page, although I am sure that the Old Irish Texts Society is doing its best.

In any event, the *northern* part of our story, as exemplified in the Saga, is rich in folklore, could we but understand it all. Chapter 20, for example, the scene between Brynhild and Sigurd on Hindarfell, takes us back into the folklore of a bygone age, in which we can recognize names but do not fully grasp the mythological or folkloristic implications. We know only that some of these, especially in their *märchen* or fairy-tale aspects, can be found over all the Indo-European terrain and elsewhere: tree worship, sea spells, traditions concerning wild animals, semi-deities, and even the gods themselves. What I am emphasizing, however, is that the northern branch of our story is richer in such imponderables than the southern, for its locales are wilder, more remote, and certainly less sophisticated than those in the southern areas. For that reason I am including a brief synopsis of both the *Nibelungenlied* and the *Thidrekssaga* at the end of the present translation.

VII

If I were to hazard a theory as to the chronology of the development of the Saga, it would be in stages something like this:

1. Oral tradition concerning individual incidents, beginning at the latest in the sixth century, starting with individual lays that tended to expand and pick up details.

2. A lost *Sigmundarsaga*, originating in the same way. Both were, of course, first oral until someone interested enough and skillful enough reduced them to writing, at first possibly in verse, but then put into prose later by him or by others.

3. The Eddic poems, those surviving as well as those lost (of which there were probably many), which came to the Saga Men, the Authors, before the Saga was written down.

4. The so-called *Meiri* and *Forna* poems hypothesized for the great gap in *The Poetic Edda*. Some of this material, of course, could be subsumed under (3) above, but in other cases it treated the Sigmund story, which does not appear in the extant Eddic poems.

5. The brief prose accounts like those in Snorri Sturluson's *Prose Edda*, which still have nothing to say about many aspects of the Saga.

6. One or even more *Ur*-Saga(s), or original prose telling(s) of the whole story.

7. The Saga itself, as we have it.
8. The material in the *Nornageststháttr*[26] and lost ballads or *rímur*.
9. A late popularization such as the *Rímur frá Völsungi hinum óborna*, which I consider to be later than the other material.

We are still, however, so much in the dark as to the popularizations of the story that it may be, as E. V. Gordon put it, that the unknown Author "collected all the stories he could find about the Völsungs, and arranged them" in a continuous narrative.[27] Some of these stories were oral, some written. He was also capable of rearranging and even of inventing, and, writing as he did rather late in the thirteenth century, when the fire of Eddic composition had begun to die down, he sometimes achieved a product quite different from the Eddic.

At the same time, I doubt very much that this Author has ever received his proper due. It was no mean accomplishment to assemble, in a generally connected, not to say fluent, prose narrative, all of the chief ingredients for one of the greatest of medieval stories, perhaps not the most significant of Norse sagas from the standpoint of sheer narrative art, but undeniably central, the most important and influential to appear in the gallery of medieval European literature, when taken in the gross. This Author's version is always readable, and although he tends to retreat from the poetic, as almost all of his critics have complained (even to the point where they see no poetry in him at all), still he is by no means a mere wooden clodhopper. It is true that his work as a whole is most uneven. He is clearly interested, however, in the careers of Sigmund and Sinfjötli, whom he treats with some humor and not a little drama. There are many little touches that should attract the reader: the rather grotesque matter of Bredi's Memorial Snowdrift; the scene around Barnstock (or Branstock); the bizarre episode of the murderous she-wolf, said to be Siggeir's mother; the moving final scene between Sigmund and Signy, their revenge accomplished; the death of Sinfjötli, much better handled, I believe, than in its Eddic counterpart; the scene between the dying Sigmund and his wife, Hjördis, on the battlefield; the chitchat over drinks in Hjalprek's hall, so reminiscent of a present-day vapid cocktail party; and many more. These are, of course, only subjective reactions, but others can no doubt find memorable scenes on their own.

The first meeting of Brynhild and Sigurd on Hindarfell, whatever its fairy-tale atmosphere or *märchen* origins, gives promise of a great romantic human love that later events cannot bring to fruition. To be sure, it is obvious that the Author has not succeeded in reconciling the two characters in Brynhild, but he manages to make her a schizophrenic, if that ugly word be permitted, and therefore all the more interesting to a modern reader. Yet the speech of Brynhild as she mounts the funeral pyre to accompany Sigurd to Hel; the drama of the battle between Atli and the Gjukings, Huns against Burgundians, including the bathetic characterization of the thrall Hjalli; the confused dream-sequences and their general misinterpretations; Gunnar in the snake pit, which brings to culmination the inevitable passing of the Gjukings (in which, as compared to the pertinent Eddic poems, the Author has brought order out of chaos); the ultimate woeful actions of Gudrun against Atli, offering a symbolic revenge for the defeat of the Burgundians by the Huns eight hundred and more years before—all these are to be credited to the Author's skill as a storyteller.

At the same time, the Author never tries to be poetic, although he quotes some poetry, and he lacks a good sense of artistic proportion. Thus, while the story of Gudrun following the murder of Sigurd is well maintained, her third marriage (this time to Jonak), with the hitching on (*Anknüpfung*) of the Legend of Ermanric and the abortive attempts of her sons to avenge the death of their half-sister Svanhild—to say nothing of the execution of Svanhild herself—are all compressed into two short chapters, and the telling is almost indecent in its haste. Yet unevenness of this kind is not unknown in other sagas. The Author manages also to make his often gory narrative sound decorous; he is never so carried away by the violence as to rejoice in the killing and the torture for their own sakes. By the same sign, objections can be made that the pace of the earlier chapters leading up to the birth of Sigurd is both too long-drawn-out and too digressive, especially chapter 9, which is virtually a *Helgaþáttr*. Yet even here the narrative is never per-functory, and much would be missed if that chapter were omitted. The resolute figures of Sigmund, Sinfjötli, and Signy lend emphasis to the fact that there is a story of the Völsungs before Sigurd.

I am persuaded also that the Author's use of Odin[28] as a kind of central motif is handled with considerable dramatic effect. He is the progenitor who gets the story of the Völsungs underway and he is there when the last of the Gjukings have been killed. No less than eleven times does he appear (all but once in the earlier part of the Saga, which tends to associate him with Sigmund and young Sigurd). This part is not at all under Eddic influence.

1. He is the originator of the Völsung line.
2. He is a befriender and rescuer of his son Sigi.
3. He is the donor of Sigmund's sword Gram by way of the sword-in-the-tree-trunk motif.
4. He gives the fructifying apple to Rerir and his wife, thereby making possible the birth of Völsung.
5. He, in the guise of a weasel and of a raven, helps Sinfjötli recover from the attack made on him by Sigmund, which the boy had brought on himself by sheer filial impudence.
6. He, in the guise of an old man in a tiny boat, takes Sinfjötli's body and disappears, presumably taking it to Valhalla.
7. He intervenes in the battle between Sigmund and Lyngvi, causing Sigmund's death and assuring him also a place in Valhalla.
8. He assists Sigurd in his choice of the steed Grani.
9. He quiets a storm for Sigurd before his battle against Lyngvi.
10. He advises Sigurd how best to protect himself in his forthcoming combat with Fafnir; and finally,
11. He brings about the destruction of Hamdir and Sörli in their attempts to kill Jörmunrek in revenge for Svanhild, thus bringing, in the Author's judgment

> (for he has forgotton about Helgi and Aslaug), the
> Völsung-Gjuki line to an end, in the approved Ger-
> manic manner, dead in combat.

To the present-day reader, Odin is thus revealed as the force that
gives and that takes away, disposing of us all, showing preference
toward some and rejecting others. This, of course, is not the
Christian way, but it would be unwarranted to look for that here,
especially in the northern version of the Saga, in which Chris-
tianity was the last creed to conquer.

In conclusion, consider the last dozen stanzas of the Eddic
poem *Gudrúnarhvöt* ("The Urging-On by Gudrun") and com-
pare them to the last paragraph of the Saga:[29]

9. Weeping, Gudrun,
   Gjuki's daughter,
   Went with reluctant steps
   To sit by the entrance
   And to relate,
   With tears of grief
   In many a way.

10. "Three fires have I known,
    Three hearths have I known,
    To three husbands' homes
    Have I been carried.
    And Sigurd was to me
    Better than all,
    He whom my brothers
    Put to death.

11. "A heavier wound
    I never knew nor saw;
    Yet more it seemed to me,
    A greater torment to me,
    When the princes
    Gave me to Atli.

12. "My keen young boys I called
    To secret talk with me.
    For my woes I could not
    Get me compensation,

Till I had hewed off
The heads of the Niblungs.

13. "I went to the shore,
   Angry at the Norns;
   I wished to hurl myself
   From their harassment.
   High waves lifted me
   Without drowning me;
   Thus on land I climbed,
   For I was fated to live.

14. "I went to bed
   (I had planned something better)
   For yet a third time
   With a great king.
   I bore him children,
   Rightful heirs,
   Sons of Jonak.

15. "And around Svanhild
   Sat her serving-women,
   Whom I of my children
   Loved best of all.
   So was Svanhild
   In my own hall,
   As if she were to look at
   As glorious as a sunbeam.

16. "I endowed her with gold
   And with costly robes,
   Before I gave her
   To the Gothic people.
   To me the cruelest
   Of all my griefs
   Is for the blonde
   Locks of Svanhild—
   They trod them in the mud
   Under the feet of horses.

17. "And the most sorrowful,
   When my Sigurd
   They stripped of triumph,
   And slew him in bed;
   And the harshest

When those gleaming serpents
Slithered toward Gunnar,
Deprived him of life,
When they flayed to the heart
That uncowardly king,
Slit him still living.

18. "Many songs I remember . . .

19. "Bridle now, Sigurd!
Your black steed,
Swift-coursing steed.
Let him come galloping!
Here sits now
No son's wife or daughter
Who can to Gudrun
Bring priceless gifts!

20. "Do you remember, Sigurd,
What we two swore
When we two in bed
Lay both together—
That you would remember me,
Proud one, and visit me
Even from Death and Hell, my hero!
And I you from this world!

21. "Build high, my lords!
That pyre of oakwood,
And pile it under heaven
Highest of all!
May it burn the breast
Most curse-filled of all!
May the sorrows melt
That weigh down my heart!"

Now, if we leave aside a brief six-line stanza that indicates that the foregoing is intended to lessen the troubles of all of us, men and women alike, because these woes have been recited, let us concede that this Eddic poem is of heroic dimensions, and the climax truly a Wagnerian brass choir indicating that Gudrun is preparing for suicide by fire, like Signy and Brynhild before her. Now place beside it the account in the Saga, the ungarnished prose of chapter 41, particularly at the point where it reaches stanza 10 of the poem:

But Gudrun went to her bower, her sorrow increasing, and said: "To three men I have been wedded: first to Sigurd Fafnisbane, and he was betrayed, and that was for me the greatest woe. Then I was given in marriage to King Atli, and my heart was turned so cruel toward him that I killed our sons in my grief. Then I went to the sea and was carried by great waves to this land, and then I was wedded to this king. Then I gave Svanhild in marriage away from here, with great treasure, and it has been for me the sorest of sorrows, next to Sigurd, when she was trodden under the feet of horses. And it was most grim for me when Gunnar was cast in the snake pit, and the keenest when the heart was cut out of Högni. For it would be better if Sigurd should come to me and bear me off in his arms. Here sits now no son or daughter to comfort me. Do you remember, Sigurd, what we two said when we entered one bed, that you would come to me and stay with me, even out of Hel itself?" Then she ended her lamentation.

We find nothing here to imply impending suicide, even though we know that the Author must know that that is the way the story should end. I wonder, however, if the Author may not be finessing the reader. At the end of chapter 38 he has told us that after the death of Atli, Gudrun did not wish to live, "but the end of her days had not yet come." Regardless of the Eddic poem, the Author is not fumbling here; he knows exactly what he is doing. For all we are ever told, Gudrun is to live in sorrow and grow old and be forgotten, as is the misfortune of most of us. This is not heroic, but rather the way things are.

Notes to Introduction

1. Since both the editor of the diplomatic text of the Saga, Magnus Olsen, and the editor of the most accessible modern edition, Ernst Wilken (Paderborn, 1877; 1912) seem to differ on the dates—Olsen dates the appearance of Codex in Denmark as early as 1641, when Christian IV was king, and Wilken *tends* to follow suit—I thought it best, because the beneficence of Bishop Sweinsson was well known, to seek the advice of the Royal Library (Det Kongelige Bibliotek) in

Copenhagen, where Codex is housed. I received a very helpful report from Dr. Tue Gad of the Library staff, of which the following paragraphs represent the gist:

Bishop Sveinsson made more than one donation of Old Icelandic manuscripts to the royal court in Copenhagen. We are interested in Codex, which appeared in 1656, and with it two more manuscripts, of which one was the *Flateyjarbók*, containing *inter alia* a version of the *Nornageststháttr*. In 1662 a total of twelve more manuscripts was added, including the priceless MS of *The Poetic Edda*.

In 1784 all these various manuscripts were given a number and entered in a written catalogue; all fifteen manuscripts were thus registered, except for that of the *Völsungasaga*, which was apparently missing. It was not until 1821 that it was located in the Royal Chamber of Arts (or Museum), where it apparently had been lying for 165 years. That is why its official designation is *Ny. kgl. Saml* (New Royal Collection), whereas all the other manuscripts (the other fourteen) are designated in *Gl. kgl. Saml* (Old Royal Collection). The miracle of this is that the Saga survived at all; it is a true nightmare for the specialist in Library Science.

2. It has yet to be determined how or even where Björner prepared his edition.

3. Anton Edzardi, trans., *Die Sage von den Völsungen und den Nibelungen* (Stuttgart, 1881), p.1. *The Saga of Ragnar Lodbrók* has been translated by Margaret Schlauch, *The Story of the Volsungs* (New York, 1930).

4. Per Wieselgren, "Quellenstudien zur Völsungasaga," *Acta et Commentationes Universitatis Tartunensis* (Tartu, 1938). In writing about the great amount of scholarly literature devoted to the study of the Saga and its relationship to the Continental (i.e., southern) form of the story, he notes the desirability of establishing a connection between the northern and southern branches, and yet "we cannot consider this matter solved. And it is a nice question indeed, whether it ever will be solved. There are so many unknown factors which call upon so many hypotheses for us to recognize the matter as settled once and for all" (p. 6).

5. Ursula Browne Dronke, ed. and trans., *The Poetic Edda*, vol. 1 (Oxford, 1969), especially pp. 107-11.

6. More detailed references to Chadwick's work are given in the bibliography, nos. 2 and 3.

7. See n. 6 above.

8. Ammianus Marcellinus, *Rerum gestarum libri qui supersunt* (Loeb Classical Library, Cambridge, Mass. and London, 1939), chap. 31, par. iii, pp. 396-97, merely states that in his discouragement Ermanric died a voluntary death (*voluntaria morte*), which sounds like suicide to me.

9. Jordanes, *De Origine Actibusque Getarum*, ed. Anton Holder (Freiburg i.P. and Tübingen, 1889), chap. 24. The question of Ermanric's suicide being something of a moot point, we compare his "voluntary death" mentioned in preceding note 8 with Jordanes's statement, in his purported continuation of the great Roman historian Tacitus, himself a Goth. Ermanric, having been badly wounded by Sarus and Amnius after the Sunilda affair, died "full of days" at the

age of 110. The implication is that the combination of his severe wounds and old age caused his death.

10. These names will be found in Louis de Solis, ed., *Monumenta Germaniae Historica: Leges* (sec.1) (Hannover, 1882), 2:43

11. Attila. There have been two useful studies of this figure. It has been proposed that his name is derived from the Gothic *atta*, a child's name for "father," with a diminutive suffix—hence "little father" or the like. But Imeljan Pritsak, "Der Titel Attila," *Festschrift für Max Vosmer* (bibliography no. 104), shows that *atta* (as in the Gothic version of the Lord's Prayer) was a Hunnish rather than a Gothic word; hence "Attila" in Hunnish would be "little father." More important, of course, is Helmut de Boor's *Das Attilabild: in Geschichte, Legende, und heroischer Bildung* (Bern, 1932), which considers three aspects of this character: (1) the churchly view of Attila as the Scourge of God; (2) the German baronial concept; (3) the role of brother of Brynhild and opponent of the Gjukings; and finds that all three of these distinctions can be traced to the account of Attila in Jordanes.

12. See Gudmund Schütte, *Sigfrid und Brünhild* (Copenhagen, 1935). He attacks the idea of Sigurd and Brynhild as mythical creations, referring to the story told in Gregory of Tours (see nn. 13 and 14 below). But with these two we are dealing with the stuff of fairy tales: sleeping beauty, father avenged, wicked mother-in-law, dragon slain, unapproachable female won, and only later, when the Author brings them back to earth, so to speak, are they mortals. I am therefore not prepared to accept Brunihildis and Sigbert of Metz as prototypes; as for Brunihildis, let her be the original of Grimhild or Kriemhild.

13. The story is told in Gregory of Tours, *Historia Francorum*, ed. Henri Omont (Paris, 1886), 3, sec. 5.

14. Gregory of Tours, 4, sec. 25.

15. The same uncertainty of date prevails here as in the case of the Huns versus the Burgundians.

16. Troyes. Although Hagen is sometimes called Hagen of Tronek, he is sometimes called Hagen of Troja, which comes near enough.

17. Geats . . . Gautar. These people, whose tribal names in the two languages are strictly cognate, have usually been identified as a Scandinavian group from the ancient Swedish province of Götarike, south of the two great lakes of Väner and Vätter. Two notable dissidents, however, have been Gudmund Schütte, "The 'Geats' of *Beowulf*," *Journal of English and Germanic Philology* 11(1912): 574–602, and Elis Wadstein, "The Beowulf Poem as a National English Epic," *Acta Philologica Scandinavica* 8 (1933–34): 273–91. Both believe them to be the Jutes, despite the fact that the initial consonant would be a Modern English *y*, and the *j* derived from the French had not yet arrived in the language—that is, in initial position. On the other hand, it seems impossible that the Geats can be the ancient nation of the Getae (see Jane A. Leake, *The Geats of "Beowulf"* [Madison, Wis., 1967]), a tribe of prehistoric Thrace, although it might be phonetically possible to wrench the word into that form. Normally, however, *Getae* would become West Saxon *Gietas*. In spite of the to me

frivolous suggestion by Robert Kaske, "The Eotenas of 'Beowulf,' " *Studies in Old English Poetry*, ed. Robert P. Creed (Providence, R. I., 1967), pp. 285–310, I concede that the study is well done, but for various reasons it fails to convince me. I agree, nevertheless, that the tribe in the Finnsburg Episode of *Beowulf* (ll. 1068–1158a) are in likelihood the Jutes.

18. "It was the duty of the *fili* of the various ranks to memorize stories, genealogies, and topographical traditions, and to master the hundreds of Gaelic metres. The *ollamh*, graduating after twelve years' study, was required to know by heart three hundred and fifty classic narratives." Aodh de Blácam, *Gaelic Literature Surveyed*, rev.ed. (New York, 1974), p. 28. There is no question but that the interrelationship of Germanic skaldic verse and Celtic bardic verse should be examined much further than it has been. The intrinsic difficulty, of course, lies in the fact that both were originally entirely oral.

19. See in particular Albert B. Lord, *The Singer of Tales* (Cambridge, Mass., 1960).

20. The translation given here is my own.

21. In other words, the name of Sigemund's ancestor should be Waels, and in the Norse story it should be Völs. The older explanation was that the word is cognate to the Gothic *walis*, to be found only in the Ulfilan translation of the Pauline Epistles Colossians 3:12; Philippians 4:3; 1 Timothy 1:2; Titus 1:4. In all of these the accepted meaning is "chosen," "respected," "faithful." The word is also applied to an ancient Slavic deity. I am not enamored of either explanation, and I doubt that many today would disagree with my reservation.

22. This matter was common knowledge among students of Old English ever since the first edition by Friedrich Klaeber (*Beowulf*; Boston, 1922), a statement that is repeated in his last edition (1957), where the formulaic structure is noted (p. lxvi). But Francis P. Magoun, in "Oral-Formulaic Character of Anglo-Saxon Narrative Poetry," *Speculum* 28 (1953): 446–67, called attention to this characteristic on an extensive scale, seeing, as it were, a "formula" behind every bush. Unfortunately, many of his disciples ignored the word *narrative* in his title and could not always agree on what a "formula" really was. In consequence, one of them was confident that he would find 4,000 formulas in *Beowulf* alone, a poem of 3,182 lines, or something better than a formula to every line. We have been hearing much less about this matter in the last quarter-century, chiefly because of the continuing indecision about what constitutes a formula. Mere repetition of a word or even a special phrase is hardly enough.

23. Gudmund Vigfusson, in *Grimm Festschrift* (Berlin, 1885), pp. 1–21. An actually more militant pioneer was Adolf Giesebrecht, "Ueber den Ursprung der Siegfriedssage," *Neues Jahrbuch der deutschen Sprache* 2 (1837) 203–34.

24. For the various works by Höfler and the theories contained therein, see bibliography, items 59, 60, and 61.

25. Bragi Boddason inn gamli, who flourished between 825 and 850, was a half-legendary poet who is considered by many the initiator of the tradition of skaldic verse. It is possible that he is the euhemeristic origin of the god of poetry, whose name was Bragi. The god is mentioned frequently by Snorri Sturluson in *The Prose Edda*.

26. The *þáttr* is defined as a story within a story.

27. E. V. Gordon, *Introduction to Old Norse*, rev.ed. (Oxford, 1957), p. 21.

28. The role played by Odin has, of course, been recognized from the beginning, and it is easy enough to say that he is a *deus ex machina* assisting the Völsungs as long as it suits his purpose to do so. One old explanation, offered by Adolf Rassmann, "Woden und die Nibelungen," *Germania* 26 (1881): 279–315, is that Odin favors the Nibelungs because of the insult visited upon him by Hreidmar, his captivity until the wergild is paid, and the harsh exaction of that same blood-money by both Hreidmar and Fafnir. The difficulty here is that Rassmann was oriented toward *The Nibelungenlied*, or at any rate toward the southern version of the story. It must not be forgotten that Odin concerns himself almost exclusively with Sigmund, Sigurd, and their forbears. See also n. 167 below. We have here another instance of the blindness to the Sigmund story in favor of the material on Sigurd as it appears in the Eddic poems, and Rassmann compounds the felony by observing that no other people in the world would think of having its highest god given the task of saving a family of heroes, a chosen group. This sounds most parochial, although in reality it is not. But did he never hear of Jehovah?

An interesting and far more recent study is that by Richard L. Harris, "Odin's Old Age," *Southern Folklore Quarterly* 33 (1969): 23–48. With the coming of Christianity, of course, Odin is gradually relegated to a minor figure even in Scandinavia: "The possibility of the Old Man is seen to be more likely when one considers . . . his degradation in the later Fornaldarsögur and . . . his mellowing in folklore to the point where he becomes a protector of the poor farmers of Iceland. He becomes a guardian of order as opposed to the spirit of disorder which he used to be." This is all very well, but Harris then applies this idea to the concept of the Old Man in Chaucer's *Pardoner's Tale*. This old man has been interpreted in various ways—as Death himself, as Experience, even as the Wandering Jew (see my *Legend of the Wandering Jew* [Providence, R.I., 1965], pp. 31–32). The point I must emphasize is that this figure in Chaucer's work is of truly epic stature and dignity, and no faded deity rambling around the countryside helping poor farmers. I see him as representing Old Age or Experience or both.

29. The translation of the stanzas from the *Gudrúnarhvöt* is mine.

The Saga of the Völsungs

Chapter 1

Here the story begins and tells us about a man who was called
Sigi, said to be a son of Odin. Another man should be named in
the story; he was called Skadi;[1] he was powerful and great in his
own right, yet Sigi was more powerful and of a more respected
family, such as men considered it in those days. Skadi had a thrall,
who is worth mentioning in the story and who was called Bredi.
He was wise in such matters as he should be wise in; he had prow-
ess of body and cleverness of mind equal to, even beyond, those
who were supposed to be of greater account.

Now we are told that one time Sigi went hunting with this
thrall and they chased wild beasts all day long until evening. And
when they had thus hunted together until evening, Bredi had a
larger bag, much more than Sigi, which displeased the latter very
much. He said that it was a wonder to him that a thrall should
have greater success in hunting than he. And so he leaped upon
Bredi and slew him and buried his body in a snowdrift.

Now Sigi went home that evening and said that Bredi had rid-
den away from him into the woods—"and he was suddenly out of
my sight, and I know nothing about him." Skadi was suspicious
of this story of Sigi's and guessed that he was being deceived, and
that Sigi must have killed Bredi. He took some men and went
looking for the latter. The search ended when they discovered
Bredi's body in a snowdrift. Skadi said that this snowbank should
be called Bredi's Snowbank from that time on, for it was a big
one.

And so it came out that Sigi had slain the thrall with
murderous intent, and so they proclaimed him a wolf in the holy
places,[2] and now he could not stay longer with his father. But

Odin followed him out of that land a long way, a very long way, and did not leave him until some ships had been found for him.

Then Sigi went warring with the company of men that his father had got for him before they parted, and he was victorious in his warring: such was his reward that he won for himself lands and a kingdom and made an important marriage, so that he became a powerful king and a great one, ruling over Hunland[3] as a very great warrior. He had by his wife a son called Rerir, who grew up with his father and became tall and valiant.

By now Sigi had become a man old in years. He had made many enemies, and these finally conspired against him—those whom he had trusted most, and they were his wife's brothers. They attacked him when he least expected it and had but few followers, and they overpowered him. In that battle Sigi fell, with all his men. His son, Rerir, had not been in that perilous adventure, but now he took so great a band of the friendly chieftains of his land that he recovered both land and kingship after his father Sigi. Now when he thought he had his kingdom well under his feet and felt secure, he remembered the feud that he had against his mother's brothers, who had killed his father. And so, as king, he gathered to himself a great troop and attacked his kinsmen with their army. (For they seem to have waged the feud first against him, although he valued their friendship but little in any case.) And so he did not leave until he had killed all of his father's slayers, even though it might be considered in every way an unfitting deed. Now he possessed land and kingship and wealth, getting for himself more than his father before him.

Thus Rerir won for himself much booty, and a wife who seemed fitting for him, and they lived together for a very long time, but they had no children or heirs. This pleased them not at all, and so they prayed to the gods with great earnestness that they might get for themselves a child.

It is said that Frigg heard their prayers and told Odin[4] what they were asking for. Odin was not without counsel, and so he took a Valkyrie[5] of his, the daughter of the giant Hrimnir,[6] and put an apple in her hand and bade her take it to the king. She took the apple and put on her crow's mantle[7] and flew to where the king was sitting on a mound. She let the apple fall beside the king's knee. He took the apple and seemed to understand what it meant. He went from the mound back to his men, found the queen, and she ate some of the apple with him.

Chapter 2

It is now to be told that the queen soon found that she was with child, and it went on for a long time that she could not give birth. Then it came to pass that Rerir had to go off to war, as is usual when a king has to protect his land, but from this expedition came the news that Rerir had been taken sick and was very near to death—and he had in mind to go home to Odin.[8] In those days that seemed to many a desirable thing.

Meanwhile it went on as before with the queen's illness: she could not give birth to her child, and this went on for six years. Now she decided that she could live no longer, and so she bade them cut out the child, and it was done as she had asked. It was a boychild, very well grown, as might be expected. It is said that the boy kissed his mother before she died. A name was given him; he was called Völsung. He succeeded his father as King of Hunland. He was very early tall and strong and bold in those things which test a man and pertain to manliness. He made himself into the greatest warrior and was always victorious in those battles he had in his war-making.

When Völsung was fully grown, the giant Hrimnir sent him his daughter Hljod,[9] who has been mentioned before; she was the one who had gone with the apple to Rerir, father of Völsung. So Völsung married her, and they were together for a long time, and their relationship was a happy one. They had ten sons and one daughter. Their oldest son was called Sigmund, and the daughter Signy—they were twins, most excellent and fairest of all children of King Völsung, in all respects. (Yet all of them were mighty in their own right, and it has long been kept alive in memory and celebrated, that the sons of Völsung were tall and proud and ahead of the greatest—as it is told in ancient poetry—both in knowledge and skill and all kinds of prowess.) Now it is said that King Völsung had built an excellent hall of such a kind that an oak stood within the hall, and the limbs of the tree stood out, fair with blossoms, over the hall-roof, while the trunk of the tree stood below in the hall. They called the tree Barnstock.[10]

Chapter 3

There was a king named Siggeir; he ruled over Gautland[11] and was a mighty king, with many followers. He came to meet King Völsung to ask for the hand of Signy. King Völsung and his sons liked his offer,[12] but she herself was unwilling. She asked for her father's advice, as she did in all matters concerning her. But it seemed to the king advisable to marry her off and so she pledged her troth to King Siggeir. Now when the wedding feast was to take place, King Siggeir went as guest to King Völsung's. The king prepared for the feast with the best of entertainment and when the banquet was all ready, the guests invited by both King Völsung and King Siggeir came on the appointed day, and King Siggeir had many worshipful men with him.

It is told also that great fires were kindled throughout the length of the hall, where the great appletree[13], Barnstock (as it is named above), was standing in the middle of the hall. Now it is said that when the men were sitting about the fire in the evening, a man came into the hall; he appeared to be a stranger. He was clothed thus: a spotted cloak over him, he was barefoot and wearing linen breeches laced at the knee, with a broad hat on his head. He was very hoary and aged and had only one eye. The man carried a sword in his hand. Going up to Barnstock, he brandished the sword and thrust it into the tree-trunk, so that the blade sank in up to the hilt. There was no greeting to this man from anyone there. So he spoke up:

"Whoever draws this sword from this tree-trunk, that man will receive it from me as a gift, and he shall prove to his satisfaction that he never bore in his hand a sword better than this one!"

After that the old man went out of the hall, and no one knew who he was or where he was going. But they stood up and did not hang back from grasping at the sword: he who first reached it would seem to have the advantage. The noblest went for it first, one after another, but none who grasped it could succeed in budging it in any way. Now Sigmund, son of Völsung the king, came up to it, and he grasped the sword and lifted it out of the tree-trunk, as if it were lying there loose for him. The weapon seemed so good that none could think of a sword as good as that. Siggeir offered to pay for it with three times its weight in gold.

But Sigmund said: "You could have taken up that sword as easily as I, while it was lying there, if it had been fitting for you to wear it. But now you will never get it, for I hold it already in my own hand—and that even if you offered me all the gold that you possess!"

King Siggeir was angered by these words, for it seemed to him a very scornful remark, but because he was very crafty, he acted as if he had not heard the speech. Yet that same evening he pondered a reward for those words, which later came to pass.

Chapter 4

Now it is to be told that Siggeir went to bed beside Signy that night, and the next day there was good weather. But then King Siggeir said that he wished to go home and not wait until the winds should strengthen or the sea become impassable. Nor is there any suggestion that King Völsung or his sons detained him, especially when they saw that King Siggeir wanted nothing so much as to leave the feasting.

But Signy said to her father: "I do not want to go away with Siggeir, nor do my thoughts about him laugh aloud. For I know, by my own foresight and by our guiding spirit, that from this marriage will come great sorrow, unless it is quickly broken off!"

"You must not say that, my daughter," he said, "because it will be a great reproach both to him and to us if we break off with him without cause. We shall have no claim to trust or friendship from him if this is truly broken off. For he will then repay us with evil as far as he can. It behooves us especially to hold up our part of the bargain."

None the less, King Siggeir prepared for his journey home, but before they left the wedding feast he invited his new father-in-law,

King Völsung, to his home in Gautland, in three months' time, and all his sons with him, and all the followers that he wished to have with him or that might be suitable to his honor. King Siggeir wished to make good for the fact that he had fallen short of his part in the wedding feast inasmuch as he had not been willing to stay there for more than one night, since it was not the custom to do thus. King Völsung therefore promised to make the journey and come on the appointed day. Then father-in-law and son-in-law parted and King Siggeir went home with his wife.

Chapter 5

Now it can be told of King Völsung and his sons that they went at the appointed time to Gautland, on the invitation of King Siggeir his son-in-law. They sailed from their land in three ships, all well manned, and they made a favorable sea-journey and came in their ships to Gautland. This was late in the evening. And that same evening Signy came, daughter of King Völsung, and called her father and brother to a place apart from the others. She straightway spoke her mind, telling of King Siggeir's intent—that he had collected an invincible band—"and he plans to betray you. Now I pray you," she said, "that you go back to your kingdom immediately and get as many men as you can and then come back here again to avenge yourselves. But do not get into trouble here now, because his treachery will not pass you by, unless you practice the strategy that I offered you."

Then said King Völsung: "All men can say in their own words that I gave my word, as an unborn child, and made this vow, that I would flee from neither fire nor iron because of fear, and so I have done even until now. And why should I not do the same also in my old age? And maidens shall not throw at my sons in mockery that they were afraid to die, because each one of us must die once, and no man can avoid death in his time. It is my counsel that we flee not at all, but do with our hands as bravely as we can. I have endured a hundred[14] battles, and I have had sometimes a greater troop and sometimes a lesser one, but I have always had victory, and it shall never be said that I would flee or sue for peace.''

But Signy wept sorely and asked that she not remain as wife to King Siggeir. King Völsung answered: ''You shall certainly go home to your husband and stay with him, however it may go with us!''

So Signy went home, and they prepared to follow her later that night. And in the morning, as soon as it was day, King Völsung ordered his men all to rise and go to land and prepare for a battle. And so they went ashore, all fully armed. They did not have long to wait before King Siggeir came with his whole troop, and between them there took place a most bitter battle. King Siggeir urged on his men to the attack most bravely, and it is said that King Völsung and his sons charged eight times through the ranks of King Siggeir's men during the day, and they hewed away with both arms. But as they were on the point of charging once more, King Völsung fell in the midst of his troops, and then all his men with him, except for the ten sons, because there was too much overstrength against them for them to withstand.

All the sons of Völsung were taken and put in bonds and led away. Signy was aware that her father had been slain and her brothers taken in hand and condemned to death. So she called to King Siggeir to speak to him alone, saying:

''I will ask this of you, that you not have my brothers slain too soon. Let them rather sit for a while in the stocks. For it has occurred to me, as the saying goes, that the eye is pleased with what it still sees. So I do not ask for anything more, for I know it would not help to do so.''

Siggeir then answered: 'You are mad and without understanding when you demand greater torment for your brothers than that they be hewed down on the spot. However, this I will grant to you, because this seems to me better that they should suffer worse and endure more agony before death.''

So he let it be done as she had asked, and a great set of stocks was taken and placed on the feet of the ten brothers at a certain place in the forest, and so they sat there all that day until night. Then at midnight there came an old she-wolf at them from out of the woods, while they were sitting in the stocks. She was both huge and horrible, and she straightway bit one of the brothers to death. After that she ate him all up and went back into the woods.

The next morning Signy sent to her brothers a man whom she trusted very much, to find out what might have happened. He came back and told her that one of the brothers was dead. It seemed to her a heavy sorrow, that they would probably all fare thus and she not be able to help them. It is a short matter to tell: nine nights in all, this same she-wolf came around midnight and straightway bit one brother to death and ate him, until all were dead except for Sigmund. But now before the tenth night came, Signy sent her trusted servant to her brother Sigmund. She put some honey in the man's hand and told him to smear it on Sigmund's face and lay some of it in his mouth. So he went to Sigmund and did what he had been told to do, and then he went home.

The next night this same she-wolf came, as was her wont, intending to bite Sigmund to death as his brothers before him, but this time she smelled the honey that had been smeared on him, and licked his face all over and reached with her tongue into his mouth. Sigmund did not let his courage fail him; rather he bit back on the she-wolf's tongue. She started back, pulling hard and bracing herself with her feet against the stock. But then the tongue of that she-wolf came out by the roots, and from that she got her death. It still is the saying of some that this she-wolf was in fact the mother of King Siggeir, who had changed herself into this shape through trolldom and witchery.

Chapter 6

Now Sigmund found himself free, and the stock shattered, so he got himself away into the woods. Signy meanwhile sent to find out what had happened to him, or whether he was indeed alive. When the messengers came, he told them all that had happened, and how it had fared with him and the she-wolf. And so they went back and told Signy what had taken place. She went out and found her brother, and they took counsel, deciding that he should build himself an earth-house[15] there in the forest. And so it went for a

time: Signy concealed him there and carried to him what he need-
ed, and King Siggeir thought that all the Völsungs were dead.

Now it happened that King Siggeir had two sons by his wife,[16]
and it was said of them that when the older was ten years old,
Signy sent him to meet Sigmund and give him help if he should
wish in some way to avenge his father. The boy went into the
forest and came, late in the evening, to Sigmund's earth-house.
Sigmund received him well and fittingly and told him to make
bread for them—"for I wish to look for firewood"—and put in
the boy's hand a bag of meal. Then Sigmund went to look for
some firewood, but when he returned, the boy had still done
nothing about his bread-making. Sigmund asked him if the bread
was made.

The boy said: "I dared not pick up that bag of meal, because
some sort of living creature lay in the meal."

Sigmund thought he was pretty sure that this boy would not be
brave enough that he should wish him to accompany him. And so
when they next met, Sigmund and his sister, Sigmund said that
he was no nearer to having a man's help even though the boy
might be with him.

Signy said: "Take him and kill him; he need not live longer!"
And so he did. The year passed, and the year after that Signy sent
her younger son to meet Sigmund. The story need not be drawn
out: it all went as before. He slew this boy too, at the bidding of
Signy.

Chapter 7

On a certain occasion it came to pass, while Signy was sitting in
her bower,[17] that there came to her a certain witch-woman greatly
skilled in sorcery. Signy said to her: "I wish that we two would
change shapes!" The witch-woman said: "That is for you to
decide." So she brought it about by her magic tricks that the two
changed shapes, and the witch-woman seated herself in Signy's
place, according to the latter's wish, and went to bed with the
king that night, but he did not discover that it was not Signy
beside him. As for Signy, she went to her brother's earth-house

and asked him to grant her lodging for the night—''because I have lost my way out of the forest and do not know where I am going.''

Sigmund said that she should stay, for he would not deny hospitality to her, a woman, and knew that she would not reward his good promise by speaking against him.[18] And so she came into his house and they sat down to eat. He glanced at her often; she seemed to be a handsome, fair woman. When they had finished eating, he told her that he wished her to share a bed with him that night. She did not refuse, and he laid her beside him for three nights altogether.

After that she went home and met the witch-woman and asked that they change back their shapes, and so she did. And when due time had passed, Signy gave birth to a boy-child. He was called Sinfjötli.[19] When he had grown up, he was both tall and strong and fair of face, very much in the likeness of a Völsung. He was not quite ten years old when Signy sent him to Sigmund in the earth-house. She had made a test of her former sons before she had sent them to Sigmund: she sewed a seam in their arms through flesh and skin. They had suffered it ill and cried out when she did it. But when she did this to Sinfjötli, he did not even wince. She stripped him out of his kirtle, so that the skin followed the sleeves. She asked him if this had not been painful, but he replied:

''Such pain seems little to a Völsung!''

So now this boy went to Sigmund, who bade him knead some bread, while he went out for firewood, putting first into Sinfjötli's hand a bag of meal. He went into the forest and when he came back after a while, Sinfjötli had finished baking the bread. Then Sigmund asked if he had found anything in the bag of meal. Said Sinfjötli: ''I am not without some suspicion that there was something alive in the meal, when first I began to knead it, but now I have kneaded into the meal whatever there was in it.'' Sigmund replied, laughing: ''I do not intend that you should eat that bread this evening, because you have kneaded into it a most venomous snake!''

(Sigmund was so powerful in his own way that he could eat poison and not harm himself, and for Sinfjötli it was allowed that poison could not harm him from without, but it was not granted him to eat it or drink it.)

Chapter 8

Now it is said that Sigmund considered Sinfjötli still too young to wreak vengeance with him, and so he decided first to accustom him to some hardship. So they ranged far and wide through the woods and killed men for their money. The boy seemed to Sigmund much like the other sons of Völsung, but he still thought he was the son of Siggeir and that he therefore had the ill-nature of his father combined with the energy of the Völsungs. Still, it seemed to him that Sinfjötli did not have much regard for his kinsmen, because he often kept reminding Sigmund of his grief and urged him very strongly to kill King Siggeir.

Now once on a certain occasion Sigmund and Sinfjötli ranged farther than ever into the woods to get riches for themselves; they found a hut and two men with heavy gold rings asleep inside the hut. They had been bewitched, because there were wolf-skins hanging over them, and only on every tenth half-day[20] could they come out of those skins. They were both the sons of kings. Sigmund and Sinfjötli put on those wolf-skins, and could not come out of them to resume their human shapes and natures, until the time described before. Now they uttered wolf-howls, yet they could distinguish each other's voices. They betook themselves into the forest, each of them going his own way. They had agreed between themselves, however, that they would attack though there were seven against them, but not more, for then he who was being attacked should utter his wolf-howl.

"Let us stick to this plan," said Sigmund, "because you are still young and rash, and so men will think it easy to hunt you."

So each of them went his way, and when they had separated, Sigmund found seven men (and perhaps more[20]); in any case he uttered the wolf-howl. When Sinfjötli heard it, he came immediately and killed all of Sigmund's opponents. Again they separated. When Sinfjötli had gone not far into the forest, he came upon eleven men and fought them, and did so well that he disposed of them all, but he was very much exhausted and went to rest under an oak.

Sigmund came up to him and asked: "Why did you not call out?"

Sinfjötli replied: "You had help in the slaying of seven men, and I am but a child in years beside you, but I did not call for help to kill eleven men!"

Sigmund leaped upon him in anger so hard that Sinfjötli staggered and fell, and Sigmund bit him in the windpipe. (That day was not one when they could come out of their wolf-skins.) Sigmund laid Sinfjötli on his back and bore him into the hut, and sat over him and bade the trolls take over the wolf-skins.

One day Sigmund noticed two weasels; one of them bit the other in the windpipe. Then it ran into the woods and brought out a leaf, which it applied to the wound, and the other weasel sprang up all whole. Sigmund went out and saw a raven flying toward him, bearing him a certain leaf. So he put the leaf on Sinfjötli's wound, and he sprang up at once all whole, as if he had never been wounded. After that they went back to their earthhouse until the time came for them to get out of their wolf-skins.[21] These they took and burned, so that they could never again bring bad luck to anyone. (In their bewitched shapes they had done many a heroic deed in King Siggeir's realm.)

Thus when Sinfjötli was full-grown, Sigmund thought he had been well tested. It was no long time thereafter when Sigmund decided to go about avenging his father, if it could be brought about. And so on a certain day they left their earth-house and came to the dwelling of King Siggeir. It was late in the evening. They went into an outer room which was in the front of the hall.[22] There were ale-vats within; there they hid themselves.

Signy and the king had two children young in years; they were playing on the floor of the hall with a gold ring. The ring rolled along the floor of the hall, and they ran after it. As the ring rolled farther and farther, they came to where Sigmund and Sinfjötli were. One of the boys started in to look for the ring when he saw two men, great and grim, sitting there. They had helmets over their faces and were wearing white byrnies. The boy leaped back into the hall in front of his father and told him what he had seen. The king realized that there must be treason against him. Signy heard what they were saying; she rose and took both children into the outer room to Sigmund and Sinfjötli and told them they had been informed on—"and I advise you to kill the children."

Sigmund said: "I will not slay your children, even though they have informed on me." But Sinfjötli did not falter and raised his sword and slew both children and cast their bodies into the hall before King Siggeir. The king now stood up and called his men, ordering them to seize the warriors who had concealed themselves in the outer room that evening. The men immediately leaped in from without and tried to lay hands on Sigmund and Sinfjötli, but they defended themselves well and manfully: the ones nearest them got by far the worst of it. After a time, however, they were borne down and seized and finally put in chains. They sat there all night.

Now the king pondered what sort of death he could give them which would be the most long-drawn-out. When morning came, he had a hollow mound built out of loose stones and turf, and when it was ready, he had a great flat stone placed in the middle of this mound, so that one surface of the stone showed above and the other beneath. This was so large that it touched the two walls inside the mound so that no one could get past it.[23] Then he had Sigmund and Sinfjötli taken and placed in the vault, each one on opposite sides of the flat stone, for he thought it worse for them if they should not be together and yet each could hear the other. While they were covering the vault with turf, Signy came to them. She had some straw in her arms which she threw into the vault to Sinfjötli, and at the same time told the servants that they should hide this action from the king. They agreed to that, whereupon the vault was closed. Then, when night came, Sinfjötli said to Sigmund:

"I do not think that we shall be short of food for a while. The queen has thrown some meat into this vault, wrapped in straw." He groped around further in the food and discovered Sigmund's sword thrust in with it. He recognized it by its hilt, for it was dark in the mound. When he told Sigmund, they both rejoiced. Then Sinfjötli thrust with the point of the sword above the slab and pulled hard. The sword bit into the stone. Sigmund took the sword-point on his side and together they sawed the rock between them, not stopping until the cutting was done, as it is told:[24]

> They cut with might the great flat stone,
> Did Sigmund and Sinfjötli with the sword.

And now they were free together, for they had cut through stone and iron in the mound and come out of that vault. They went back to the hall. The men there were all asleep. Sigmund and Sinfjötli carried wood to the hall and laid fire to it. Those within wakened from the smoke and saw the hall in flames above them. The king asked who started the fire. "We two here, myself and Sinfjötli, my sister's son," cried Sigmund, "and we intend to let you know that not all the Völsungs are dead!"

He bade his sister come out and receive from him good esteem and much honor, for he wished to make good her troubles.[25]

But she answered: "Now you must know how I have held against King Siggeir the slaying of King Völsung. I let our children be killed because they seemed to me too slow to avenge my father. And I went into the woods to you in the shape of a witch-woman, and Sinfjötli is our son. He has therefore great might, for he is the son of both a son and a daughter of King Völsung. I have worked to this end in every way: that King Siggeir should be brought to death. I have striven so much to come to this revenge that under no conditions will life be livable hereafter. I will now die willingly with King Siggeir, whom I married under compulsion!"

Then she kissed her brother Sigmund and Sinfjötli and walked into the fire, bidding them farewell. There she received death, along with King Siggeir and all his troop.

* * * * * *

The kinsmen[26] got themselves men and ships. Sigmund held his heritage and drove out of the land the king who had set himself up after the death of King Völsung.

Sigmund then made himself into a king both rich and famous, wise and ambitious. He took a wife named Borghild. They had two sons: one was called Helgi and the other Hámund. When Helgi was born, the Norns[27] came and made him a prophecy. They said he would become most famous of all kings. Sigmund had come from a battle and went to see his son with a leek,[27] and therewith he gave him the name Helgi and these gifts at his natal feast:[28] Hringstadi and Solfjöll and a sword. He bade him have good success and grow as one of the Völsung family.

Helgi became in time great-hearted and happy in his friends and best among all men in all accomplishments. It is told that he undertook a war-expedition when he was fifteen years old. Helgi became chief over the men in arms, and Sinfjötli was also entrusted with that duty. Both ruled over the band of warriors.

Chapter 9

Now it is told that Helgi met a king in his warring whose name was Hunding. He was a mighty king with many followers who ruled over many lands. It came to battle between them, and Helgi pressed hard on Hunding. The day of battle ended by Helgi's coming away with the victory, and King Hunding falling, with a great part of his band. Helgi now thought that he had grown great, since he had slain so mighty a king. But the sons of Hunding called out an army to meet Helgi and try to avenge their father. They had a hard battle, but Helgi charged through the ranks of the enemy and sought out the standard of the sons of King Hunding, slaying these sons of Hunding: Alf and Eyjolf, Hervard and Hagbard. Thus he got himself a famous victory.

While he was coming from battle, he met by a forest many women of noble appearance, yet one exceeded them all as they rode along in their fine attire. Helgi asked their leader for her name. She called her Sigrún and said that she was the daughter of King Högni.[29]

Helgi said: "Come over here to me and welcome!"

Then the king's daughter replied: "I have another task to do before I drink with you!"

Helgi asked: "What task is that, king's daughter?"

She replied: "King Högni has promised me to Hoddbrod, son

of King Granmar, but I have sworn that I would as soon marry a young crow as marry him, and yet this will come to pass unless you can prevent him by going against him with warriors and then taking me away, for I have no wish to live with any other king than you.''

"Be happy, king's daughter," he said. "Much better that we should try each other's valor than that you be married to him, you who excel others. I will lay my life on it.''

After that Helgi sent men with gifts of money to summon his warriors and called all his troops together at Raudabjarg. There Helgi waited until a great fleet had come to him from Hedensey and a mighty army from Norvasund,[30] with fine large ships. Then King Helgi called to his steersman named Leif, and asked if he had counted their host. He replied: "It is not easy to count them, my lord. The ships that have come from Norvasund have on them twelve thousand men, and the others half as many more.'' King Helgi told him that they should turn into the fjord called Varinsfjord, and so they did.

Now a great storm came upon them, and so heavy a sea that the sound of the waves dashing against the sides of the ships was as if mountains were crashing together in sport. Helgi told them all not to be afraid and not to reef their sails, rather to set them higher than before. Even so they were near to going over before they came to land. Then Sigrun, daughter of King Högni, came down from the land above with a large retinue, and guided them into a good harbor called At-Gnipalund.[31] The men on land watched these happenings, and the brother of King Hoddbrod, who ruled there, also came down from the land above, which is called Svaringshaug. He shouted to them, asking who was in command of this great army. Sinfjötli stood up; he had on his head a helmet polished like glass and wore a byrnie white as snow; he held a spear in his hand with a splendid banner on it, and before him was a gold-striped shield. He knew how to talk with kings.

He spoke thus:[32] "When you have finished feeding your swine and your hounds, tell your wife that the Völsungs have come here, and one will find King Helgi in the host, if Hoddbrod wishes to meet him. It will be his pleasure to fight bravely while you are kissing maidservants by the fire.''

Granmar replied: "You cannot know much worthwhile speech, or much of ancient things, you who tell lies about princes. It would be more accurate to say that you must have fed yourself out in the woods on wolf's food and killed your brothers. It is indeed remarkable that you dare to come in the same army with brave men, you who have sucked the blood from many a cold corpse."

Sinfjötli answered: "You cannot clearly remember now when you were a witch-woman in Varinsey and said you wanted to have a man and chose me for that service. Later you were a Valkyrie in Asgard,[33] and it almost happened that everybody had to fight on account of you. I begot on you nine wolves in Laganess and was indeed the father of them all."

Granmar answered: "You certainly know how to lie! I doubt that you could be anyone's father, for you were castrated by the giant's daughter on Thorsness, and you are the bastardly 'stepson' of King Siggeir, and ran out in the woods with wolves, and you committed all kinds of shameful deeds. You killed your brothers and made yourself notorious for your wickedness."

Sinfjötli replied: "Do you remember when you were a mare with the steed Grani,[34] and I rode you at a gallop on Bravell.[35] Later you were a goatherd for the giant Golnir."

Granmar remarked: "I would rather sate birds with your corpse than have anything more to do with you."

Then King Helgi interrupted: "It would be better for you both, and wiser counsel, to fight than to say such things, which are a shame to hear. The sons of Granmar are no friends of mine, and yet they are brave men."

Granmar then rode away to meet with King Hoddbrod at the place called Solfjöll. Their steeds were called Sveipud and Sveggjud. They met at the gate of Hoddbrod's stronghold and talked over reports about the war. King Hoddbrodd was wearing a byrnie and had a helmet on his head. He asked who these invaders might be—"and why are you so angry?"

Granmar replied: "The Völsungs have come here; they have twelve thousand men on the shore and seven thousand on the island called Sok, and there at the place called Grind is the greatest force of all. I think that Helgi intends to fight us now."

The king said: "Let us summon men from our whole kingdom and prepare to meet them! Let no one who can fight sit at home! Send word to the sons of Hring and to King Högni and to Alf the Old; they are great warriors!"

They met at a place called Frekastein and began a bitter fight. Helgi charged through the ranks; there was great slaughter. Then they saw a large band of shield-maidens who appeared as if they were afire. With them was the king's daughter, Sigrún. Helgi attacked King Hoddbrod and killed him beneath his banner.

Then Sigrún said: "Have thanks for that brave deed! These lands must now be changed! For me this is a very lucky day, and you will receive from this honor and glory, for you have slain so mighty a king!"

Thus King Helgi took over the kingdom and dwelt there a long time. He married Sigrún and made himself into a famous king and well-known, but hereafter he has nothing to do with this Saga.

Chapter 10

The Völsungs now went home, having added much to their fame. Sinfjötli betook himself once again to making war. He saw a fair woman and wished very much to wed her, but a brother of Borghild, the wife of King Sigmund, had already asked for this woman. This forced matters to a fight, and Sinfjötli slew that prince. He now went harrying far and wide in many battles, and always won a victory. He became the most famous and glorious of men. In the autumn he came home with many ships and great booty. He told his father what had happened, and Sigmund reported it to the queen. She ordered Sinfjötli out of the kingdom, saying that she did not wish to see him again. But Sigmund told him not to go away, offering to make good to her the killing of her brother with gold and great riches, even though he had never before offered amends to anyone. He said that it did no good to quarrel with a woman. She could not bring about what she desired, so she said: "It is up to you, my lord, to decide what is fitting."

So she now made ready a funeral feast for her brother, with the consent of the king. She prepared the feast with the best of means and invited many important guests to it. Borghild brought drinks to the men. She came before Sinfjötli with a great drinking-horn, saying to him: "Drink now, stepson!"

He took the horn and looked into it and said: "This drink is bewitched!"[36] Sigmund said: "Give it to me!" He drank of it. The queen said: "Why should other men drink their ale before you?"

So she came again with the horn: "Drink now!" And she taunted him with many words. He took the horn and said: "This drink is treacherous!"

Sigmund said again: "Give it to me!"

A third time she came and bade him drink up, if he had the courage of the Völsungs.

Sinfjötli took the horn and exclaimed: "Poison is in this drink!"

Sigmund said: "Let your moustache strain the drink, son!" He said this when he was very drunk, and that is why. Sinfjötli drank and immediately fell dead. Sigmund rose up, and his grief was such that it brought him near to death. He took the body in his arms and bore it into the forest, coming finally to the shore of a firth.[37] There he saw a man in a little boat, who asked if he wished to be ferried over the firth. But the boat was so small that it could not hold them all, and so the body was floated off first, while Sigmund went along the shore of the firth. And soon thereafter the boat and the man also disappeared from Sigmund's sight, and so he turned back home. He drove away the queen, and in a little while she died.

King Sigmund ruled still over his kingdom and is considered to have been the greatest warrior and king in former times.

Chapter 11

There was a mighty and famous king named Eylimi. His daughter was called Hjördis, fairest and wisest of all women. King Sigmund heard of her and decided that she was suitable for him, and no other. So he paid a visit to King Eylimi, who prepared a great feast for him, understanding that he did not come as an enemy. Messages passed between them, and everything passed in friendship, not in hostility. The feast itself was prepared with the best means, and many guests were invited. For King Sigmund a market was set up nearly everywhere,[38] and other comforts for traveling. When they came to the feast, both kings were assigned to one hall.

Lyngvi, son of King Hunding, also came there; he too wished to become the son-in-law of King Eylimi. It was clear to Eylimi that the two, Sigmund and Lyngvi, could not both be successful, and he felt instinctively that fighting would be imminent if the matter did not come off well.

So the king said to his daughter: "You are a wise woman, and I have told you that you are to choose a husband for yourself. Make your choice between these two kings, and I will agree with your decision."

She replied: "This business is difficult for me; however, I choose the king who is more famous, and that is King Sigmund, although he is much advanced in years." Therefore she was married to Sigmund, and King Lyngvi departed. Each day following that there was a bigger feast and more guests than before. Afterward King Sigmund went back to Hunland with King Eylimi, his new father-in-law, and Sigmund once more took care of his kingdom.

King Lyngvi and his brother, however, gathered an army for themselves to go against King Sigmund, because they had always had the worse in such affairs,[39] and again the matter had been decided against them, and besides, they wanted to overcome the pride of the Völsungs. So they came into Hunland but sent word ahead to King Sigmund that they had no intention of taking him unawares but that they were sure he would not flee from them. King Sigmund agreed that they would come to battle. He too drew up his forces, and Hjördis was sent into the forest with a maid-servant, and much treasure went with them. She stayed there while they fought.

The vikings leaped from their ships in an invincible band. King Sigmund and King Eylimi set up their battle-standards, and the war horns blew. King Sigmund called for the horn that his father had possessed and urged on his men. He had a much smaller force, but he joined now in a hard battle, and although he might be old, still he fought hard and was always the foremost of his men; no shield nor byrnie could hold against him, and he charged continually against the band of his enemies all day long. Indeed, none could see how things were going. Many a spear was in the air there, and many an arrow. And Sigmund's guardian-women[40] protected him so well that he was not wounded, and no one knew the count of those many men who had fallen before him. Both his arms were bloodied to the shoulders.

When the fight had lasted for this long a time, there came a man into the fight wearing a broad hat and a blue cloak; he had but one eye, and a spear was in his hand.[41] This man came toward King Sigmund and lifted up his spear before him. When King Sigmund hewed hard with his sword, it met the spear and broke asunder into two parts. After that the slaughter changed sides, and King Sigmund's good fortune disappeared, and many of his band fell in front of him. The king made no effort to protect himself but urged on his troops most valiantly. But now, as it is said, "None can avail against the many." In this battle finally fell King Sigmund and his father-in-law, King Eylimi, in the front rank of their followers, and the greater part of their men.

Chapter 12

King Lyngvi now sought the king's dwelling, intending to take away the King's daughter,[42] but in that he failed—he got for himself neither woman nor wealth. So he traveled about the land, dividing the kingdom among his men. He thought that he had now killed all the Völsungs and was sure no man need fear them any more.

Hjördis went by night to the field of the slain after the battle and came to where King Sigmund lay. She asked if he could be healed, but he answered:

"Many a man keeps living although there is little hope, but my good fortune has left me. So I will not let myself be healed; Odin does not wish me to draw my sword again, for it is now broken. I have had my battles while it pleased him.''

She said: ''Nothing would be lacking for me, if you could only become healed and avenge my father.''

The king said: ''That is destined for another. You go now with a boy-child. Bring him up well and carefully, and the boy will become famous, the most distinguished of our family. Preserve as well these sword-fragments, from which can be made a good sword that will be called Gram. Our son will bear it and will accomplish many mighty deeds with it, the memory of which will never grow old, and his name will be exalted as long as the world endures. Now be content with that. Now my wounds have exhausted me, and I will now seek my kinsmen who have gone before.''

Still Hjördis sat over him until he died, and it grew light in the dawn. Then she saw many ships coming close to land and said to her maid-servant: ''Let us change our clothes, and you shall be named by my name and call yourself the king's daughter.'' And they did so.

The vikings on their arrival took a look at the great slaughter of men, and they saw also the two women going into the woods. They decided that this must be a matter of some importance, and so they leaped ashore. This band was led by Alf, son of King Hjalprek of Denmark. He had been sailing along the coast with his troop. Now they looked once more at the battlefield where they saw the great slaughter of men. The prince now ordered the band to seek out the women, and so they did. He asked who they might be, but things did not quite turn out as expected. The maid-servant had an answer for both of them and told of the fall of King Sigmund and King Eylimi and of many another brave man, and told also who had been responsible for all this. The prince asked whether they knew where the king's treasure had been concealed. The maid-servant answered: ''It is rather to be expected that we should know,'' and showed them the treasure. There they found great riches, so much that the men thought they had never seen so much gathered in one place, or more costliness. They carried it off to Alf's ship; Hjördis followed, and also the maid-servant.

Then Alf went home to his kingdom, acknowledging that the

kings who had fallen there were most distinguished. The prince seated himself in the stern of the ship, and the women amidships. He conversed with them and paid attention to what they said. Soon the prince came home to his realm with the great treasure. Alf was the most accomplished of men. When they had been home for a short time, the queen his mother asked him: "Why has this beautiful woman fewer rings and poorer clothes? It certainly seems to me she must be the higher in social rank whom you have taken to be the lower."

He answered: "I have suspected that there is not the quality of a maid-servant in her, for when we met she greeted me easily in her welcome to a nobleman. Now I shall make a test." Soon came a time for drinking. Then the prince entered into conversation with the women and said:

"What do you have to mark the passing of time when the night grows old, if you cannot see the stars in the heavens?"

The maid-servant answered: "We have this sign for that: in my youth I was accustomed to drink much at dawn, but since I have left off drinking, I awaken still at the same time, and that is my sign."

The prince smiled and said: "That was a bad habit for a king's daughter."

Then he sought Hjördis and asked her the very same question. She answered: "My father gave me a little gold ring of such a nature that it grows cold on my finger at dawn. That is my sign thereof."

The prince replied: "There was enough gold there, for the maid-servants were wearing it, but you have concealed the truth from me long enough! I should have acted towards you as if we two were both of us children of a king if only you had told me. But I shall trust you now even better, for you shall be my wife, and I will pay you a marriage-dowry when you have borne your child."

She answered him by telling him the whole truth about her situation. Thenceforth she was held in great honor and considered the noblest of women.

Chapter 13

Now it must be told that Hjördis gave birth to a boy child, and this boy was brought up by King Hjalprek. The king himself rejoiced when he saw the bright eyes that the child bore in his head, saying that no one would be in any way like him or even equal to him. The child was sprinkled with water and given the name of Sigurd. All have said the same about him: that in breeding and stature none was his peer. He was reared there by King Hjalprek with great love, and when the most famous men and kings in the ancient sagas are all named, Sigurd will stand first as to strength and skill, bravery and doughtiness, which he possessed above every other man in the northern regions of the earth.

Meanwhile Hjalprek betrothed Hjördis, and Prince Alf was given her hand.

Regin was the name of Sigurd's foster-father;[43] he was the son of Hreidmar. He taught him various crafts, chess, runes,[44] and many tongues to speak, as was customary for the son of a king, as well as many other things. Once, when the two of them were together, Regin asked Sigurd if he knew how much treasure his father had possessed and who was guarding it. Sigurd answered that the kings[45] were taking care of it.

"Do you trust them that much?" asked Regin.

Sigurd replied: "It is only fit and proper that they should guard it until it becomes useful to me, because they know how to watch over it better than I."

Another time Regin came talking to Sigurd, saying: "It is strange that you should be a stable-boy of the king's and go about looking like a tramp."

Sigurd answered: "That is not so, because I take counsel with them in all matters, and whatever I want is granted me."

Regin said: "Ask him to give you a horse!"

"It will be at once as I wish," answered Sigurd.

So Sigurd went immediately before the king. Hjalprek said to him: "What is it that you want from us?"

"I want a horse for my pleasure," replied Sigurd.

The king said: "Choose yourself a horse, whichever one you wish, from our possessions."

The next day Sigurd went into the woods and met an old man with a long beard who was a stranger. He asked Sigurd where he was going.

"I am going to choose a horse," said Sigurd. "Give me a suggestion."

The man said: "Let us go and drive all the horses to the river, which is called Busiltjörn."

So they drove the horses into deep water, and all but one of them headed for shore. He was the one Sigurd took: he was gray in color and young in years, grown large and fair. No one had mounted him yet.

The bearded man observed: "This horse is sprung from Sleipnir,[46] and he must be carefully brought up, because he is to become better than any other horse." Then the man disappeared.

Sigurd called the horse Grani, and the horse was excellent. It was Odin whom he had met.

Now Regin said to Sigurd: "You have far too little wealth. I am sorry to see you running around like the village-boys. It happens, however, that I know of a magnificent opportunity for treasure that I can tell you about. For there is great honor in seeking it and even greater if you could attain it." Sigurd asked where it might be and who was guarding it.

Regin answered: "He is named Fafnir, and he lies a short distance from here at a place call Gnitaheath. When you go there, you will have to admit that you never saw more riches in gold in one place. You would never need more, though you became the oldest and most famous of kings."

Sigurd replied: "I have heard of the nature of this dragon, though I may be young, and I have learned that no one dares go against him because of his size and his wickedness."

Regin replied: "That is not so; his size is about that of a lingworm,[47] made out to be much greater than it really is, and that is how it would have appeared to your kinsmen before you. Although the blood of the Völsungs is in you, you do not seem to have their spirit, because they are accounted foremost in all things."

Sigurd replied: "Maybe I do not have much of their bravery or skill, but I see no reason for you to taunt me, for I am scarcely out of my childhood. Why are you egging me on so much?''

Regin answered: ''There is a tale to be told, and I will tell you.''

Sigurd said: ''Let me hear it!''

Chapter 14

''This is the beginning of my tale: my father was called Hreidmar, a great man and rich. His son was named Fafnir, and another was named Otr, and I was the third, least in accomplishments and appearance. I could work in iron and silver and gold, and I made all sorts of things that might be useful in any way. My brother Otr had another occupation and another nature: he was a great hunter and surpassed other men in this, and he could also assume the likeness of an otter by day, when he was always in the water catching fishes in his mouth. He would bear his catch to his father and was a great help to him. (This shape of an otter was often on him.) He would come home late and eat by himself, blinking his eyes because he could not see well on dry land. Fafnir was by far the biggest and grimmest of us, and he considered everything that was, to be his own.

''There was a dwarf named Andvari''—continued Regin— ''who was always in a waterfall called Andvarafors. There he assumed the likeness of a pike and got his food, because there was a mass of fish there in the waterfall. My brother Otr also went into the waterfall and caught up fish in his mouth and always laid them on the bank.

''One time Odin, Loki and Hœnir[48] went their way and came to Andvarafors. Otr had taken a salmon and was eating it, blinking as usual, on the bank of the river. Loki took a stone and struck Otr and killed him. These Æsir thought themselves very lucky in their quarry and flayed the otter. That evening they came to Hreidmar's and showed him their trophy. Then we took them all captive and laid on them payment of blood-money and ransom. They were to fill the hide with gold and cover it on the outside with red gold. So they sent Loki to find them the gold. He came to Ran[49] and fetched her net; then he went back to Andvarafors and

cast the net before the pike, and it leaped into the net.
''Then Loki said:

Reginsmál, stanza 1	'What is this fish that runs in the flood And cannot guard itself against punishment? Will you redeem your head from Hel[50] And fine me the flame of waters'[51]
Reginsmál, stanza 2	'Andvari I am called, Oinn my father Into many a waterfall have I fared For me, luckless, in days of yore, The Norn decreed I should swim in water.'

''Loki saw the gold that Andvari possessed. But when he had counted and weighed this gold, he had a ring left over, and Loki took this from him. The dwarf went into a hollow stone and said that it would be death for whoever should own that gold ring, to say nothing of the gold itself. The Æsir counted out the treasure for Hreidmar and stuffed up the otter's hide and then set it on its feet. Then the Æsir also piled up gold beside it and covered it from the outside, and when that was done, Hreidmar went up to it and saw one whisker, and bade them cover even that. Then Odin took a ring, Andvaranaut, from his hand and covered that whisker. Then Loki said:

Reginsmál, stanza 6	'Gold is now yielded you, and you have paid Much for my head. To your son No good fortune is shaped; it is death to you both!'

''Afterwards Fafnir slew his father,'' said Regin, ''by murder, and I gained nothing from the treasure. He behaved so badly that he finally took himself off, and still later he became a very evil dragon. Now he sits on the treasure. Later I went to the king and became his smith. Now that is the gist of my story, how I lost my father's heritage and my brother's wergild. The gold has ever since been called Otr's Ransom, and it has served as an example.''

Sigurd replied: ''You have lost much, and your kinsmen have been very wicked. Now make me a sword with your skill, better than any other, and I will perform a mighty deed, if my spirit avails. Do this, if you want me to kill that mighty dragon.''

Regin said: "That will I do, and with confidence, for you will be able to slay Fafnir with this sword."

Chapter 15

Regin made the sword and put it in Sigurd's hand. He grasped it, saying: "This is your smithing,[52] Regin!" When he hewed down on the anvil, the sword broke; he threw the blade aside and told him to forge a better one. So Regin made another sword and brought it to Sigurd. He looked at it. "This one should please you," said Regin, "but it is a hard thing to be your smith!" Sigurd tested the sword, but it broke like the first one.

Then he said to Regin: "You must be like your kinsmen before you—unreliable!"

So he went to his mother. She received him affectionately, and they talked and drank together.

Then Sigurd said: "Is it true what I heard, that King Sigmund gave you the sword Gram in two pieces?"

"That is true," she answered.

Sigurd said: "Put the pieces in my hand; I want them."

She said that he was very likely to win fame from them and brought him the sword-fragments.

Then Sigurd met Regin again and ordered him to make a sword from the pieces, as good a one as possible. Regin grew angry, but went to the smithy with the fragments. He thought that Sigurd was over-anxious about his smithing, but he made a sword, and when he bore it from the hearth of the forge, it seemed to his apprentices that fire was flaming from the edges. He bade Sigurd take the sword, saying that he would not know how to make a better one if this one should fail.

Sigurd struck on the anvil with the sword, and it clove the anvil all the way to its base without breaking or shattering the blade in any part. He therefore praised the sword highly and went down to the river with a shred of wool. This he cast into the stream, and it came asunder when he held the blade against it. This sent Sigurd home happy.

Regin said: "Now you must fulfill your promise, and go meet Fafnir, for I have made a sword for you."

Sigurd replied: "I will do it, but not before my father is avenged."

(Sigurd was beloved by all as he grew older, and every child was especially inclined to him in devotion.)

Chapter 16

Gripir was the name of Sigurd's mother's brother. A little while after the sword was finished, Sigurd went to visit Gripir, because he had knowledge of the future and knew beforehand the fate of every human being. Sigurd was seeking to learn how his life would go. Gripir, however, took a long time before answering and finally replied to the earnest entreaty of Sigurd and told all his future, even as it came to pass afterward. Then, when Gripir had told these things, as Sigurd had wished him to do, Sigurd rode home. Soon after that he and Regin met again.

Regin said: "Slay Fafnir, as you promised!"

Sigurd replied: "I shall do that, but another thing first: to avenge King Sigmund and my other kinsmen who fell in that battle!"

Chapter 17

Now Sigurd went to the king and prince[53] and told them: "I have been here with you for quite a time, and I am indebted to you for your favors and attention given me. But now I wish to go from this land and seek out the sons of Hunding, for I want them to know that the Völsungs are not all dead. I shall have need of your support." The king and the prince said that they would give him all that he might ask for. Thus a large army was gathered, and everything as well prepared as possible, ships and all kinds of equipment, so that his expedition would be more splendid than any before. Sigurd steered the sea-drake, [54] which was very large and stately. Its sails were carefully wrought and magnificent to look upon.

They sailed away with a favoring wind, but when a few days[55] had passed, there was a great storm and tempest, and the sea was reddened as if with blood. Sigurd ordered them not to reef their sails, rather to set them higher than before.

And when they were sailing past a certain rocky headland, a man called out from it to the ship, asking who was leading this expedition. They told him that their chieftain was Sigurd Sigmundson, who was now the most famous young man alive.

The man answered: "All say the same about him, that no kings' sons can be compared to him. I would like you to lower the sails on one of your ships, so that you can take me with you." They asked him his name.

He replied:

Reginsmál,   "Hnikar[56] they called me when I gladdened Huginn,[57]
stanza 18   O young Völsung! and when I fought, [58]
          For now you may call this man of the cliff
          Feng or Fjölnir; [59] I would fare along with you."

They turned to land and took the man aboard Sigurd's ship. Then the storm abated, and they went along until they came to the land of the kingdom of the sons of Hunding. There Fjölnir disappeared. At once the men let pour forth fire and iron; they killed men and burned dwellings and laid waste wherever they went. Everyone fled thence to King Lyngvi and told him that an army had come to land and was wreaking great destruction. They had never seen anything like it before. They said that the sons of Hunding had not been far-sighted when they said that the Völsungs were no longer to be feared, "for it is Sigurd Sigmundson who is leading that array."

King Lyngvi now sent throughout his whole kingdom to summon an army, for he refused to take to flight. He called to him all who were willing to come and serve him. So now he went to meet Sigurd with a very great host, and his brothers with him, and the hardest of battles took place between the armies. There could be seen many a spear in the air, and many an arrow, axes raised mightily, shields cloven and byrnies slit, helmets riven, skulls split, and many a warrior knocked to earth. Finally, after the battle had gone on for a long time, Sigurd penetrated as far as Lyngvi's battle-standard, holding in his hand the sword Gram. He hewed down men and horses, charging through the ranks with both arms bloodied up to the shoulders. Wherever he came, the warriors fled. Neither helmet nor byrnie could hold him back. None had seen such a fighter before. Still the battle continued, with fierce attacks and slaughter of men. Yet, as it seldom happens that a man's leadership does not finally come forward and assert itself, so it was here. So many warriors fell before the sons of Hunding that no man will ever know the number. In the end, with Sigurd at the forefront of his army, the sons of Hunding came to attack him. Sigurd aimed a blow at King Lyngvi and clove his helmet and split open his head and his byrnied belly, and then he hewed Hjörvard, Lyngvi's brother, asunder in two halves and followed this up by killing all the sons of Hunding who were still alive, as well as the greater part of their band.

Therefore Sigurd went home with a decisive victory and much wealth and fame gained in the adventure. Feasts were prepared to greet him at home in his kingdom. Now when he had been home but a short time, Regin came to talk with him and said: "Now you should be willing to cast off the head of Fafnir, [60] as you promised, because you have now avenged your father and all your other kinsmen." Sigurd said: "In this matter I shall accomplish that which I promised, for I have not forgotten it."

Chapter 18

Now Sigurd and Regin went riding up on the heath to the track along which Fafnir was in the habit of creeping when he went to the water to drink. It is said that the cliff on which he lay to drink the water was thirty fathoms high.

And so Sigurd said: "Regin! You said that this dragon would be no greater than a lingworm, but his tracks seem to me very large."

Regin said: "Make a pit and sit in it, and when the dragon crawls up to the water, strike him in the heart and thus give him his death. You will get yourself great glory that way.''

Sigurd said: ''How will that help, if I get into trouble because of the dragon's blood?''

Regin replied: ''No counsel can advise you if you are afraid of anything and everything. You must lack the courage of your kinsmen!''

Nevertheless, Sigurd rode to the heath, while Regin moved away, much frightened.

Sigurd made a pit, and while he was at this task an old man with a long beard came up to him and asked him what he was doing there. Sigurd told him. Then the old man answered: ''That is not a good idea. Make some more pits and let the blood run into them, while you sit in one of them and lay the sword into that dragon's heart.''

And then the old man disappeared. Sigurd dug more pits accordingly, as he had been told.

Now when the dragon crept down to the water, there was such a great earthquake that the whole earth in the neighborhood trembled. He spewed forth poison all the way before him, but Sigurd never showed fear or terror for all that din. When the dragon crawled over the pit, Sigurd drove home the sword under its left shoulder, so that it went in up to the hilt. Then Sigurd leaped out of the pit and snatched out his sword and had his arms all bloodied up to his shoulders. And when this great dragon felt this mortal wound, it lashed about with head and tail so that everything in front of it was broken apart.

So Fafnir, having received his death-wound, asked: ''Who are you, and who is your father, and what is your family, you who have been so bold that you dared bear arms against me?''

Sigurd answered: ''My family is unknown to man; I am called the Noble Beast, and I have no father or mother, and I have come alone.''[61]

Fafnir replied: ''If you have neither father nor mother, by what miracle were you born? For though you do not tell me your name on my death day, you know well that you are lying.''

He answered: ''I am named Sigurd, and my father Sigmund.''

Fafnir replied: 'Who urged you on to this deed, and why did you let yourself be urged? Had you not heard that all are afraid of me and of my helmet of terror?[62] You bright-eyed boy, you had a brave father!''

Sigurd answered: ''To this deed my hardy spirit urged me and supported me so that this could be accomplished, and this strong hand and this sharp blade, with which you are now acquainted. For few are brave when old if they are weak when young.''

Fafnir said: ''I know that if you had grown up among your kinsmen, you would know how to fight in anger, but it is to me a greater wonder that a captive should have dared to fight me, because a prisoner of war is seldom brave in battle.''

Sigurd said: ''Do you reproach me that I am far from my kinsmen? For though I have been a prisoner of war, I have not been in fetters, and now you have found that I was indeed free.''

Fafnir answered: ''You are taking whatever I say as words of hate. But that gold treasure which I have possessed will become your death!''

Sigurd replied: ''Every man wishes to keep all his wealth until his last day, and yet each man will die some time.''

Fafnir spoke: ''You clearly will do nothing according to my counsel. But you will drown if you go to sea without precautions. Wait rather on land until it is calm.''

Sigurd said: ''Tell me this, Fafnir, if you are so very wise: Who are the Norns that choose sons from their mothers?''

Fafnir answered: ''They are many and of different kinds: some are of the race of Æsir[63]; some are of the race of elves; some are the daughters of Dvalin.''[64]

Sigurd asked: ''What is the name of the island where Surtr[65] and the Aesir mix blood together?''

Fafnir replied: ''It is called Óskapt.'' [66] And then he added: ''My brother Regin has brought about my death; and it gladdens me that he will bring about your death, for it will happen even as he has wished.'' And again he spoke: ''I have borne a helmet of terror to frighten all people while I lay on my brother's heritage and blew venom before me everywhere along the way, so that none dared come near me. And I feared no weapon, and never did I find a man, however great, before me that I did not know myself to be much stronger, and everyone has been afraid of me.''

Sigurd said: ''That helmet of terror which you spoke of gives victory to few, because he who meets with many will find out some time that no one is bravest of all alone.''

Fafnir answered: ''I advise you at once to take your horse and ride away as quickly as you can, because it often happens that he who carries his death-wound will avenge himself.''

Sigurd said: ''So much for your advice! I will indeed not take it! I will ride to your lair and take the great gold treasure there, which your kinsmen have possessed.''

Fafnir replied: ''When you ride there, you will find so much gold that it will do you all your days, and that same gold will become the death of you and the death of any other who owns it!'

Then Sigurd stood up and said: ''I will ride away now, though I should pass up that great treasure, if I knew that I should never die. But every brave man wishes to be master of all wealth until his last day. As for you, Fafnir, lie there in your death-struggles until Hel receives you!''

Then Fafnir died.

Chapter 19

After that Regin came up to Sigurd and said: ''Hail, my lord! You have won a great victory, for you have killed Fafnir, and no one before you has been so daring as to venture to sit in that dragon's path. This heroic deed shall be exalted while the world endures!''

But then Regin stood still and looked down at the ground for a long time, and then suddenly spoke in great anger: ''You have killed my brother, and I cannot be thought innocent of this deed!''

Meanwhile Sigurd took the sword Gram and dried it on the grass and said to Regin: ''You ran far off while I did this deed and I tested with my strength the power of this dragon, while you were lying in the heather and did not know which was heaven and which earth!''

Regin replied: ''This dragon might have lain long in his den if you had not made use of this sword which I wrought for you with my own hands, and neither you nor any other could have done this deed alone.''

Sigurd answered: ''When men come to fight, a good heart is better for them than a sharp sword!''

But Regin continued in a troubled mood: ''You killed my brother, and I can scarcely be considered innocent of this deed!'' Then Regin[67] cut the heart out of the dragon with a sword called Ridill. He drank the blood of Fafnir and said: ''Grant me, as a boon that will mean little to you, that you go to the fire with this heart and roast it, and give it to me to eat!''

Sigurd went and roasted it on a spit, and when it was bubbling, he tested it with his finger and lifted his fingers to his mouth, and the heart-blood of the dragon came upon his tongue. After that he could understand the language of birds. He heard some nuthatches chattering in the bushes near him. [*Translator's note:* At this point in the parchment MS Codex Regius b 1824 4°, there is a large initial thorn before the next word (*þar*), on the basis of which Olsen, editor of the diplomatic edition of the Saga, began a new chapter 20.]

''There Sigurd is sitting and roasting the heart of Fafnir'' [*sang one of them*]: he should rather be eating it himself; then he would be wiser than any man.''

Another said: ''There lies Regin; he will deceive the one who trusts him.''

Then said the third: ''Better he should hew off his head, and then he will rule that great treasure alone.''

Then said the fourth: ''He would be wiser if he did what you suggested and rode after that to Fafnir's lair and took the great treasure which is there, and then rode up to Hindarfell, where Brynhild is sleeping. Then he would learn great wisdom. He would be wise to take your advice and think about his own needs. For I can expect a wolf when I see wolf's ears.''

Then said the fifth: ''He is not so clever as I had thought if he spares Regin, since he has already killed his brother.''

Then said the sixth: ''It would be a good idea for him to kill Regin and rule the treasure alone.''

Then Sigurd said to himself: ''The evil fates will not have it that Regin should slay me; instead, both brothers shall travel one road!'' He snatched up the sword Gram and hewed off Regin's head. Then he leaped on his horse and rode along the trace of Fafnir up to his dwelling. He found that it lay open, and the doors were all of iron, and all the fittings of the doors also, and all the posts in the house were of iron, dug well down into the earth. Sigurd found there a great heap of gold as well as the sword Hrotti. He picked up there also the helmet of terror and a gold byrnie and many other costly things. He found so much gold there that it would take no fewer than two or three horses to carry it. Then he took his horse, Grani, by the reins. The horse would not move and it did no good to whip him, but Sigurd soon saw what the horse wanted. He leaped onto Grani's back and touched him with his spurs, and the horse ran as if it were free of any load.

Chapter 20 (Olsen 21)

Sigurd now rode a long way ahead until he came up on Hindarfell and had made his way south towards Frankland.[68] He saw before him on a mountain a great light, as if a fire were burning, and it shone up into the heavens. When he came up to it, there stood before him a rampart of shields and above that a banner. He climbed this rampart of shields and saw a man sleeping there who lay in full war-gear. First Sigurd took the helmet from his head and discovered that it was a woman. She wore a byrnie, and it was so tight that it seemed grown into her flesh. He slit it from the head-opening on down to the bottom and also down both arms, as if it were nothing but cloth. Sigurd told her that she had been sleeping much too long. She asked what was the mighty thing which had cut her byrnie—''and roused me from sleep, or has Sigurd the son of Sigmund come here, who holds Fafnir's helmet and his slayer[69] in his hand?''

Then Sigurd answered: ''It is one of the Völsung family who has done this deed. And this I have heard, that you are the daughter of a mighty king, and I have heard also about your beauty and your wisdom, and I shall see for myself as to both.''

Brynhild told him that two kings had fought each other. One

was named Hjálmgunnar; he was an old man but a very great fighter, and Odin had promised him victory. The other was Agnar, brother of Audi. "I felled Hjálmgunnar in battle, and for that Odin stung me with a thorn of sleep in punishment, and said that I was to be married. But I swore this vow: I would marry no one who could know fear."

Sigurd said: "Teach me wisdom in all important matters!"

She answered: "You should know better, but I will gratefully teach you, if there is something I might know that would please you, in runes or in other things that concern man's lot. But first let us drink together, and may the gods give us two a good day, that you may have use and fame from my wisdom, and afterwards remember what we two have talked about."

So Brynhild filled a goblet and brought it to Sigurd, saying:[70]

Sigrdrifumál, stanza 5

"Beer I bring to you, wielder of byrnie-things,[71]
Mixed with power and mighty fame.
'Tis full of song and pleasing charms,
Good magic words and merry runes.

Sigrdrifumál, stanza 6

"Victory-runes shall you know, if you would be wise,
And cut on sword's hilt and blade's back
And on weapon's point, and call twice on Tyr.[72]

Sigrdrifumál stanza 9

"Surf-runes shall you make, when you would be saved
On the sail-horse[73] in the sea. On its prow shall they be cut
And on the rudder-blade, and fire laid on the oar,
That broad breakers slay you not, nor blue-back waves,
And you may come safe from the sea.

Sigrdrifumál, stanza 11

"Speech-runes shall you know if you will,
That no man may hatefully pay you back harm.
One winds them and one weaves them,
One sets them all together at the Thing,[73]
When the folk shall fare unto full judgment.

Sigrdrifumál, stanza 7

"Ale-runes shall you know, if you will, lest another's wife
Betray you in your trust, if you put faith in her.
On the horn shall you cut them, and on the back of your hand,

And Naud shall be marked on your nail.[74]
The cup shall you bless[75] against peril at sea,
And cast a leek in the water.[76] Then shall I know
That never shall your mind be mixed with misfortune.

Sigrdrifumál,   "Travail-runes shall you get, if you would be saved,
stanza 8   And release child from woman. In the palm it shall be cut
                  And spanned through limb. Pray help from goddesses.

Sigrdrifumál,   "Branch-runes shall you know, if you would be leech,
stanza 10   And learn to look at wounds. In bark they shall be cut,
                  And on tree's twig, whose limbs point to the east.

Sigrdrifumál,   "Thought-runes must you take if you wish to be
stanzas 12   Than any man more doughty of spirit.[77] Hroptr[78] has read them
    & 13   And cut them and pondered them.

Sigrdrifumál,   "On the shield were cut for him who stands before shining god[79]
stanza 15   On Arvark's ear and on Alsvin's hoof,[80]
                  And on the wheel under Rognir's chariot,[81]
                  On Sleipnir's teeth[82] and on straps of sleigh.

Sigrdrifumál,   "On forepaws of bear and on Bragi's[83] tongue,
stanza 16   On claw of wolf and on beak of eagle,
                  On bloody wings and on bridge's end,[84]
                  On loosening palm and on comfort's traces,[85]

Sigrdrifumál,   "On glass and on gold and on fine silver,
stanza 17   In wine and in beer and on witches' bench,[86]
                  On Gungnir's point[87] and on giantess's breasts,
                  On nail of the Norn and beak of the owl.

Sigrdrifumál,   "All have been scored that thereon were cut
stanza 18   And stirred in sacred mead and sent on far ways.
                  They are with elves and some with the Aesir,
                  Some with the Vanir,[88] and some humans have.

Sigrdrifumál,   "These are the book-runes and help-runes,
stanza 19   And all ale-runes and proud strength-runes.
                  To each who knows clear and unspoiled

To keep them for safety. Enjoy them if you take them
Till the power of the gods is overthrown.[89]

Sigrdrifumál,
stanza 20
''Now you shall choose; all choice is offered you,
Brave weapon-tree![90] Speech of silence,
Keep in mind for yourself. All words must be weighed!''

Sigurd replied:

Sigrdrifumál,
stanza 21
''I would not flee, though you knew me doomed;
I have not been born with fear,
Your loving counsel I will have all,
As long as I shall live.''

Chapter 21 (Olsen 22)

Sigurd said: ''A woman will never be found in this world wiser
than you. Teach me more counsel!''

She answered: ''It has been allowed me to do your will and give
good counsel, according to your wishes and your desire for
wisdom.'' And then she added: ''Do well by your kinsmen and
avenge but little[91] their enmities toward you, but bear with en-
durance, and you will get long-lasting praise for it. Guard yourself
against evil chance, against both love of a maiden or of a man's
wife, whence come often evil things. Do little disputing with ig-
norant men at the folk-meetings; they often speak worse than
they know, and at once you will be called a coward, and so it may
be accounted true. But kill the man some other day and make him
pay for his angry words. If you travel a road where evil creatures
dwell, be wary; take no lodging near a path, if night should come
upon you, because wicked folk often live where men wander. Do
not let fair women deceive you, though you see them at the feast
so that it stands in the way of your sleep or you get disturbed in
heart. Do not entice them to you with kisses or other signs of
friendliness. If you hear foolish words from drunken men, quarrel
not with those who are tipsy with wine and have lost their wits.
Such things can become for many a great trouble and even death.

"Fight rather with your foe than be burned,[92] and do not swear a false oath, because grim vengeance can follow a breaking of peace. Deal carefully with dead men, whether dead from sickness or dead from the sea or dead from weapons; prepare their bodies properly. And trust not the man whose brother or other near kinsman you have killed, though he be young. 'Often a wolf is in a younger son.'

"Beware of the wily advice of your friends. Yet I can see little of your life ahead. Still, you must not let the hatred of your wife's kin come upon you."

Sigurd said: "No man will ever be found wiser than you, and this I swear: that I will have you, for you are after my own heart!"

She replied: 'I would take you first, though I had all men to choose from!'" And this they bound with oaths.

Chapter 22 (Olsen 23)

Then Sigurd rode away. His shield was marked in this way: it was bathed in red gold and a dragon was painted on it. It was dark above and bright red beneath. And in the same way were marked his helmet and his saddle and his tunic. He wore a gold byrnie, and all his weapons were adorned with gold. In the same way a dragon was marked on all of his weapons, so that whoever saw him as he passed by, would know by asking that this man had slain the great dragon whom the Vaerings[93] called Fafnir. Therefore his weapons were decorated with gold and brown color, because he was superior to other men in manners and in noble bearing and in all other things. And so, when all the greatest warriors and the most glorious chieftains are counted, then he must be counted even the first, and his name will go about on the tongues of all men north of the Greekland Sea, [94] and so it will be while the world endures.

His hair was brown in color and fair to look at and grew in long locks; his beard was thick and short and of the same color. His nose was high; he had a broad face and was large-boned. His eyes were so keen that few dared look under his brows. His shoulders were so broad that he seemed to be two men at whom one was looking. His body was shaped altogether in height and breadth as could best be fitting. And this is a sign of his height—when he had girded on the sword Gram (and that was seven spans high) and went striding through a full-grown field of rye, the sheath of the sword would knock down the top of the grain. His strength was greater than his size.

Well could he wield sword and shoot spear and cast shaft and push shield and hold it, span bow or ride horse; and many kinds of courtliness he had learned in youth. He was a wise man, and he knew about things to come. He knew the language of birds, and from this skill few things happened to him unawares. He was fluent and expert in speech, and so he never took a matter to discuss that he could not end his discussion in such a way that no one could accept it in any other way than as he had urged. And this was his particular pleasure, to give help to his men and to test himself in all great undertakings, and to take wealth from his foes and give it to his friends. He was never short of courage, for he was never afraid.

Chapter 23 (Olsen 24)

After leaving Brynhild, Sigurd rode until he came to a great homestead. There a great chieftain ruled; he was called Heimir. He had wed a sister of Brynhild whose name was Bekkhild,[55] because she stayed at home and had taken up handwork, while Brynhild went forth with helmet and byrnie and took to warring, and so she was called Brynhild. Heimir and Bekkhild had a son, who was named Alsvid, most courtly of men.

The men of the homestead were playing outside, but when they saw this man ride up, they stopped their play and wondered at him, because they had never seen such a man. They went out to meet him and were well pleased that he had come. Alsvid invited him to stay there and receive such things from him as he might need. Sigurd accepted the invitation. It was ordered that he be most honorably served. Four men lifted the gold from his horse; the fifth took care of Sigurd. They saw there many gold treasures and rare; they were delighted to gaze upon byrnies and helmets and great rings and wonderful great gold goblets as well as all kinds of war-gear.

Sigurd stayed there a long time in great honor. His famous deed was noised about throughout the land, that he had killed the monstrous dragon. He and Alsvid came to like each other well, and each was loyal to the other. They had for their mutual sport making ready their weapons and putting shafts to their arrows and going hunting with their hawks.

Chapter 24 (Olsen 25)

By this time Brynhild had come home to her foster father, Heimir. She sat in a bower with her handmaidens. She knew more skills than other women: she laid a tapestry with gold and embroidered on it the great deeds that Sigurd had done—the slaying of the dragon, the taking of the treasure, and the death of Regin. Now a day or so after her return, it is told that Sigurd went riding in the forest with his hounds and hawks and many retainers, and when he came back, his hawk flew up to a high tower and settled down by a window. Sigurd went after his hawk. There in the tower he saw a beautiful woman whom he recognized as Brynhild. It appeared to him that both were equally fair, her beauty and the tapestry on which she was working. He returned to the hall and would have little to do with anyone.

Then Alsvid asked: "Why are you so silent? This behavior of yours troubles me, to say nothing of your friends also. Why will you not be more cheerful? Your hawks are drooping, as well as your steed Grani. It will take a lot to make amends for this to me!"

Sigured replied: "Good friend, hear what is in my mind! My hawk flew up into a tower, and when I went to fetch him, I saw a beautiful woman. She was sitting beside a gold tapestry and embroidered it all with my deeds past and done."

Alsvid answered: "You were looking at Brynhild, Budli's daughter, who is a very noble person."

Said Sigurd: "That may be true, but how did she come here?"

Alsvid answered: "It was a short time between her coming and yours."

"That I have known for a few days since," said Sigurd. "This woman seems to be the best in the world."

Alsvid said: "Pay no attention to a woman, such a man as you are. It is an ill thing to grumble about what a man cannot attain."

"I will meet her," said Sigurd, "and give her gold and gain pleasure from her and exchanges of love."

Alsvid answered: "He will never be found in life, the man to whom she will grant a place beside her or give ale to drink. She wishes rather to go to war and win fame of all kinds."

"I know not whether she will respond to me or not," said Sigurd, "let alone grant me a seat beside her."

So the next day Sigurd went up to the tower, but Alsvid stayed outside, sharpening his arrows.

Sigurd said: "Hail to you, my lady! and how fare you?"

She answered: "I fare well; our kinsmen and friends are alive, but there is doubt what fortune men will have until their last day!"

He sat down beside her. Then four women entered with great table-beakers made of gold and within them the best of wines, and they stood before them.

Then Brynhild said: "That seat should be granted to few, unless my father were here!"

He answered: "Now it is granted to one who pleases me!"

The room was hung with most costly tapestries, and the whole floor was carpeted.

Sigurd said: "Now has come to pass that which you promised me."

She answered: "Welcome here!"

Then she rose up and the four handmaidens with her, and came before him with the golden cup and bade him drink. He reached out for the golden goblet, but caught her arm and drew her down beside him. He put his arms about her and kissed her and said: "No woman has ever been born more beautiful than you!"

Brynhild said: "It is a wiser idea never to place trust in the power of a woman, because they always break their promises."

He said: "May the day be the best for us, when we can enjoy each other!"

But Brynhild answered: "We are not fated to live together. I am a shield-maiden,[96] and I wear a helmet among the princes of battle; I must help them, and I am never averse to combat!"

Sigurd replied: "That would delight me most, if we were living together, and it is sharper to suffer the woe that lies therein than the pain from a keen weapon."

Brynhild answered: "I must inspect the band of warriors,[97] and you will marry Gudrun, Gjuki's daughter."

Sigurd replied: "No king's daughter will beguile me; I am not of two minds about that, and I swear by the gods that I will possess you or no other woman!"

She swore the same.

Then Sigurd thanked her for her words of encouragement and gave her a gold ring. They swore their oaths anew, and he went back to his men and stayed there for a time in great honor.

Chapter 25 (Olsen 26)

Gjuki was the name of a king who ruled a kingdom south of the Rhine. He had three sons, who were called Gunnar, Högni, and Gutthorm. Gudrun was the name of his daughter; she was a most renowned maiden. The children surpassed other kings' children in all accomplishments, beauty, and stature. The sons were always in battle and wrought many famous deeds. Gjuki had married Grimhild, who was wise in magic.

Budli was the name of a king who was mightier than Gjuki, and yet both were strong and rich. Atli was the name of Brynhild's brother; he was a grim man, great and swarthy and yet noble, and a very great warrior. Grimhild was a cruel woman. The authority of the Gjukings stood in full flower, but lay most in the children, who were altogether most distinguished.

One day Gudrun told her handmaidens that she was most unhappy. One of the women asked her what was causing her sorrow. She answered: "I have not been lucky in my dreams, and they are making great trouble in my heart. Interpret the dream for me after you have heard it."

The woman replied: "Tell it to me, and let it not worry you, because one always dreams in bad weather.''

Gudrun answered: ''But this is not bad weather! I dreamed that I was holding a fair hawk on my arm; his feathers were of golden hue.''

The woman replied: ''Many have learned of your beauty, wisdom, and good breeding. Some king's son will be asking for you.''

Gudrun continued: ''Nothing pleased me better than that hawk, and I would rather have lost all my wealth than have lost him.''

The woman answered: ''He who wins you will be well brought up, and you will love him very much.''

Gudrun answered: ''It vexes me that I do not know who he will be, and so I shall visit Brynhild. She will know.''

So they made them ready with gold and great adornment. Then Gudrun and her maidens went to the hall of Brynhild. This hall was all adorned with gold and stood on a mountain. When their coming was observed, it was reported to Brynhild that many women were driving to the hall in golden wains.

''That will be Gudrun, Gjuki's daughter,'' said Brynhild. ''I dreamed about her last night. Let us go out to meet her! A fairer woman has never before come to visit me.''

They went out to meet the visitors and greeted them well as friends. Then they went into the fair hall, which was painted within and decorated with much silver. Carpets were spread under their feet, and all were served; they had many kinds of entertainment.

But Gudrun spoke few words. Brynhild said: ''Why can you not show some happiness? Do not be like that! Let us all be cheerful together and speak of mighty kings and their great deeds!''

''Yes, let us do that!'' exclaimed Gudrun. ''Now who do you think has been foremost among kings?''

Brynhild answered: ''The sons of Hamund, Haki and Hagbard; they wrought many a famous deed of war.''

Gudrun observed: ''They were great and renowned, and yet Sigar took one of their sisters and burned another in her house, and they were slow to avenge.[98] And why did you not name my brothers, who are considered now to be distinguished men?''

''Well, said Brynhild, ''that is a good point, but they have not yet been much tested, and I know one who far surpasses them, and that is Sigurd, son of King Sigmund. He was only a child when he killed the sons of King Hunding and avenged his father and Eylimi, his mother's father.''

''What importance,'' asked Gudrun, ''was there in that? Did you say he was already born when his father fell?

''His mother went to the battlefield,'' Brynhild answered, ''and found King Sigmund badly wounded and tried to bind his wounds, but he told her he had fought as one in old age,[99] and bade her take comfort in the fact that she would give birth to the greatest of sons. That was the prophecy of a wise man. And after the death of King Sigmund she escaped with the help of Prince Alf, and Sigurd was brought up there in great honor, and he performed many a great deed every day and now is the most renowned man in the world.''

Gudrun said: ''You have remembered all this information about him out of love for him! But I came here to tell you about my dreams, which have brought me much trouble of mind.''

Brynhild answered: ''Do not let such things distress you! Stay with your kinsmen, who all want you to be happy!'' [*Translator's note*: A very large capital Þ before *that* has led Olsen to start a new chapter here.]

''I dreamed,'' said Gudrun, ''that I went from my bower, with my handmaidens, and saw a great hart; he was far superior to other deer, for his fur was of gold. We all tried to capture that deer, but I did so all by myself. That deer seemed better than anything else. But after that you shot the deer before my knees.[100] For me that was such a grief that I could hardly bear it. Later you gave me a wolf-whelp, and it spattered me with the blood of my brothers.''

Brynhild said in reply: ''I shall advise you how things are going to happen. Sigurd will come to you, the one whom I chose for husband. Grimhild will give him mead mixed with evil, which will bring us all into great strife. You will have him and quickly lose him. Then you will marry King Atli. You will lose your brothers and then you will kill Atli.''

''This is a great sorrow for me to hear,'' answered Gudrun, ''and to learn such things!'' Then she and her handmaidens went away, home to King Gjuki.

Chapter 26 (Olsen 28)

Sigurd rode away from Heimir's home with his great treasure. He and his friends parted; he rode Grani, with all his war-gear as a burden, until he reached the hall of King Gjuki. He rode into this stronghold, and one of the king's men saw him and said: "I think that one of the gods has arrived: this man is all bedecked with gold. His steed is much bigger than other steeds, and his weapons are extraordinarily beautiful. He himself surpasses other men by far and bears himself accordingly."

King Gjuki went out with his retainers, asking him in greeting: "Who are you who come riding into this dwelling when no one has dared to come in here without the permission of my sons?"

He answered simply: "My name is Sigurd, and I am the son of King Sigmund."

King Gjuki said: "You are welcome here. Receive here such things as you desire." So Sigurd went into the hall, and all seemed small beside him and all served him, for he was in great favor. All three princes rode out together, Sigurd and Gunnar and Högni, and yet Sigurd was ahead of them in all feats, though they were all mighty men in their own right.

Grimhild the queen discovered how much Sigurd loved Brynhild and how often he spoke of her. She thought to herself that it would mean better fortune to them if Sigurd should settle down there and marry the daughter of King Gjuki, because she realized that none could be Sigurd's equal. She saw also what security lay in him, and saw that he had a great deal of wealth, much more than men had known of. The king acted toward him as toward his own sons, and they honored him more than themselves.

One evening, while they were sitting at drink, the queen rose and stood before Sigurd and addressed him, saying: "Your being here is our pleasure, and we wish to give you all good things. Take here this drinking-horn and drink!" He took it and drank of it.

Grimhild continued: "King Gjuki shall be your father and I your mother; your brothers, Gunnar and Högni and all who will swear an oath, and no one will be found equal to you!" Sigurd took this well.

But with that drink he remembered Brynhild no longer.

He stayed there for some time. Then one day Grimhild went up to King Gjuki and put her arms about his neck and said: "Now the greatest warrior in the world has come to us. Great security lies in him. Give him your daughter, with such great wealth and lordship as he may wish, and let him find enjoyment here!"

The king, however, answered: "It is unusual to offer one's own daughter. Still, there is greater honor in offering her than in having others bid for her."

So one evening it was Gudrun who poured the drinks. Sigurd saw that she was a beautiful woman, most courtly in every way.

Five half-years [101] Sigurd stayed there, so that they became settled in honor and affection.

Finally King Gjuki spoke to Sigurd, saying: "You have brought me much good, Sigurd, and have strengthened my kingdom very greatly."

Gunnar said also: "We will do everything to have you stay with us a long time. We offer you both the realm and our sister, and no other could get that even if he asked!"

Sigurd replied: "Thank you for your favor, which I shall accept!"

They then swore blood-brotherhood, as if they had been born brothers. And so a splendid feast was prepared, which lasted many days. Sigurd then drank the bridal draught with Gudrun.[102] There one could view all kinds of games and entertainment, and each day of feasting was observed to be better than the one before.

Then they went far and wide about the land and accomplished some great deeds: they slew many kings' sons,[103] and no man did such great deeds as they, and they finally came home with much booty.

Sigurd gave Gudrun a piece of Fafnir's heart to eat, and after that she was much grimmer and wiser than before. Their son was named Sigmund.

Once Grimhild went to her son Gunnar and said: "Your estate is now most prosperous, except for one thing: you have no wife. Woo Brynhild! That would be a great match, and Sigurd can ride with you on your wooing!"

Gunnar replied: "She is indeed beautiful, and I am not

uneager!'' He told his father and his brothers and Sigurd, and they all encouraged him.

Chapter 27 (Olsen 29)

And so they prepared carefully for the journey and rode over hill and valley to King Budli, bearing a formal proposal. He accepted it, providing she would not say no, as she had a right to do. They rode over to Hlymdale, where Heimir received them well. Gunnar told him his mission. Heimir pointed out that the choice was Brynhild's to marry whom she wished. He said that her hall was a short way from there, and he added that he believed she would wed only that man who would ride through the flickering flame burning around her hall.

They found the hall and the fire and saw there a stronghold with a golden roof-top, and the fire was burning outside all around it. Gunnar was riding Goti, and Högni Helkvi. Gunnar drove his horse toward the flame, but it drew back.

Sigurd asked: ''Why do you draw back, Gunnar?''

He answered: ''My horse will not leap,'' and he then asked Sigurd to loan him Grani.

''That is permitted!'' said Sigurd.

Gunnar tried again to ride through the fire, but Grani would not move, and so Gunnar failed again. Then the two changed shapes, Sigurd and Gunnar, as Grimhild had taught them, whereupon Sigurd rode over and held Grani with his hand while he bound golden spurs to his feet. Then Grani leaped forward to the fire when he felt those spurs. Now there came a great din, and the fire began to flame up, and the whole earth began to shake. The fire rose to the very heavens. No man had dared to do this before, and it was as if he were riding into darkness. Then the flames subsided, and Sigurd went from his horse into the hall. As it is told

> The fire took to roaring and the earth to shaking,
> High rose the flames up to the heavens.

> There none had dared, heroes of the princely band,
> To ride through the flames and over those paths.
>
> Sigurd urged on Grani with point of sword;
> The flames slackened before the prince,
> All the fire dropped before him eager for praise,
> His harness glistened, which Regin had owned.

When Sigurd came in through the fire, he found a fair dwelling, and Brynhild was sitting in it. She asked who this stranger might be. He called himself Gunnar Gjúkason—"and you are granted to be my wife, with the consent of your father and foster father, if I should ride through the flickering flames, provided of course that you will have me."

"I hardly know what I am to answer to this," she said.

Sigurd stood on the floor of the dwelling upright, but leaning a little against the hilt of his sword, as he spoke to Brynhild: "For you I will pay in return a great dowry of gold and costly gems."

She answered from where she was sitting, with a heavy heart, like a swan on the wave and holding a sword in her hand. (She was wearing a helmet on her head and had on a byrnie also.)

"Gunnar!" she exclaimed: "Speak not of such things to me, unless you are a better man than I think you are. For you must kill those who have tried to woo me, if you have the courage to do so. I was in battle with the king of the realm of Gard,[105] and my weapons have been colored with men's blood! And this way of life I still desire!"

He answered: "You have done many a mighty deed, I know, but you must recall your promise: if these flames should be ridden through, you must go with him who did it!"

Now when she found his answer to be true, and had made due note of his speech, she stood up and seemed glad to see him. He stayed there three nights, and they occupied one bed. He took the sword Gram and laid it naked between them. She asked what that might mean. He said that it had been decreed him that he should accept thus his bridal night, in respect to his wife, or else receive his death. He took from her the ring Andvaranaut, which he had given her, and fetched for her now another ring from Fafnir's heritage.

After that he rode away through that same fire to his companions. They changed their shapes back again and rode from there to Hlymdale and told how things had gone.

That same day Brynhild went home to her foster father and told him in secret that a prince had come to her—"and rode through my flickering flame and said that he had come to marry me, and he called himself Gunnar. And I said that Sigurd alone could do what he said he had done—Sigurd, to whom I swore oaths on the mountain, and he is my first husband."

Heimir said that now things would have to be settled as they would be settled.

Brynhild also said: "Our daughter Aslaug, Sigurd's and mine, must be brought up here by you."[106]

The princes now went home, and Brynhild returned to her father. Grimhild received the warriors well and gladly and thanked Sigurd for his help. Then a feast was prepared, to which came a large company of guests. There came King Budli with his daughter and his son, Atli. This feast lasted many days, and when it was finished, Sigurd suddenly remembered all those oaths which he had made to Brynhild. But he kept quiet about them. Brynhild and Gunnar sat together at the feasting and drank good wine.

Chapter 28 (Olsen 30)

There came a day when they went to the river to bathe, Brynhild and Gudrun together, and Brynhild waded farther out in the water, alone. Gudrun asked what that might mean.

Brynhild said: "Why should I make myself equal to you in this matter, to say nothing of anything else? I think that my father is richer than yours, and my husband has done more valiant deeds. He rode through burning fire, while your spouse was a thrall of King Hjalprek!"

Gudrun retorted in anger: "Indeed, you would be wiser to keep silent than to abuse my husband! It is said by all men that never has such a person come into the world (from any point of view), and it is not proper for you to insult him, because he was your first husband and slew Fafnir and rode through the flickering flames, when you thought it was Prince Gunnar, and he lay beside you and took from your hand the ring Andvaranaut. You have got to recognize these facts!''

Brynhild looked at the ring and recognized it. She turned pale, as if she were dead; then she went home and did not speak a word that evening. When Sigurd came to bed, Gudrun asked: ''Why is Brynhild so gloomy?''

Sigurd answered: ''I am not quite sure, but I rather suspect that we shall soon find out that something has happened.''

''Why is she not satisfied with her good fortune and well-being and the praise of all men,'' asked Gudrun, ''for she has taken the man she most desired?''

Sigurd asked in turn: ''Where was she when she said that she thought she had married the most valiant man or the one she most desired to possess?''

''I shall ask about that in the morning,'' said Gudrun, ''and find out whom she had most wished to wed.''

''That I forbid you.'' Sigurd replied, ''for you will be sorry if you do that.''

In the morning they sat together in the bower, and Brynhild was still silent.

So Gudrun said: ''Cheer up, Brynhild! Did our talk vex you? Or what else stands in the way of your good humor?''

Brynhild answered: ''Evil alone moves you to this; you have a cruel heart.''

''Be not like that!'' exclaimed Gudrun. ''Tell me about it!''

Brynhild replied: ''Ask only those things which are better for you to know, that befit a noblewoman. Better be satisfied with a good lot, while everything else is going as you wish.''

''It is too early to boast,'' answered Gudrun, ''but this must be some kind of prophecy. Why do you keep goading me? I have done nothing to vex you!''

''You are going to pay for this,'' said Brynhild, ''for you married Sigurd, and I resent your enjoying both him and that great treasure!''

Gudrun replied: ''I did not know of your speech together, but my father could well have arranged another marriage for me even though you might not be concerned at all.''

''We have not had secret conversations here,'' Brynhild answered, ''and yet we two, Sigurd and I, have sworn oaths, and you knew well that you were betraying me, and that I must avenge!''

''Indeed,'' answered Gudrun, ''you are married better than you deserve, and your pride will bring you to a bad end, and many will pay for it!''

''I might have been content,'' said Brynhild, ''if you did not have the nobler husband!''

Gudrun flashed back: ''You have so noble a husband that it is still not certain who is the greater prince, and you have wealth and power enough!''

Brynhild's answer was: ''Sigurd slew Fafnir, and that is worth more to me than all this kingdom of King Gjuki, as it has been said:[107]

> 'Sigurd killed the dragon, and that will be
> Unforgotten while the world endures,
> And your brother dared not ride
> Through the flames or over the paths!' ''

Gudrun responded: ''Grani did not run through the flames under Prince Gunnar, but Gunnar dared to ride, and one need not question his bravery!''

''I cannot deny that I do not think well of Grimhild,'' was Brynhild's answer.

''Do not blame her,'' replied Gudrun, ''because she is to you as to her own daughter.''

Brynhild flared back: ''She has manipulated the whole beginning of this evil which is gnawing at me: she bore to Sigurd that wicked ale, so that he could not remember my name.''

Gudrun's only reply was: ''You are speaking many evil words, and every one is a great lie!''

Brynhild retorted: ''May you have pleasure of Sigurd only in so far as you have not deceived me. Your rule together is unworthy; it will go with you as I know it will!''

''May I have more pleasure,'' said Gudrun, ''than you may

wish. No one, however, has supposed that he had it all too good with me—not once!''

Brynhild answered: ''You speak ill, and you will regret it when your desire passes from you. But now let us stop exchanging hateful words!''

Gudrun came back at her: ''You were the first to cast hateful words at me. Now you suggest that you can make up for them, and yet cruel things lie underneath!''

''Let us drop all this useless chatter,'' said Brynhild. ''I have kept silent for a long time about the sorrow that lies in my heart, but I will love your brother alone, so let us begin talking about something else.''

Gudrun said: ''Your mind looks too far ahead!''

From this talk, however, there arose great trouble, when they had gone down to the river, and Brynhild had recognized the ring, for the quarrel was over that.

Chapter 29 (Olsen 31)

After this talk Brynhild lay down in bed, and the news came to Prince Gunnar that Brynhild was truly sick. He went to see her and asked what her trouble might be, but she gave him no answer and lay as if she were dead. But when he pressed her hard in his questioning, she answered: ''What did you do with that ring that I gave you, which King Budli gave me at our last parting, when you Gjukings came to him and threatened to make war on him and burn him,[108] unless you obtained me? At that time Budli led me aside to talk and asked whom I would choose among those who had come. And I offered myself, to protect our land and be leader of one third of our army. There were two choices at hand: that I should be married to the one he wished, or go without all my wealth and his friendship as well. Then he said, however, that his friendship might avail me better than his anger. So I took counsel with myself, whether I should listen to his desire or kill many a man. I seemed incapable of arguing with him. Thus it came about that I promised myself to him who should ride the steed Grani with Fafnir's heritage and should come through my flickering fire and kill those men whom I had mentioned.[109] Now no one dared to ride except Sigurd alone. It was he who rode through the flames, for there was no lack of courage in him; he had killed the dragon and Regin and five kings—and you did not, Gunnar! You turned as pale as a corpse, and you are neither king, prince, nor warrior! But I swore an oath at home with my father that I would love only him who should be born famous, and that is Sigurd. Now I am an oath-breaker, for I do not possess him, and therefore I shall be planning your death, and I shall render a cruel repayment to Grimhild. There is no woman more cowardly or treacherous than she!''

Gunnar answered so that few[110] heard him: "You have spoken many false words, and you must be a woman of wicked thoughts, since you have placed the blame on this queen, who is much better than you. She loved her husband no less than you do yours. She did not torture dead men[111] nor did she murder, and she lives in good reputation.''

"We have not had secret meetings," answered Brynhild, "nor have we done wicked deeds, and my own nature is not to do so, but I may for that reason be the more ready to kill you!''

After that she tried to slay Gunnar, but Högni put her in chains.

Gunnar objected: "I do not want her to be placed in chains!''

She answered: "Do not mind that, because you will never see me happy in your hall from now on, for I will not drink, nor play chess, nor speak my thoughts, nor embroider good gold on cloth, nor give you counsel!'' She repeated that it was the greatest sorrow for her that she could not have Sigurd. She sat up and struck the tapestry so that it tore asunder, and she had the doors of her bower opened, so that her cries of grief could be heard a very long way. Her sorrow was great, and one could hear it throughout the whole town.

Gudrun asked her bower-maidens why they were so silent and sad—"and what ails you, and why do you go about like witless folk, and why do you babble in panic?''

Then a lady of her retinue explained; she was called Svafrlod: "This is an unlucky day; our hall is full of woe.''

So Gudrun said to her friend: "Arise! We have slept too long.

Wake up Brynhild! Let us get busy with our tapestry-making and be cheerful!''

"That I cannot do," said Svafrlod, "to awaken her or to talk to her. For many days now she has drunk neither mead nor wine; she has felt the wrath of the gods."

Whereupon Gudrun said to Gunnar: "Go see her, and tell her that her unhappiness is ours also."

Gunnar answered: "It is forbidden me to see her or to share her wealth."

Nevertheless he went to see her and tried in many ways to talk to her, but he got no answer. So, as he went away, he found Högni and asked him to go see her, but Högni said that he was not eager to do so. Still, he too went in, but got nothing out of her. Finally, Sigurd was asked to go see her. He did not even reply, and so it went throughout the evening.

But next day, when Sigurd had returned from the hunt, he met Gudrun and said: "This is the way it seems to me with her: a chill of anger[112] has come upon her, and I fear that Brynhild will die."

"My lord!" answered Gudrun. "Great spells must have come over her. She has slept now for seven days, and no one has dared to waken her."

"She is not asleep," Sigurd observed. "She is spinning fearful plans against us two."

Weeping, Gudrun said: "This is a great sorrow, even to think of your death. Now go in and see her and find out if her anger has passed. Give her gold and thus allay her wrath!"

Sigurd went out and found the hall-door open. He thought Brynhild was asleep, and lifted the covers from her, saying: "Get up, Brynhild! The sun has been shining all over town, and you have slept too long. Push away from yourself this sorrow, and be more cheerful."

She only said: "What does your boldness mean, that you dare to come see me? No one has acted worse than you in my betrayal!"

"Why do you not speak to people?" asked Sigurd. "And what is angering you?"

Brynhild replied: "I will tell you the cause of my anger."

Sigurd remarked: "You have been bewitched if you think my

feelings toward you are unkind. For your husband is the one you chose.''

''No!'' she exclaimed. ''Gunnar did not ride through the fire to me, and he never paid my dowry of slain warriors.[113] I wondered at the man who came into my hall, and yet I could not clearly discern him, because of the cloud that lay over my guardian spirit. Still, I thought I recognized your eyes.''

Sigurd said: ''I am not more noble than the sons of Gjuki. They slew the king of the Danes and another chieftain, brother of King Budli.''

Brynhild had a reply to that: ''I have many a wrong to charge up to them![114] But do not remind me of other troubles. You, Sigurd, struck the dragon dead and rode through fire for my sake, and the sons of Gjuki were not there.''

''I was not your husband,'' Sigurd reminded her, ''nor were you my wife, but a famous king paid for your dowry.''

Brynhild answered: ''I have never seen Gunnar in such a light that my heart rejoiced at his sight, but now I feel very grim toward him, although I conceal it from others.''

''It is strange,'' said Sigurd, ''that you cannot love such a prince. But what is vexing you most? It seems to me that his love should be better for you than gold.''

Brynhild answered: ''This is to me the sorest of my griefs: that I cannot find a way for a sharp sword to be reddened with your blood!''

Sigurd replied as best he could: ''Do not worry about that! We shall have but a short time to wait before a sharp sword will stand in my heart, and you will pray for no worse for yourself, because you will not live after me. Few will be the days of our lives hereafter.''

Brynhild answered in wonder: ''Your words come from no little bitterness! Since you have betrayed me and taken away all my joy, I do not care about living.''

''Live and love Prince Gunnar and me,'' answered Sigurd, ''for all my wealth I shall give to you if you do not die.''

Brynhild complained: ''You do not really know me at all! You surpass all other men, yet no woman has become more hateful to you than I!''

''The truth is otherwise,'' said Sigurd. ''I love you more than myself, though I became the victim of treachery, and now it cannot be changed, because, since I paid any attention to my own wits, it grieved me that you were not my wife, but I bore it as well as I could, because I was in a king's hall. But I was nevertheless pleased when we were together. Still, it may happen that it will be as was foretold before, and I shall surely not mind that!''

Brynhild replied: ''You have told me too late that my grief bothers you, and now we shall find no comfort.''

''I have desired very much,'' said Sigurd, ''that we should both go to bed, and even that you should be my wife.''

Brynhild exclaimed: ''Such a thought is not even to be uttered, for I will not have two princes in one hall. I would sooner leave life than betray Prince Gunnar.'' Then she reminded him of the time when they found each other on the mountain and swore oaths—''but all is changed now, and I do not wish to live.''

''I did not remember your name,'' said Sigurd, ''and I did not recognize you when you were married, and that is my greatest grief.''

Then said Brynhild: ''I made an oath to have the man who should ride through my flickering fire, and that oath I will keep or die else.''

''Rather than have you die, I will take you and leave Gudrun behind,'' said Sigurd, and so swollen were his sides[115] that the rings of his byrnie came apart.

''I do not want you now,'' said Brynhild, ''nor any other man!''

Sigurd went away, as it says in the *Sigurdarkvida:*[116]

> Out went Sigurd when their talk was done,
> The loyal friend of princes, all sorrowful,
> So that the combat-eager's iron-woven sark
> Came apart from his armored side.

When Sigurd came back into the hall, Gunnar asked whether he knew what had caused Brynhild's sorrow and whether or not she had recovered her speech. Sigurd said that she could talk. So Gunnar went to see her again, asking what her grief might mean and whether any remedy could have any effect on it.

''I do not want to live,'' said Brynhild, ''because Sigurd has betrayed me and no less you, when you let him come to my bed. Now I will not have two men at the same time in one hall, for that must be the death of Sigurd and you and me, because he has told it all to Gudrun, and she is having fun with me!''

Chapter 30 (Olsen 32)

After that, Brynhild went out and sat by the wall of her bower and made much lamentation. She said that everything was hateful to her, both land and wealth, because she did not possess Sigurd. Then Gunnar came up to her.

Brynhild greeted him with: ''You shall forfeit both kingdom and wealth, your life, and me, and I will go home to my kinsmen and sit there sad in spirit, unless you kill Sigurd and his son. Do not bring up a wolf's whelp!''

Hearing this, Gunnar became very sick at heart, for he did not seem to know what was best for him to do, because he was bound by oaths to Sigurd. Many thoughts played about and shifted in his mind. But it seemed to him especially that it would be the greatest kind of disgrace for his wife to go away from him.

Finally he said: ''Brynhild, you are altogether dear to me, and you are the most renowned of all women, and sooner would I lose life than lose your love.'' But he called his brother Högni to him, saying: ''A great problem has come upon me.'' He said that he wished to kill Sigurd because he had broken faith with him—''then we two can rule the treasure and the whole kingdom.''

Högni said, however: ''It is not fitting for us two to break our oaths with a blood-feud. Sigurd has been a great help to us. No kings can be our equal as long as this king of Hunland[117] lives, and we shall never again have such a brother-in-law. Now consider how good it will be to continue to have such a brother-in-law and sister's son.[118] Now I see how all this has come about: Brynhild has been watching and planning, and her advice to us comes as a great shame and disgrace.''

Gunnar answered: ''Nevertheless this must be done, and I think I have a plan: let us egg on Gutthorm, our brother. He is young and knows little and is outside all our oath-swearing.''[119]

Högni protested: ''Such an idea still seems to me ill-advised, for even though it should come to pass, we would have to make great payment for betraying such a man.''

Gunnar replied: ''Either Sigurd shall die or else I will die!''

So he bade Brynhild rise and be happy. She stood up, saying however, that Gunnar was not to come into the same bed with her until the deed was done.

The brothers then talked together. Gunnar said that the reason for killing was justified, for Sigurd had taken Brynhild's virginity—''so let us urge Gutthorm to do the deed!'' They called him to them and offered him gold and much wealth to win him over to the task. They took a snake and some wolf's flesh and had them boiled together and given Gutthorm to eat, as the skald has said:[120]

> Some wood-fish[121] they took, some wolf-flesh they cut;
> Some they gave to Gutthorm, some flesh from Gera,[122]
> To go with beer and parts of many things
> To wreak the magic spell . . .

And with this food he became so violent and covetous and subject to the persuasion of Grimhild that he promised to do that deed, and they promised him great honor in return. Sigurd had no inkling of their treachery, but he could not have struggled against his fate or his destiny, nor did he think he deserved such treachery from them.

Gutthorm came in to Sigurd along toward morning, while he was resting in his bed, and when Sigurd looked at him, Gutthorm dared not make any attack on him, and so he turned away and went out again. And so he came and went a second time. Sigurd's eyes were so bright and keen that few ventured to look in them. But the third time Gutthorm went in, and found Sigurd asleep. Gutthorm raised his sword and laid it into Sigurd, so that the sword-point[123] went into the bolster under him. Sigurd awakened from the wound, and Gutthorm went out toward the door. But Sigurd took the sword Gram and threw it after him, and it entered his back, cutting him asunder in the middle, so that his feet and legs fell one way, and his head and arms another way, back into the room.

Gudrun had been asleep in the arms of Sigurd, and she awoke in unspeakable grief, for she was floating in his blood. She lamented with weeping and with words of anguish, so that Sigurd rose up against his pillows and spoke:

"Do not weep," he said; "your brothers are alive to make you happy. But I have a son too young to know how to defend himself against his foes, and they have provided poorly even for themselves. They will not have a brother-in-law more likely to ride into battle with them, nor such a sister's son, if he should succeed in growing older. Now it has come to pass, what was long before prophesied—and I have concealed the fact from myself—that no man can struggle against his fate. For it is Brynhild who has planned this, she who loved me more than any other man. And this I will swear, that I never did wrong to Gunnar, and I respected our oaths, and I was not too good a friend to his wife. And if I had known of this before, I would have got up on my feet with my weapon. Then many would have lost their lives before I died, and all your brothers would have been killed, and it would have been more difficult for them to have killed me than to kill the greatest of bisons and wild boars!"

Sigurd now left his life.

Gudrun breathed painfully; Brynhild heard that and laughed. Then Gunnar spoke: "You are not laughing at this because your heart-roots are rejoicing, else why do you lose color? You are indeed a monster, and it is very likely that you are doomed. Nothing would be more fitting than to see King Atli slain before your very eyes, with you having to stand beside him! So how are we to sit beside brother-in-law and brother's slayer?"

She replied: "No one can complain that there has not been enough killing, but King Atli cares neither about your threats nor your anger, and he will live a longer life and have greater power than you!"

Högni spoke: "Now has come to pass what Brynhild prophesied, but for this evil deed we can never make good!"

Gudrun said: "My kinsmen have killed my husband. Now you

can ride at the head of the army, and when you come to battle, you will find that Sigurd is not at your other hand, and you will realize that Sigurd was your good fortune and your strength, and if he had had a son like him, you would have had support against those who will come after and against his kinsmen.''

Chapter 31 (Olsen, continuing 32)

Now no man seems to know how to explain why Brynhild had ordered laughing what she lamented weeping. Yet she said: "I dreamed, Gunnar, that I lay in a cold bed. For now you will ride against your enemies, and all your family will fare badly, because they are oath-breakers, and you remembered little that you two, you and Sigurd, mixed your blood together when you betrayed him. And you have evilly repaid all that he did well for you when he let you be foremost. He proved, when he came to me, how he kept his oaths, for he laid between us two the sharp-edged sword that was tempered with poison. But you soon decided to do harm against both him and me. When I was at home with my father, I had everything that I desired, and I did not think that any of you would be mine, when you three princes came riding to my dwelling. Afterwards Atli led me aside to talk and asked if I wished to marry him who was riding Grani. That man was not like you. For I had promised myself to the son of King Sigmund and to no other. Now no good can come to you from this, even though I die.''

Gunnar then arose and put his arms about her and told her she must live and partake of her wealth, and all the others tried to keep her from dying, but she pushed away each of them who came to her and said that it would not avail to keep her from what she had in mind.

Whereupon Gunnar called to Högni and asked his advice, bidding him go and find out if he could get her into a calmer mood. He said that it was very important to soothe her sorrow until it should pass.

But Högni answered: "Let no man prevent her dying, because

she has never been any good to us or to any man since she came here.''

Now Brynhild told them to help themselves to the gold and come to her—all who desired to get riches. Then she took a sword and struck herself under her arm, and leaned back against the pillows, saying: ''Now let him take the gold, whoever wishes to enjoy it!''

All were silent. Brynhild then spoke: ''Take the gold and use it well!''

And again she spoke, this time to Gunnar: ''Now I will tell you in a short space what is going to happen after this. You and Gudrun soon will be reconciled through the devices of Grimhild, the wise in magic. The daughter of Sigurd and Gudrun will be called Svanhild; she will be born most beautiful of all women. Gudrun will be married to Atli against her will.[124] You will desire to marry Oddrun,[125] but Atli will forbid it, and so you two will have secret meetings, and she will love you. Atli will betray you and put you in a snake pit, but later Atli will be killed, as well as his sons. Gudrun will slay them all. Afterwards great waves will carry her to the stronghold of King Jonak. There she will bear famous sons. Svanhild will be sent from the land and wedded to King Jörmunrek.[126] The counsels of Bikki will sting her to death, and then all your family will have passed away, and the sorrows of Gudrun will be all the greater.'' [*Translator's Note*: Here Olsen begins chapter 33.]

''Now I ask of you, Gunnar, a final boon: have a great funeral pyre built on a level plain for all of us—for myself and Sigurd and those who were slain with him.[127] Let the hangings over it be dyed with the blood of men, and burn me there on one side of the Hunnish king, and on the other side my retainers, two at the head, two at the feet, and two hawks with them. Thus it will all be equally divided. Lay there between us the drawn sword as before, when we two entered one bed and were called by the name of man and wife. The door of Hel will not close on his heels[128] if I follow him, and our funeral will be not unhappy if there attend him the five maidens and eight slaves whom my father gave me, and if also were burnt there those who were slain with Sigurd. I would say more if I were not sorely hurt, for now the wound gapes and gushes. Yet I have told the truth.''

Now the body of Sigurd was prepared according to the ancient custom, and a great pyre was built, and when the fire was well kindled, then was laid upon it the corpses of Sigurd Fafnisbane and of his three-year-old son, whom Brynhild had killed, and of Gutthorm. And when the pyre was all aflame, Brynhild went out on it. She told her bower-maidens to take all the gold that she wished to give them. And after that Brynhild died and was burned there with Sigurd. Thus their lives ended.

Chapter 32 (Olsen 34)

Now whosoever hears these tidings will say that no man will be found like Sigurd in this world, and never again will such a man be born such as Sigurd was, anywhere or at any time, and his name will never grow old on a German[129] tongue or in the Northland, while the world endures.

It is told that one day, while Gudrun was sitting in her bower, she said: ''My life was better when I had Sigurd; so much did he surpass all other men, as gold above iron or a leek[130] above other herbs, or a hart above other beasts, so that my brothers envied me such a husband, who was more distinguished than they. They could not sleep until they had slain him. Grani made a great noise when he saw the wounds of his master; then I talked to him as to a man, but he bent himself to the earth, for he knew that Sigurd had fallen.''

After that Gudrun went away into the forest and heard on all sides the howling of wolves, and she thought she would be happier if she could die. She went on until she came to the hall of King Hálf,[131] where she stayed with Thóra, Hakon's[132] daughter, for seven half-years in Denmark, having been greeted there with great welcome. There she wove a tapestry and wrought upon it many great deeds and fair sport, as was frequent in those times—swords and byrnies and all kinds of kings' trappings, and King Sigmund's ships as they sailed out from land. And she wove there also the fight of Sigar and Siggeir in the south at Fjon.[133] Such was their pleasure, Gudrun and Thóra, and Gudrun got some comfort from her grief.

But Grimhild found out where Gudrun had settled. She summoned her sons to talk, asking how they wished to make good to Gudrun for her son and husband. She told them that their payment was due. Gunnar spoke up, saying that he was quite willing to give her gold to recompense her for her wrongs. He then sent for his friends, and they prepared their horses, helmets, shields, swords, and byrnies and all kinds of war-gear, and prepared for the journey in the most courtly manner. No warrior considered great stayed at home. Their steeds were armored, and each knight wore a helmet either golden or brightly burnished. Grimhild decided to go the journey with them, for she said that their mission must be fully accomplished, and so she could not sit at home.

There were five hundred men in all, and many famous warriors among them: Valdemar of Denmark and Eymod and Jarisleif. These were they who came to the hall of King Hálf. There were Lombards, Franks, and Saxons; they came with all their war-gear and wore red fur cloaks, as it is told:[134]

Gudrúnarkvida II,	Short byrnies, hammered helmets they had,
stanza 20	Short swords, those keen dark-haired ones.

They wished to bestow on their sister good gifts, did the Gjuking brothers, and they spoke pleasantly to her, but she trusted none of them. Then Grimhild brought her a harmful drink, and she had to take it, and after that she remembered nothing: the drink was mingled with the powers of earth and sea and the blood of swine,[135] and on the drinking-horn were cut letters of all kinds reddened with blood, as it says here:[136]

Gudrúnarkvida II,	There were on the horn staves of all sorts
stanza 23	Cut and reddened—I could not read them—
	Long lingfish[137] from the land of the Haddings,[138]
	Uncut ear of grain and entrails of beasts.

Gudrúnarkvida II,	There were in that beer many evils together,
stanza 24	Roots of all trees and acorns burnt,
	Soot of the hearth and sacrifical bowels,
	Swine's liver boiled, to confound all strife.

And after that, when their wills were reconciled, there arose much mirth. Grimhild spoke, when she caught sight of Gudrun: "Well be to you, daughter! I give you gold and all kinds of treasure to enjoy after your father, precious rings and bed-hangings by most noble Hunnish maidens. These are recompense to you for your husband. Now I will marry you to King Atli the mighty. You will have power over his wealth; but do not forget your kinsmen for the sake of a husband. Do rather as I bid!"

Gudrun answered: "I never will wed King Atli, for it is not right for us to increase our family through him!"

Grimhild replied: "You shall not brood over your hatred now, but if you do have sons, act as if Sigurd and Sigmund were still alive!"

"I cannot stop thinking about Sigurd," answered Gudrun. "He was better than all others!"

"You are destined to marry this king," said Grimhild, "and you are not to marry another."

"Do not offer me this king," pleaded Gudrun, "for nothing but evil to our family will come of it, and he will treat your sons badly, and after that it will be cruelly avenged on him!"

Grimhild was annoyed by her reply and said: "Do as I tell you, and for that you will get much honor and my love and those places which are called Vinbjörg and Valbjörg." Her words had such effect that the matter was settled.

"This shall be done, then," said Gudrun, "but still against my will, and little good will come from it, rather much harm!"

They all mounted their steeds, and the ladies were set in wains, and so they went four[139] days on horseback, and another four in ships, and a third four over land-ways, until they came to a high hall. Here many people came to meet Gudrun, and a splendid feast was prepared, as had been agreed upon among them, and it passed with much honor and pride. At this feast Atli drank the bridal-draught with Gudrun, but her heart never allowed her to feel kindly toward him, and little of their life together was happy.

Chapter 33 (Olsen 35)

Now it is to be told that one night King Atli awoke from sleep and said to Gudrun: "I dreamed that you struck at me with a sword." Gudrun interpreted that dream, saying that it meant fire when one dreamed of iron—"and your mistake is that you think yourself more important than anybody else."

"Again I dreamed," said Atli, "that two reeds were growing here, which I did not wish ever to be burned. Then these were torn up by the roots and reddened with blood and carried to the board and offered to me to eat. Again, I dreamed that two hawks flew from my arms and were without prey, and so went to Hel.[140] It seemed to me that their hearts were mixed with honey, and I seemed to be eating them. Afterwards it seemed that fair whelps lay before me, yelping loudly, and I ate their flesh, though against my will."

"Those dreams," replied Gudrun, "are not good, for later they will come to pass. Your sons will be doomed, and many hardships will come upon us."

"Once more I dreamed," he said, "that I lay on a sickbed, and my death was certain."

Now this passed, yet their life together remained unfriendly. Meanwhile King Atli began to wonder where the great treasure (which Sigurd had possessed) might be hidden away. Only Gunnar and his brother knew that. Now Atli was a great king and a mighty one, a wise ruler with many followers. He sought advice from among his men on how to proceed in this business. He knew that Gunnar and his brother had much more wealth, and that no other men could be compared with them in that respect. So he made the decision to send men to visit the brothers and invite them to a feast, and to honor them in many ways. The man who was chosen leader of these was named Vingi.

The queen knew of their plans and suspected that there might be an intrigue against her brothers. So she made runes and took a gold ring and attached to it a wolf's hair, then carried it to the king's messengers. Afterwards they went on the king's errand, but before they came ashore, this Vingi looked at the runes and changed them, so that it seemed from these runes that Gudrun was urging them to come and visit King Atli.

Thus they came to King Gunnar's hall and were well received, and great fires were built for them, and they drank the best drinks with great joy.

Vingi then said: "King Atli is the one who has sent me here. He wishes you two , Gunnar and Högni, to visit him at his home and receive from him much honor, helmets and shields, swords and byrnies, gold and fine garments, warriors and steeds and many gifts, and to you two he would be willing to grant his whole kingdom."

Gunnar lifted up his head and said to Högni: "How are we two to receive this invitation? He is offering to let us two partake of much wealth, yet I know of no two kings possessing as much gold as we two, because we have all that gold that lay on Gnitaheath, and we have great chambers full of gold, and the best weapons with which to strike, and all kinds of war-gear. I know my steed to be the best, and my sword the sharpest, and my treasure the most famous."

Högni replied: "I am surprised at his invitation, because he has seldom[141] done this before. I think it would be ill-advised to go visit him. I wondered also, when I was looking at the treasures that King Atli had sent us two, because I saw a wolf's hair bound about a gold ring. Thus it may be that Gudrun knows he has a wolf's reputation toward the two of us, and so she does not want us to come."

Vingi now showed them the runes that, he said, Gudrun had sent. Then most of the people went to sleep, but a few of the men remained to drink. Now it happened that Högni's wife, called Kostbera, fairest of women, went and looked at those runes. (Gunnar's wife was called Glaumvör, a very stately woman. They were both pouring drinks.) The kings had become very drunk.

Vingi noticed this and said: "It is no secret that King Atli is too old and infirm to defend his kingdom, and his sons are too young and not yet worth much. For that reason he will be willing to give you rule over his kingdom while the boys are so young, and he will grant you full enjoyment of it."

Now both these things happened at the same time—that Gunnar was very drunk, and that a great kingdom had been offered him. He could not contend against circumstances; therefore he promised to make the journey, and so informed Högni his brother.

"Your promise," said Högni, "will have to stand, and I will follow you, but I am not eager for the journey."

Chapter 34 (Olsen 35 continued)

When the men had drunk as much as they wanted to, they went to sleep. Kostbera took the runes to look at and read the letters, but she saw that something had been cut on them different from what was underneath, and that the runes were written wrong. From her own knowledge, she made a decision and after that went to bed beside her husband.

When they awoke, she spoke to Högni: "You are planning to go from home, but that is not advisable. Go rather some other time! For you cannot be skilled in runes if you believe that your sister has invited you at this time. I have read those runes, and I am surprised that so wise a woman should have written them so wrong. For it is so written underneath as to concern your being killed. It must have been either that she lacked the letters or else others have written them wrong. And now you must hear my dream. [*Translator's note:* Again, on the basis of a large initial thorn in *pat*, Olsen has begun a new chapter (chapter 36)]. This is what I dreamed: it seemed to me that a great river came rushing in, breaking the beams of the hall."

Högni answered: "You often have evil forebodings, but I do not have the nature to deal evilly with men unless it is deserved. Atli will receive us well."

"You can try it," she said, "but friendship is not behind this invitation. And again I dreamed that another river came rushing in here and roared terribly, breaking up the dais in the hall[142] and fracturing the legs of both you and your brother. And that must mean something."

He replied: "These mean grain-fields waving in the wind when you think of rivers, for when we go through a field, the grain-tops often touch our legs."

"I dreamed," said she,[143] "that your bed-covers were burning, as fire leaped up from the hall."

He answered: "I know clearly what that means: our clothes lie here unheeded; they must have been burning here when you thought it was the bed-clothes."

"I thought a polar bear came in," she said, "and broke up the king's high seat and shook his paws at us, so that we all grew frightened, and he had us all in his maw at one time, so that we could do nothing, and great terror prevailed.''

''There will be a great storm,'' he said, ''if you thought of a white bear.''

''Then it seemed to me that an eagle flew in here,'' she continued, ''and through the hall, and sprinkled me, and then all of us, with blood, and that must be an evil sign, because it seemed to me that this eagle was in the shape of King Atli.''

He answered: ''Often we have had great slaughter and great hewing down of cattle for our sport, and it means oxen when one dreams of eagles. Atli will be well disposed toward us.''

Chapter 35 (Olsen 37)

Now as to Gunnar, it is said that when he awoke, he heard the same kind of talk, in that Glaumvör, his wife, told of her many dreams, which meant to her some likely treachery. Gunnar, however, interpreted them all to the contrary.

''This was one of them,'' she said. ''It seemed to me that a bloody sword was brought here into the hall, and you were struck by that sword, and wolves howled at both ends of it.''

Gunnar responded: ''Small dogs will bite, and often the yelping of hounds will be betokened by weapons covered with blood.''

''Again, it seemed to me,'' she said, ''that women came in here, and they were sad-faced as they chose you for husband. It may be that they were your goddesses.''[144]

He answered: ''That is difficult to interpret, but no one can save himself from the end of his life, and it is not unlikely that we have but a short time left.''

In the morning they all arose, intending to leave, while others tried to hold them back.

Gunnar said to the man whose name was Fjörnir: ''Arise and get us good wine to drink from great goblets, because it may be that this will be our last feasting. For now the old wolf will come by the treasure, if we die, and the polar bear will not spare biting with his tusks!''

After that the warriors led them out of the hall, all in tears. Högni's son said: ''Farewell, and have good fortune!''[145]

The greater part of their troop stayed behind. Solar and Snaevar, the sons of Högni, came along, and a great fighter whose name was Orkning; he was the brother of Bera. The people all followed them to their ship, and all of them tried to prevent their going, but it was to no avail.

Glaumvör then spoke: "Vingi," she said, "it is very likely that great misfortune will come from your coming here, and heavy news will be heard from your going!"

But all he said was: "This I swear, that I am not lying, and may the high gallows and all the powers of evil take me if I have spoken any word falsely." But he had little to lose with such words.

Then said Bera: "Farewell, and good fortune!"

Högni responded: "Be joyful, whatever may befall us!"

With that their destinies parted company.

Then they rowed so fast and with such great strength that more than half of the ship's keel came loose. They pulled hard on the oars with mighty backward sweeps, so that the handle and the pegs of the rudder broke, and when they came to land they did not make fast their ship. Then they rode with their famous steeds through a dark forest[146] for a time. At last they came to Atli's stronghold, where they heard a great din and clattering of weapons, and they saw there a host of warriors and the great preparations they were making. All of the gates were filled with men. They rode up to the dwelling, but it was locked. Högni broke open the gate, and now they rode into the stronghold.

"You might have left that deed undone," was Vingi's sour comment. "Now wait here, while I look for a gallows-tree to hang you. I asked you to come here with good cheer, but treachery lay underneath. Now it will be but a short time until you are all hanging aloft!"

Högni made a short answer: "We will not yield, and I think that one should cringe but little when one must fight. It is no use to try to frighten us, for it is going to go hard with you."

They knocked him down and beat him to death with the butts of their battle-axes.

Chapter 36 (Olsen 38)

And so they rode to King Atli's hall. The king had drawn up his warriors for battle, and the two bands were arranged in such a way that there was a kind of courtyard between them.

"You are welcome!" cried Atli.[147] "Now give me that great treasure which is due me, the wealth that Sigurd possessed and that Gudrun now owns!"

Gunnar replied: "You will never have that treasure, and if you offer us war, you will have met brave men here before they give up their lives! It may be that you are preparing a feast in noble fashion, but with little unhappiness for the eagle and the wolf."[148]

"For a long time I have had this in mind," said Atli,[149] "to take away your lives, to rule over your treasure, and to repay you for your villainy when you betrayed your very great brother-in-law. Now I will avenge him!"

Högni answered: "It will be hard for you to maintain this purpose for any length of time, because you are not yet prepared."

Nevertheless it now came to a fierce battle. First there was a shower of arrows. And now Gudrun heard about what was happening, whereupon she became greatly excited and cast off her mantle. Then she went out and greeted those who had just arrived and kissed her brothers and showed them affection, and this was their very last speech together.

She said: "I thought I had decided that you were not to come here, but none can contend against fate." She added: "Will anything avail to bring about peace?" All obstinately said no to that. She saw that the game was going sorely against her brothers. She thought fierce thoughts now, and so she got into a byrnie and took a sword and fought on the side of her brothers and behaved as the bravest of warriors. All said alike that hardly any one made a better defense there. Now came great slaughter, and yet the attack of the Gjuking brothers was surprising. The battle lasted long through the middle of the day. Gunnar and Högni both charged through the ranks of King Atli, and it is told that the whole battlefield was awash with blood. The sons of Högni also pressed hard.

Then King Atli spoke up: "I had a great host, and a fine one, with strong warriors, but now many of them have fallen, and we have a bad account for you to settle: nineteen of my warriors killed, and only eleven left."[150]

And so a truce was made in the fight.

Then said King Atli: "We were four brothers, and I am now the only one left. I achieved a good relationship through marriage, and I believed it would be an advantage to me. I had a wife beautiful and wise, great-hearted and keen-minded, but I could not make use of her wisdom, because we were seldom in agreement. Now you have slain many of my kinsmen, and cheated me out of kingdom and wealth, and betrayed my sister,[151] and that is to me the greatest injury."

Högni retorted: "Why bring up such matters now? You were the first to break the peace. You took my kinswoman and tried to starve her to Hel,[152] thus to murder her, and to take over the treasure, and that has not been kingly on your part. And so it seems to me laughable that you should recount your wrongs. I will thank the gods if things go badly for you!"

Chapter 37 (Olsen 39)

King Atli now urged on his men to make another fierce attack. And so they fought bravely, but the Gjukings pressed them so hard that King Atli fled into his hall, and then they fought inside, a very heavy battle indeed. The combat went on with much loss of life and ended thus: all of the Gjuking brothers' troops had fallen, so that only the two were still on their feet, but not before many a man had gone to Hel through their weapons. But now they attacked Gunnar, and by reason of their greater strength he was seized and put into fetters. Still Högni continued fighting with great valor and manliness, killing twenty of King Atli's warriors.[153] He pushed many into the fire that was burning in the hall. All agreed that one could hardly find another such man. Yet at the end he was borne down by greater numbers and seized.

King Atli said: "It is a great wonder to me how so many men have perished before him. Now cut out his heart, and let that be his death!"

Högni replied: ''Do as you please; gladly will I await here that which you wish to do, and you will realize that my heart is not afraid. For I have experienced many a hard lot before, and I have been ready to endure the test of a man whenever I was whole and unwounded. But now I am much hurt, and you alone rule over my fate.''

A counselor of King Atli then spoke: ''I see a better way: let us take instead the thrall Hjalli and spare Högni. This thrall is ripe for death: he will never live so long that he will not always be wretched.''

The thrall heard this and cried out loudly, running around to wherever there seemed to be a chance for shelter. He said that he had had an evil lot, what with all their fighting, and nothing but trouble to repay him. He said that it was an evil day when he had to die and leave his good condition and his swine-keeping. Nevertheless they seized him and struck at him with a knife. He yelled loudly before he even felt the point.

Then Högni said, as it befits few who have come into such peril, that he wished to have the thrall's life spared, and he said also that he did not want to hear such screams, and that he had no desire for them to proceed with this grisly sport. The thrall was therefore allowed to live.[154]

So now they were both in fetters, Gunnar and Högni. Then King Atli said to King Gunnar that he should tell about the treasure, if he wished to continue enjoying life. Gunnar answered: ''First I will see the heart of my brother Högni all bloody!''

So now they seized the thrall a second time and cut out his heart and bore it to Gunnar. He remarked: ''This can be only the heart of Hjalli the cowardly, for it is not like the heart of Högni the brave, because it is now quivering too much—half as much as when it lay in his breast!''

So after that, at the urging of King Atli, they went to Högni and cut out his heart. So great was his strength that he was laughing while he was suffering this torment, and all wondered at his spirit, which must be remembered ever since.

They showed the heart of Högni to Gunnar. He observed:[155] ''Here we may see the heart of Högni the brave, and it is unlike the heart of Hjalli the cowardly, because it now quivers but little, and even less while it lay in his breast. And so, Atli, you will leave your life as we leave ours, for I alone know where the treasure is, because Högni cannot tell you. I was uncertain in my mind about it while we both were living; now I have a single purpose before me. Now the Rhine shall rule the gold before the Huns can get it in their hands!''

King Atli said: ''Take this captive away!'' And so it was done.

Now Gudrun called the men to her and then met King Atli, saying: ''May it go ill with you ever hereafter, according as you have kept your word to me and to my brothers!''[156]

Then King Gunnar was placed in a snake pit. There were many great serpents in it, and his hands were bound fast. Gudrun sent him a harp, and his skill showed itself (for he played the harp with great art) in that he touched the strings with his toes, playing so well and so beautifully that few thought he had played it that well with his hands. And moreover he played so well that all the snakes fell asleep, except for one large and ugly adder[157] that crept up to him and dug him with its snout, so that it cut into his heart. And then he left his life, with great courage.

Chapter 38 (Olsen 40)

King Atli now thought that he had won a great victory, so he said to Gudrun with some mockery, as if in boast: ''Gudrun, you have now lost your brothers, and you brought it all about yourself!''

She answered bitterly: ''It pleases you now to speak of this slaughter in my presence, but it may be that you will repent it when you experience what is bound to come after! The heritage surviving longest is a grimness not to be suppressed, and it will not go well with you so long as I live.''

''Let us two now be reconciled,'' he answered, ''and I will make good to you for your brothers with gold and costly gifts, according to your wishes.''

She replied: ''For a long time I have not been easy to deal with, and I could bear up only as long as Högni was alive. You can never make good to me for my brothers in any satisfactory way, but often we women are forcibly borne down by your power. Now all my kinsmen are dead, and you alone will rule over me. I must accept that. Meantime let us now have a great funeral-feast, for I wish thus to honor my brothers and also your kinsmen.''

So she made herself blithe in words, yet she was the same underneath as before. She was obedient in speech, and he trusted her words, while she made herself compliant in speaking.

So Gudrun now did honor to her brothers, and King Atli did the same to his men, and the feast was indeed tumultuous. Still, Gudrun pondered her wrongs and waited her chance to do the king some great outrage. In the evening she took the sons of herself and King Atli, while they were playing around with a block of wood.[158] They boys were startled and asked what she wanted them to do.

She answered fiercely: "Do not ask that! It is to be death for you both!"

They replied: "You can do with your children as you like, of course. That no man forbids you, but it is a disgrace for you to be doing this!"

Nevertheless she cut their throats.

Afterward the king asked where his sons were. Gudrun told him: "I will tell you and gladden your heart. You aroused great grief in me when you killed my brothers. Now you must listen to my words: you have lost your sons, but their skulls are here, to be used as goblets, and you have drunk their blood mingled with your wine. Then I took their hearts and roasted them on a spit, and you have eaten them.''

King Atli merely replied: "You are a cruel woman, you who murder your sons and give their flesh to me to eat, and you allow but a short time between your evil deeds.''

Gudrun replied: "It would be my desire to do you a truly great injury, for it cannot go hard enough with such a king!''

Atli answered: "You have done something worse than men have example of; there is great folly in such rashness. It would be fitting that you be burned alive on a pyre or sent to Hel by stoning, for you deserve that much, the way you have gone.''

"Prophesy that for yourself!" she shot back. "I shall achieve another kind of death!'' They spoke many hateful words to one another.

Högni had a son who survived him; his name was Niflung;[159] he held great hatred toward King Atli and told Gudrun that he wanted to avenge his father. She was pleased to hear this, and they made plans together. She said that it would be a great happiness to her if revenge could be done. And so in the evening, when the king had drunk, he went to sleep, and while he was asleep Gudrun and the son of Högni went in to him. Gudrun took a sword and struck into the breast of King Atli. (They were both involved in this, she and the son of Högni.) King Atli wakened from the wound, saying: "There is no need to bind or to make preparations here. Who has done me this injury?"

Said Gudrun in triumph: "I did some of it, and with me the son of Högni!"

"It was most unfitting for you to do this, although there might have been some cause for it. You were married to me, however, by the will of your kinsmen and I have paid a dowry for you: thirty good knights and seemly maidens and many other men, and yet you conceded nothing to your expected duties unless you could rule over the lands that King Budli possessed, and you have often let your mother-in-law sit weeping."[160]

Gudrun replied: "You have told me many a lie, and I have not paid attention to them all; often, indeed, I was unfriendly, and that added much to our dislike of each other. There has often been much tumult here in your dwelling. Often kinsmen and friends fought, and one would provoke another. It was a far better life for me when Sigurd killed hostile kings and ruled over their possessions and granted peace to those who wanted it, and those princes came into our power, and we let them rule, who so wished. But later I lost him, and it seemed nothing to hear the name of widow. Yet it vexed me most when I came to you, I who had once been married to the most famous of kings. You never came from battle without having played a lesser, meaner part!"

"That is not true," answered King Atli, "but the lot of neither of us is made better by such talk, because I am defeated. Deal with me in honorable fashion, and let my body be prepared in a noble way!"

"That I will do," she said; "I will have an honorable grave made for you, and a worthy stone coffin, and I will wrap you in fair burial clothes and keep in mind all that is needed.''

Soon after, King Atli died, and she did as she had promised. Then she had fire kindled in the hall. When the warriors awoke in terror, the men could not endure the fire and began hewing each other, and so they all came to their deaths. There ended the lives of King Atli and all his men. After this deed Gudrun did not want to live, but the end of her days had not yet come.

(The Völsungs and the Gjukings, so men say, were the most haughty and noble men, and so it is told in all the ancient lays. Now their feud was brought to an end in this way and by this happening.)

Chapter 39 (Olsen 41)

Gudrun had had a daughter by Sigurd who was called Svanhild. She was the most beautiful of all women and had keen eyes like her father, so that only a few dared look under her brows. She far surpassed other women in beauty, as the sun outshines other heavenly bodies.

One day Gudrun went down to the sea, taking stones in her arms, and then walked into the water, intending to do away with herself. But great waves lifted her up out over the sea, and with their help she floated at last to the stronghold of King Jonak, who was a mighty king and had many followers.

He took Gudrun in marriage, and the sons they had were Hamdir, Sörli, and Erp.[161] Svanhild was reared there.

Chapter 40 (Olsen 42)

Jörmunrek[162] was the name of a mighty king in those days. His son was named Randver. The king summoned his son one day and said to him: "You are to go on a mission for me to King Jonak, along with my counselor named Bikki. It is there that Svanhild, daughter of Sigurd Fafnisbane, has been reared. I know her to be the most beautiful maiden under the sun. I want her in marriage above all others, and you shall woo her in my name."

Randver replied: ''Lord, it is fitting that I should go on your errand!''

So he made proper preparations for the journey, and then they traveled until they came to King Jonak. They saw Svanhild, and her beauty seemed very much as reported. Randver called the king aside to talk with him, saying: ''King Jörmunrek wishes to offer himself in marriage to your family. He has heard about Svanhild and prefers to choose her as his wife. It is unlikely that she could be given to a mightier man than he.''

Jonak agreed that this would be an honorable marriage, for Jörmunrek was very renowned.

Gudrun observed, however: ''Fortune is an unsafe thing to trust in, for it may turn out badly!'' Nevertheless, because of the urgent wish of King Jörmunrek and all that was involved in it,[163] it was decided. And so Svanhild went aboard a ship with a worshipful retinue, and sat in the raised deck at the stern, beside the king's son.

Then Bikki remarked to Randver: ''It would be more suitable for you to have so attractive a wife than for so old a man!''

That remark pleased Randver well, and he talked merrily with Svanhild, and she in turn with him. They came home to land and met with Jörmunrek.

But Bikki said: ''Lord, you need to know what has happened, although it is hard for me to tell it, for this is a deceitful business, since your son has received the full love of Svanhild, and she is his mistress. Now do not let such a thing go unpunished!''

Much evil counsel had Bikki given him before, yet this bit deeper than his other evil counsels. The king listened to his many wicked speeches and said that he could not possibly quiet his anger and that he would have Randver seized and hanged on the gallows.

Now when Randver was being led to the gallows, he took a hawk and plucked from it all its feathers, ordering that it be shown to his father.

And when the king saw that, he said: ''It must now seem to him that I am in a way as bereft of honor as this hawk is bereft of feathers!'' And he commanded them to cut Randver from the gallows. But in the meantime Bikki had set his treachery to work, and Randver was dead.

Again Bikki said: ''No one is more to blame than Svanhild; let her die a shameful death!''

The king agreed: ''I will take your advice!''

So Svanhild was bound by the gate of the stronghold, and horses were sent to leap upon her. But when she opened her eyes, the horses refused to trample her. When Bikki saw that, he said that a bag should be drawn over her head, and so it was done, and after that she left her life.

Chapter 41 (Olsen 43)

Gudrun now heard of the death of Svanhild and told her sons: ''Why should you sit so quiet, speaking merry words, when Jörmunrek has killed your sister and has had her trampled shamefully under the feet of horses? You two do not have the spirit of Gunnar or Högni. They would have avenged their kinswoman.''

Hamdir answered in protest: ''You praised Gunnar and Högni very little when they killed Sigurd and you were reddened with his blood, and you took an evil revenge for your brothers when you slew your sons. Perhaps we all together may be able better to kill Jörmunrek; besides, we cannot stand these reproaches that are urging us on so hard!''

Gudrun went off laughing and gave them to drink out of great goblets, and after that she chose for them byrnies good and strong, with other equipment for battle.

Hamdir, however, said: ''Now we shall part for the last time, and you will hear news, and you will drink at the funeral-feast for Svanhild and us.''

And so they went journeying forth. But Gudrun went to her bower, her sorrow increasing, and said: ''To three men I have been wedded: first to Sigurd Fafnisbane, but he was betrayed, and that was for me the greatest sorrow. Then I was given in marriage to King Atli, and my heart was made so cruel toward him that I killed our sons in my hatred. Then I went down to the sea and was carried by great waves to land, where I was wedded to this king. And I gave Svanhild in marriage away from this land, with great treasure, and it has been for me the sorest of sorrows, next to Sigurd, when she was trodden under the feet of horses. And it was most grim for me when Gunnar was set in the snake pit, and the keenest when the heart was cut out of Högni. Indeed, it would be far better if Sigurd could come to me and carry me off in his arms. Here no son or daughter sits to comfort me. Do you remember, Sigurd, what we two said when we entered one bed, that you would come to me and stay with me, even from Hel itself?''

Then she ended her lamentation.

Chapter 42 (Olsen 44)

Now it is to be told concerning the sons of Gudrun that she had so prepared their armor that no iron could bite through it, and she told them not to harm stones or other large things, and she told them that it would be unlucky for them if they did not do just as she had said.

So when they set out on their way, they met their brother Erp and asked him how he could help them.

He answered: ''As much as hand helps hand, or foot helps foot.''

It seemed to them that that was no answer at all, and so they killed him.[164]

When they had gone on their way a little while, Hamdir stumbled.[165] He stretched out his hand, however, and said: ''Erp must have spoken the truth; I would have fallen now if I had not supported myself with my hand.'' A little later Sörli stumbled too, but raised his foot and thus steadied himself, remarking: ''I too would have fallen now, if I had not steadied myself with both feet.'' They agreed that they had done wrong to their brother Erp.

And so they traveled until they came to King Jörmunrek's, and they went before him and attacked him. Hamdir hewed off both his hands and Sörli both his legs.

Then said Hamdir: ''The head would have come off by now if our brother Erp, whom we slew on the way, had only been here and alive! We have seen this too late, as it is told:[166]

Hamdismál,   ''The head would be off, were Erp now alive,
stanza 26   Our battle-keen brother, whom we slew on the way!''

Thus they had broken their mother's commands, in that they had harmed stones. Now men attacked them, but they defended themselves well in manly fashion, bringing many men to harm, for no iron could bite them. Then there came a man tall and aged, with but one eye,[167] who said:

''You are not wise fellows if you do not know how to bring about the deaths of these men!''

The king asked: ''Give me advice if you know the answer!''

The old man answered: ''Stone them to Hel!''

And so it was done, and then stones flew at them from all sides, and that was the end of the lives of Hamdir and Sörli.

End Note

At this point in Codex there comes a chapter 43. Over it is a heading entitled (in translation) the *Saga of Ragnar Lodbrók*. In effect, then, chapter 43 of our Saga is chapter 1 of a new saga, very possibly by the same Author.

The *Saga of Ragnar Lodbrók* is somewhat longer than the *Völsungasaga* and appears to have been intended as a sequel to our Saga. It refers the reader to Aslaug, the daughter of Sigurd and Brynhild, who is identified briefly near the end of chapter 27 of the Saga (see n. 106 below). It will be remembered that here Brynhild committed her as-yet-unborn (?) child to the care of her own foster father and brother-in-law, Heimir.

Later, when Heimir has heard of the deaths of Sigurd and Brynhild, he fears for the safety of the little three-year-old girl, and flees with her into the forest. When he seeks shelter with a peasant couple, he is murdered for his gold, which he has brought with him, and Aslaug is brought up by the couple under the name of Kraka. Eventually, in Cinderella fashion, she becomes the second wife of Prince Ragnar of Denmark, who has heard reports of her great beauty from some of his retainers. There is a considerable amount of Germanic (and probably Celtic) *märchen* material in this Saga, but it is chiefly an account of the exploits of Ragnar and his sons by Aslaug (Kraka), which tend to link up the *Völsungasaga* with the historical lines of Norwegian and Danish kings.

In short, it is clear that the Author of the *Völsungasaga* is trying to keep the narrative going in order to show (to quote the words of Sigmund and Sigurd) that the Völsungs are not all dead. But since the *Saga of Ragnar Lodbrók* as a whole is totally irrelevant to our Saga, it has been omitted in the present translation.

Explanatory Notes,
the *Völsungasaga*

1. *Skadi*. The Old Norse common noun *skaoi*, meaning "damage," "destruction," is a masculine noun, but is identical in form with the *jötunn* or giantess whose amusing marriage to the god Njörðr is recounted in Snorri Sturluson's *Gylfaginning*, chapter 23, the first section (after the Prologue) of the *Prose Edda*. In spite of the distinctly feminine nature of this giantess, who became goddess of skiing, I see no reason for doubting the authenticity of this male name, which was pointed out a hundred years ago (Karl Müllenhoff, "Die alte Dichtung von den Nibelungen" *Zeitschrift für deutsches Altertum* 23(1878) 113–73, esp. p. 117). In fact in the balladlike *Rímur frá Völsungi hinum óborna*, referred to in the general introduction, allusion is made in stanza 53 to the goddess and in the very next stanza to the thane. From Bredi's point of view, of course, his companion is well named.

2. *wolf in the holy places*. The wolf is in Old Norse a symbol for an enemy. Since Sigi has killed Bredi out of sheer envy and cruelty and not for the usual respected motive, revenge, he has definitely sinned against "the holy places," which cannot, of course, be read in any Christian context. (Of course, the Author, being presumably Christian, may have had some kind of Christian coloration in mind.) The phrase undoubtedly means that Sigi is to be named an outlaw, which was the usual punishment for egregious cases of what was politely known as "manslaughter." Sigi must therefore be exiled for an indefinite period, although the sentence was usually for three years. If, during that period in which he was outlawed, a man should be found in the territory from which he had been exiled, he was liable to be killed by anyone who met him. Moreover, this did not preclude his being slain later by some member of the murdered man's family or supporters of the deceased, even when the term of his outlawry had expired. On the other hand, capital punishment decreed by the *thing*, the judicial-legislative assembly, was not the rule.

3. *Hunland*. No doubt the name of the Huns was originally restricted to the Asiatic tribes who made vast depredations in Europe during the later fourth and early fifth century, especially when related to their ruler Attila (d.453). But by the time of the composition of the *Völsungasaga*, it is hardly likely that there was any such fine distinction in the minds of the authors, whose knowledge of geography was minimal, particularly in relation to the lands south of the Baltic. Thus Sigurd is referred to later as ruler of the Huns; see note 117 below.

4. *Frigg . . . Odin.* Frigg was in Norse mythology the wife of Odin, king of the Æsir, or gods in Asgard (another and probably older family of gods were the Vanir (or Wanes); see note 88 below). Snorri Sturluson, in his *Prologue* to the *Prose Edda*, puts Odin, king of the Æsir as the eighteenth in line of descent from Priam of Troy. This is evidently an attempt on Snorri's part to rationalize the existence of these pagan deities in a Christian world, at a time when Troy was favored over the Greeks. The result of such rationalizing, of course, is to make all of the Norse gods the product of euhemerism—that is, the traditional or mythological explained by real persons and events, which may or may not be the actual case. As for Frigg, she may once have been a solar goddess (although Snorri gives her name also as Frigida, which hardly sounds solar). She appears, like her husband, to be able to see the future; perhaps she also has the power to heal. She was a general manager and hostess in Asgard. She is further noted for her tendency to disagree with her husband (as Hera often quarreled with Zeus, though for different reasons). In the case of Rerir, however, they are in complete agreement.

As for Odin (Woden), his role in the Saga has already been pointed out; see introduction. His name has been connected with the O. N. *vaða,* and the concept of advancing—the ineluctable force that brings about all change, the one permanent thing in life, and controls destiny.

5. *Valkyrie.* The Valkyries were warlike young women appointed by Odin to assist his chosen warriors in battle and, if they fell notwithstanding, to bear the honored slain in battle to Valhalla. The name signifies "chooser of the slain." Since the Valkyries fulfilled the wishes of Odin, they were sometimes known as "wish-maidens." They might sometimes wear the coats of swans or other birds (cf.n. 7 below), in which case they might be referred to as "swan-maidens" or "crow-maidens" or the like. In such circumstances, however, humans could get them into their power by stealing their bird-coats. Other terms applied to them were "shield-maidens" and "spear-maidens," for they could participate in battle with full war-gear.

6. *Hrimnir.* The term *giant* is used to translate *jötunn* (plural *jötnar*). The giants coexisted with the Æsir and the Vanir; their abode was Jötunheim. They were usually in conflict with the Æsir, but not always. Compare the "giants" of Genesis 6:4 and the Titans of the classical mythology. Hrimnir appears to have been the leader of the Jötnar.

7. *crow's mantle.* See note 5 above.

8. *to go home to Odin.* For a chosen warrior, to die.

9. *Hljód.* See note 5 above. Her lineage is important, for with Odin as the father of Sigi and the marriage of Hljód to King Völsung, the family is descended from a union of the gods and giants.

10. Despite the undoubted reading of *Barnstokk* in Codex, I suspect that the original reading (pre-Codex) must have been *Branstokk*, for the latter, meaning "sword-trunk," is much more appropriate than "children's trunk."

11. *Gautland.* The home of the Gautar, between Lakes Vennern and Vättern in the old province of Götarike, Sweden. They would correspond to the Anglo-Saxon Gēatas, the tribe to which Beowulf belonged. It is always a question, of course, of how specific the Author intended to be.

12. *liked his offer*. Literally, the Old Norse text would read: "The king took well to this proposal, and his sons also." Compare the dialectal English "to take to" meaning "to like."

13. *apple-tree*. This is the literal translation of *apaldr*. It is evident, however, that the word could be used for any fruit- or nut-bearing tree, and the first mention of this one is specifically of an oak. Incidentally, the appearance of the "stranger" a few lines below indicates that it is clearly Odin—the rather informal costume, somewhat disreputable, and the one eye are unmistakable bits of evidence. (Odin gave an eye to the water-spirit Mimir in exchange for a knowledge of his future doom. The story is told in chapter 15 of Snorri Sturluson's *Gylfaginning*.)

14. *hundred*. The Old Norse *hundrað* meant 120 rather than 100; the usual expression for 100 was *tíu tigir* ("ten units of ten"), for the system of numerals was based originally upon a sexagesimal (60) rather than a decimal (100) plan. This was true of the other Germanic languages and indeed of many other Indo-European languages. It has been for centuries the basis of all measurements of the circle. Some surviving traces of this sexagesimal system will be seen in the use (particularly in England) of important fractions or multiples of 60—three, a dozen, fifteen, twelve inches to a foot, three feet to a yard, twelve pence to a shilling, twenty shillings to a pound, and so on. The customary number of a warrior's *comitatus* was twelve (or fifteen); there were twelve disciples of Christ. An armed band often comprised fifteen men, and a youth arrived at his majority when he became fifteen years old.

In considering numbers higher than a dozen, it is therefore important to keep the original meaning of *hundrað* in mind. But by the time of our Saga, it would be pendantic to insist upon the original idea of 120.

15. *earth-house*. An underground chamber.

16. *two sons by his wife*. It is to be presumed that Signy was the mother of these two boys, because her purpose in sending them to Sigurd was to avenge her father and their grandfather. Two sons represent a favorite number in folklore, as here; later King Gjuki has two sons (and another by a different marriage); Gudrun has two sons by Atli. A third son, however, as Gudrun had by Jonak, is a different matter (see note 164 below). Incidentally, to allow for the gestation, birth, and growth of these offspring is to suspend disbelief, and one should take no account of elapsed time in dealing with a folktale.

17. *bower*. The *skamma*, thus translated, was a small house separate from the main building (*höll* or *skáli*). It was intended for the mistress of the establishment, or *burg* (stronghold), and her handmaidens. Here she sat, received and entertained visitors, and did the spinning, weaving, and tapestry-making. When not occupied, the *skamma* was often used as a storehouse.

18. *speaking against him*. She would not betray his whereabouts to any one who might wish to harm or kill him, nor denounce him to the king or to an enemy of any kind.

19. *Sinfjötli*. The "Fitela" of *Beowulf*, ll. 879 and 889. The name means perhaps "yellow-spotted," a possible reference to the subsequent episode told in chapter 8, in which Sigmund and Sinfjötli are for a time werewolves running in

the forest. The incestuous union of Sigmund and Signy, initiated by Signy herself, indicates that she considers a son of pure Völsung extraction more capable of avenging his grandfather, Völsung. Social and moral scruples would be subordinated to the overriding desire to avenge her father.

20. *every tenth half-day*. In other words, every fifth day. There is much uncertainty, however, about the exact meaning of the word *dœgr* (*dægr*). It is usually interpreted as obviously not the same as *dagr*, the usual word for "day." Rather *dœgr* means a twelve hour period, whereas *dagr* is the general term for the day-and-night twenty-four-hour span. In measuring distances at sea, for example, *dœgr* indicates not only time but also distance covered. Since the Vikings rarely sailed at night (except on their transoceanic voyages to Iceland, Greenland, or Finland and parts south), *dœgr* is estimated to have been anywhere from 75 to 100 or even 120 miles, depending upon sailing conditions.

It should be added that a few lines below, Codex is in poor condition, and the space left before *menn* is reflected in the "'seven men (and perhaps more)'" of the translation; we supply the number on the basis of Sinfjötli's statement and the paper-manuscripts. It happens that the number seven has been suggested, though there may have been more. There is a considerable gap a few lines farther on in the manuscript; indeed, everything from *oak* to *have help* has been restored with the aid of the paper-manuscripts.

21. *time . . . wolf-skins*. That is, until the next "tenth half-day" or "fifth day" had come around.

22. *front of the hall*. Either a small room to the right or left of the entrance to the hall, or a vestibule or possibly an outhouse near the entrance; in view of the action in this scene, probably the first of the possibilities.

23. *get past it*. The "mound" or "vault" (*haugr*) thus constructed is difficult to visualize. The great flat stone (*hella*) would be placed in a deep depression in the earth either vertically or horizontally. It would be large enough to divide the hole into two sections, side by side if the stone was placed vertically, or one above the other if it was placed horizontally. My own preference is for a horizontal position of the stone, but in either case the hole or depression containing the stone would be covered over, so that the victims would die of either asphyxiation or starvation.

24. *as it is told*. The verse following, like several others that I call Völsung Fragments, is not to be found in any of the Eddic poems. These lines, however, may well come either from a long poem of popular nature covering the material of the putative *Sigmundarsaga* or from some lost *ríma*.

25. *make good her troubles*. She would receive compensation for the loss of her father and the killing of her sons, to say nothing of the ignominy imposed upon her by having married her father's slayer. Incidentally, the reader should calculate that Sigurd was in his earthhouse some twenty or more years, for note that Signy has two sons by Siggeir and after she had allowed them to be killed (no compensation for them) she has two more. See note 16 above.

26. *The kinsmen*. Sigmund and Sinfjötli.

27. *the Norns*. There were three chief Norns, "maidens mighty in wisdom," who bestowed life upon men and women and set their destinies throughout their

142   *The Saga of the Völsungs*

whole existence. They correspond in many ways to the *Parcae*, or Fates, of classical mythology. Their names are *Urth* ("Past"), *Verdandi* ("Present"), and *Skuld*, ("Future"). We are told later, however, (see note 40 below) that there are many minor Norns, some protective divinities or guardian-norns; some are from the gods, some from the elves and dwarves. See the Eddic poem *Fáfnismál*, stanza 13. As for the *leek*, mentioned a few lines below, it was the symbol of growth, fertility, and health. It had special magical and medicinal properties, and is referred to more than once as superior to other plants and vegetables. See the interesting article by Winfred P. Lehmann, "*Lín* and *laukr* in the Edda," *Germanic Review* 30 (1955), 131–47.

28. *natal feast*. This is not to be understood as a Christian baptismal ceremony; the details given here are characteristic of the pre-Christian recognition of an important birth. Later, however, at the natal feast of Sigurd (chapter 13), the child is "sprinkled with water," which is a Christian detail preferred by the Author to call special attention to his greatest hero.

29. *King Högni*. Not to be confused with Högni the Gjuking, who plays an important part in the later chapters of the Saga.

30. *Norvasund*. The name usually refers in Old Norse tradition to the Straits of Gibraltar (?), which is hardly likely here. Yet the Vikings would know the Straits, for they were in the Mediterranean before our Saga was composed. Still, I prefer the interpretation that this is a misreading for Orvasund (Modern Danish Öresund, off Seeland), which is mentioned in the Eddic poem *Helgakvida Hundingsbana I*, stanza 25, since all the other place names mentioned here have approximately the same locale. Again, however, one must not trust the Author's geography.

31. *At-Gnipalund*. This place name indicates "a grove on a towering peak." The preposition was often prefixed to topographical names; cf. the Modern English Atwater, Atwell, Atwood, et cetera.

32. *He spoke thus*. What follows is an exchange of insults between Sinfjötli and Granmar (according to the Eddic poem *Helgakvida Hundingsbana I*, stanzas 37, 42, 51, it is Sinfjötli and Gudmund), common in both early Germanic and early Celtic traditions. Its literary descendant is the "flyting" or "scourging" literature of the later Middle Ages, as the fifteenth-century *Flyting of Dunbar and Kennedy*, which in more sophisticated form blends with the classical satire, as in Dryden's *Macflecknoe* or Pope's *Dunciad*. Personal invective is, of course, universal.

I have chosen the older reading, which indicates that the contest is between Sinfjötli and Granmar. I wish merely to call attention to the fact of the contest, for it is immaterial who the interlocutor may be. Note that Helgi, the leader, cuts the contest short when it threatens to become too abusive.

33. *Asgard*. The home of the Æsir, the ruling order of gods. To reproach a man with having once been a woman, and particularly to say that he then bore offspring, was the highest kind of insult.

34. *Grani*. A slightly anachronistic reference to Sigurd's steed.

35. *Bravell.* The site of an important battle fought between the Danes under King Harald Hilditönn ("Battle-tooth") and his nephew King Sigurd (H) ring in the neighborhood of Bravik in the province of Österhötland, Sweden, some time around the year 750. It is something of a landmark in Scandinavian history, for it tends to separate the eventual kingdoms of Denmark and Sweden.

36. *bewitched,* the O.N. *gjöróttr* suggests muddy, bewitched, or even poisoned.

37. *firth.* An estuary or arm of the sea, not so long or narrow or with such steep banks as a fjord. The man in the boat is, of course, Odin.

38. *market . . . everywhere.* Thus affording opportunities to buy, sell, or exchange gifts or goods.

39. *worse . . . affairs.* They had never been successful in this kind of competition.

40. *guardian-women.* The minor Norns; see note 27 above. They would be present at a wedding, a birth, even a death, assigning their subject a personal destiny, meanwhile taking care of him as best they could.

41. *spear in his hand.* Here is Odin again. He is intervening to bring about the death of Sigmund and to prepare the way for Sigurd to assume the role of protagonist.

42. *king's daughter.* Hjördis.

43. *foster father.* A man who brought up a boy or girl who was not his son or daughter was known as a *fóstri.* Thus Hjálprek and Álf might be called Sigurd's foster fathers, but Regin is clearly a teacher as well as a father substitute; he devoted himself to the boy's upbringing and his schooling. In short, the term is used rather loosely for the male equivalent of a governess. It will soon be learned that Brynhild herself had a *fóstri,* her brother-in-law, Heimir.

44. *runes.* The term *rune* is applied to anything mysterious or arcane or magical; thus it comes to mean anything secret, esoteric, or erudite. Later it designated a letter in the so-called Runic alphabet (*Fuþark*, from the order of the first six letters), an alphabet adapted from the Roman, cut wherever possible against the grain of bark. There was some Greek influence, and some native Germanic. As used here, it means instruction in knowledge. But in chapter 20, where Brynhild offers to teach Sigurd in specialized knowledge, the term covers the specialty. Sigurd thus learns from Brynhild various kinds of special, particularized knowledge of various branches of learning—something he would not have learned from Regin.

45. *the kings.* Hjálprek and Álf, king and prince respectively. It is evident that the Old Norse *konungr* was applied to either a king or a prince, or any one directly related to him—son, grandson, or brother.

46. *Sleipnir.* According to the *Gylfaginning* in Snorri Sturluson's *Prose Edda* (chapter 42), a giant (*jötunn*) appeared before the gods (Aesir) and offered to build them an impregnable stronghold. He was to receive in return the rather exorbitant payment of Freyja, the goddess of love and beauty, with the sun and the moon thrown in. The gods, persuaded by Loki, accepted, provided that the task

was accomplished in one winter, but if any day of the next summer was needed to complete the task, the contract would be null and void. The giant agreed to this, provided in turn that he could have the help of his horse Svadilfari. Loki, the perpetual trouble-maker of the Æsir (actually the power of evil in the world), induced the gods to grant the giant's request. But the giant then made such progress that when it was only three days away from summer (the Thursday that fell between the 9th and 15th of April), the stronghold was all but finished. Not wishing to lose Freyja and the sun and the moon, the gods threatened Loki with bodily harm unless he could find a way to thwart the giant. Loki turned himself into a mare and managed to seduce Svadilfari by running with him into the forest, where they remained for a time long enough to prevent the completion of the building. Freyja, the sun, and the moon were saved, but Loki became pregnant and subsequently foaled Sleipnir, the great eight-legged steed that became the special mount for Odin. His memory is retained in the eight-legged hobby-horse of the kindergarten.

47. *lingworm*. a small grass-snake, so-called from its frequent presence on a heath (*lyng*) or in heather.

48. *Hœnir*. Not much is known about this god, although he seems to have traveled about much with Odin and Loki. According to the Eddic poem *Völuspá* (''The Wise Woman's Prophecy''), Odin gave soul to the dwarves, and Hœnir gave them understanding. In the same poem, after the account of Ragnarök, the cataclysmic doom of the gods, it is told that Hœnir survived and became a prophet in the new, more beautiful world.

49. *Ran*, or Ron. Wife of the sea-god Aegir; her great net draws down drowning men. The ensuing verses, as indicated, are from the Eddic poem *Reginsmál*, stanzas 1, 2, and 6.

50. *Hel*. the dire goddess of the dead, daughter of Loki and the giantess Angrbotha. Her realm, Niflheim, is deep down in the bottom of the universe, under the longest root of the great world-tree Yggdrasil; it is a cheerless place of murkiness and mist, with two dangerous rivers, Hron and Hrith. The name of Hel is synonymous with Death, but not, as it became when it was drawn into the Christian sphere, a place of sadistic punishment for sinners. It was, rather, a kind of foggy limbo.

51. *flame of waters*. Gold. This is a notable example of a *kenning*, a short, highly metaphorical descriptive phrase common in most Germanic poetry of pre-Christian times, which in many cases (as in Old English) persisted into the Christian era. The same is true of Old Norse, in both the skaldic and Eddic poems. In this particular instance, the kenning is derived from the story that Ægir, a sea-god, decorated and illuminated his underwater dwelling with gold.

There are one or two matters of interest furnished by these two stanzas from the *Reginsmál*. As for *Oínn*, he is Andvari's father, but nothing is known about him. He is not Odin, but is generally accepted as a dwarf. *Andvaranaut*, which appears more than once in the story, signifies the ''gift of Andvari.'' *Wergild* represents the fine, or monetary compensation, exacted for a crime, especially murder, paid to the immediate relatives of the victim of said crime.

52. *smithing.* One reading here is "bad smithing"; another "your smithing." In either case Sigurd is showing his distrust of Regin's motives, to say nothing of his skill.

53. *king and prince.* Hjálprek and Álf, respectively.

54. *sea-drake.* Sea-dragon, another effective kenning (see n. 51 above) for "ship," suggested no doubt by the dragon's head often carved on the curving prow of an Old Norse ship of war as a figurehead. The original purpose was to frighten away evil spirits when venturing into unknown seas.

55. *few days.* For the significance of *dœgr* as a unit of both time and distance, see note 20 above.

56. *Hnikar.* Another name for Odin. Over thirty such additional names for the god are mentioned in the Eddic poem *Grimnismál*, stanzas 46–50. See also Snorri Sturluson's *Skaldskaparmál*, chap. 2.

57. *Huginn.* The name of a raven in the service of Odin. On the other hand, this may be a common noun meaning something like "the wise one." Some have combined the ideas and refer to "the wise raven of Odin." Still more see a reference here to the birds of prey on a battlefield after a battle (the so-called Beasts of Battle motif), and the two lines could be read: "Hnikar they called me when I gladdened the raven—O young Völsung!—and I was in battle." In other words, Huginn, Odin's raven, is generalized to refer to any raven.

58. *when I fought.* It is obvious that this represents still another appearance of Odin in the Saga, and as usual he is not recognized. Nor is it clear whether he is here alluding to some specific battle or is merely indicating his general availability or usefulness in the enterprise being undertaken.

59. *Feng or Fjölnir.* Additional names for Odin (see n. 56 above). *Fjölnir* is mentioned in the Eddic poem *Grimnismál*, stanza 47; *Feng* does not appear elsewhere.

60. *cast . . .Fafnir.* A periphrastic and euphemistic expression for "kill," but the reference may be to Fafnir's "helmet of terror" mentioned later (see n. 62 below).

61. *I have come alone.* According to the interspersed prose narrative in the Eddic poem *Fáfnismál*, between stanzas 1 and 2, Sigurd conceals his identity because it was believed that the words of a dying man might have great power to harm, if he was able to curse his enemy by name.

62. *helmet of terror.* A helmet the sight of which inspires fear in an enemy.

63. *Æsir.* The gods in Asgard; see note 4 above.

64. *daughters of Dvalin.* Dvalin was the chief of the dwarves. He is said to have given them a knowledge of runes (see n. 44 above), which would account for their skill in arts and crafts.

65. *Surtr.* Ruler of the world of fire (*Muspellheim*). He was one of the leading attackers of the gods in the final battle leading to the destruction of the Æsir, as told in the Eddic poem *Völuspá* and in the prose account of the *Gylfaginning*.

66. *Óskapt.* Literally "unshaped," "formless." It would seem to be another name for Vigrith, mentioned in the Eddic poem *Vafþruðnismál* ("Ballad of Vaf-thruthnir"), stanza 18, as the place of the final battle in the Twilight of the

Gods, or Ragnarök, the Armageddon of the North.

67. *Regin.* In at least one manuscript, it is Sigurd who does the cutting.

68. *Frankland.* Land of the Franks, probably the present-day Rhineland. It probably should not be understood so exactly, however, for the Norse legend-writers are notoriously vague in matters of geography. Still, one can assume that the term could apply to anywhere in the neighborhood of the River Rhine not occupied by Saxons, Frisians, Burgundians, or some other Germanic tribes. In any event, the reference here is of interest because it echoes the memory of the probable Burgundo-Frankish origins of the figure of Sigurd.

69. *slayer.* The sword Gram.

70. *to Sigurd, saying* . . . The verses that follow are, as indicated, from the Eddic poem *Sigrdrifumál*; the stanzas have been numbered. The likelihood has been recognized for over a hundred years now (see Sijmons's seminal study, item 124 of bibliography) that *Sigrdrifa* is a kenning for Brynhild the Valkyrie. Brynhild is here laying out a kind of curriculum of advanced studies (beyond Regin's level) of various fields of knowledge (trees, ale-making, childbirth, etc.).

71. *byrnie-things.* Those *things* which would concern the byrnie, or corslet; it is really a kenning for "battle."

72. *Tyr.* The sword-god, or god of war, the parallel of the classical Ares or Mars. From an older genitive form of the name, *Tys,* comes the name of the day of the week, Tuesday, (cf. French *mardi*). The name is given also to the runic letter corresponding to T (↑).

73. *sail-horse.* Another kenning for "ship." In the next stanza, *Thing* refers to the popular assembly and tribunal, where all legal problems concerning matters of the kingdom or republic were adjudicated. The term is applied later to a parliamentary body. The semantic development to Modern English *thing* is one of the most remarkable examples of generalization of meaning on record; see the Oxford English Dictionary under *thing*, with particular attention to the dates of examples.

74. *Naud . . .on your nail. Nauð* ("need") is the name of the runic representation of the letter N (↑). In view of the context of this stanza, it is probably correct to believe that the letter Naud offers a phallic significance, especially in association with "nail."

75. *bless.* In the sense of giving a saving protection; it is not necessarily to be assigned a Christian connotation.

76. *leek in the water.* For the curative and protective magical properties of the leek, see note 27 above.

77. *doughty of spirit.* In the *Sigrdrifumál*, there is a break in stanza 12, which consists of but two lines.

78. *Hroptr.* Another name for Odin, pronounced Hroftr. It is mentioned in the Eddic poem *Völuspá*, stanza 62 and in the *Lokasenna* ("Loki's Wrangling"), stanza 45.

79. *shining god.* The sun. According to the Eddic poem, *Grimnismál*, stanza 38, the sun had in front of it a cooling shield, Svalin.

80. *On Arvark's ear and on Alsvin's hoof. Arvark* ("early Waker") and *Alsvin* ("All-Swift") are the horses that draw the chariot of the sun. They are named also in the *Grimnismál*, stanza 37.

81. *Rognir's chariot.* Rognir is apparently another name for Odin, but the name is found only here in *Sigrdrifumál,* stanza 15, and the manuscript is in such bad condition that the reading is conjectural. A possibility exists that the reading should be Hrungnir, the name of a giant killed by the god Thor. But Odin has a chariot, and the likelihood remains that Thor is not to be considered here. Odin's chariot has been identified astronomically as the constellation of Ursa Major (the Big Dipper), which would be an obvious mark, particularly for mariners in the north, since it is essential to locate Polaris, the North Star.

82. *Sleipnir's teeth.* The teeth of Odin's steed; cf. note 46 above.

83. *Bragi's tongue.* Bragi was the god of poetry, perhaps derived euhemeristically from Bragi Buddason *(fl.ca.* 750), the most famous of ancient Norse skalds.

84. *bridge's end.* There is a possible allusion here to the rainbow bridge Bifrost, which led from the world here (Midgard) to Asgard, the home of the gods. But it is more likely that in this stanza we are being told of the various and sundry dangers that confront a man, including crossing a bridge into alien or enemy territory, or conversely of the safety which comes from crossing back into one's own land. Cf. Robert Burns's *Tam O'Shanter.*

85. *On loosening palm and on comfort's traces.* In this line it has been suggested that the "loosening palm" (literally, "the palms of loosening") represents the hand of a midwife freeing the child from the mother's body, and "comfort's traces" would signify the footprints of someone bringing aid and comfort. On the whole, however, these allusions are obscure; the words themselves are definite enough, but their combined meaning is not.

86. *witches' bench.* The bench on which the witch or prophetess sat while she made her prophecy.

87. *on Gungnir's point.* Gungnir was the name of Odin's spear, which he sometimes loaned to his favorite warriors. In this reading, however, there is a variation from the text of the *Sigrdrifumál* (stanza 17) in this same line: the Eddic poem has "Grani's breast" rather than "giantess's breasts," and the reference is certainly more appropriate.

88. *the Vanir.* The Wanes, originally another family of gods (see n. 4 above), whose cult arose among the seafaring peoples of the Baltic and southern coasts of the North Sea, and then spread into Norway, in oppposition to the cult of the Aesir. At first the two groups were "at war," but by agreement the conflict was resolved, and the two "families" blended by marriage and tradition and were worshiped in common. The most famous of the Vanir were Njörd and his two children, Freyr and Freyja.

89. *overthrown.* Another allusion to Ragnarök, the twilight and destruction of the gods, as it is recounted in the Eddic poem *Völuspá* and paraphrased, with excerpts from that poem, in the *Gylfaginning,* chapter 51.

90. *weapon-tree.* A kenning for "warrior"; in this case, Sigurd.

91. *but little.* Generally speaking, such understatements are to be taken as definite negatives: "to avenge but little" would then mean "to avenge not at all." It is a matter of understatement, or litotes, which is an important ingredient in Old Germanic humor. In this case, however, there is some inconsistency with the advice a few lines below that one should not openly resent an insult, but

rather "kill him another day." Yet this merely means that revenge is a prime motive for deadly action here and elsewhere is Old Norse society. This sequence of counseling speeches by Brynhild is typical of the kind of didactic, gnomic process, drawn from ancient habits and customs, well exemplified in the poem *Hávamál*, once in the Eddic canon, but now rejected. It is also an example of the ancient lore that goes to make up the *Forna* material hypothesized to fill in the gap left by the famous lacuna in the Codex Regius of the *Poetic Edda*. It actually has little enough to do with Brynhild.

92. *be burned.* The ultimate revenge in the Old Norse tradition is to burn one's enemy in his own house, as Sigmund did Siggeir in chapter 8 above, or Gudrun did Atli as told in chapter 38. Such action is a dramatic feature in what most consider the greatest of the Norse sagas, that of Burnt Njal. In addition to giving a cruel personal satisfaction, it was also a formal punishment frequently visited on one who had been adjudged an outlaw and had been caught in forbidden territory.

93. *Vaerings.* This name was applied specifically to Norse mercenaries in the employ of the Emperor in Byzantium. Probably it is used here as a name for all Scandinavian peoples. A Vaering adventurer, Rurik, became the founder of the first royal dynasty in Russia (9th century); cf. also the French word for "Viking," *Varègue.*

94. *Greekland Sea.* Probably the Mediterranean, although, in view of the preceding note 93, the Aegean has been suggested, or even the Black Sea. It is interesting to note that this chapter 22 is the only one to transport us to southern or southeastern Europe; it has generally been recognized as a transcription from the *Thidrekssaga.*

95. *Bekkhild.* The word *bekkr* ("bench") indicates that the lady preferred to stay at home rather than go abroad like her warlike sister Brynhild.

96. *shield-maiden.* Here, as several times elsewhere in the Saga, a Valkyrie.

97. *inspect the band of warriors.* In order to determine those warriors Brynhild would be carrying off to Valhalla, fulfilling Odin's wish.

98. *slow to avenge,* etc. The exact circumstances referred to here are obscure. Hakon and Hagbard were the sons of King Hamund of Denmark, as it is told by the thirteenth-century Danish chronicler Saxo Grammaticus in his *Gesta Danorum,* Book 7. Hagbard, having made a treaty with the sons of Sigar, seduces Sigar's daughter Signe. Meanwhile, a certain "Teuton" by the name of Hildigisl, who had been rejected by Signe, started trouble between the sons of Sigar and the sons of Hamund, and Hagbard killed the sons of Sigar. He is then betrayed by Signe's handmaidens and is hanged by Sigar's men. Signe immolates herself, together with her handmaidens. Hagbard's brother, Hakon, being on the point of attacking the Irish, is reluctant to turn his sword upon fellow Danes; hence his revenge is "slow"; indeed, it does not take place at all. The question in the Saga is whether *Haki* is Hakon; the names otherwise correspond. A more difficult problem, however, is whether or not the Author is writing with a full knowledge of the old story, or whether he is familiar only with the names and the burning of the women, and makes up his own version. Besides, one cannot be

sure that the Sigar referred to here is necessarily the same as the one in Saxo Grammaticus, although the grouping fo the same names here is rather striking. There is also, moreover, another Sigar, referred to in the two Eddic poems dealing with Helgi, the *Helgakvida Hundingsbana* I and II.

99. *as in old age.* It will be recalled (see chapter 11 above) that Sigmund was on the point of winning his battle against Lyngvi when Odin interfered and broke Sigmund's sword. At the same time, Hjördis had chosen Sigmund over Lyngvi, "although he is much advanced in years." The tradition is maintained that Sigmund, like Beowulf, undertook his last battle when he was too old.

100. *before my knees.* A curious variant of "before my eyes."

101. *half-years.* The Old Norse *misseri* and the Old English *missera* are of disputed etymology, but the context usually indicates that *half-year* is the probable meaning. Thus in *Beowulf*, 1. 1769, the statement is made that Hrothgar has ruled over the Danes for a hundred *missera*, which is taken to mean fifty years.

102. *bridal draught with Gudrun.* As we have seen, the drinking of wine by the bride and groom was the climactic point in the pre-Christian Norse wedding ritual. They drink, of course, from the same cup, and in poorer families, ale or mead could be substituted.

103. *kings' sons.* It is to be presumed that such slain princes were hostile, and that the killings took place in battle, as appointed by Odin; see note 97 above.

104. *As it is told.* The verses following make up another of the so-called Völsung Fragments, but this time it may well be from some *Meiri* poem lost in the lacuna (see introduction above); in other words, from the *Meiri* fragment.

105. *realm of Gard.* Generally taken to be Russia, or a land inhabited by Slavs; see note 94 above.

106. *Aslaug,* etc. An interesting variant in the Saga and still quite mysterious. This daughter of Sigurd and Brynhild is mentioned in Snorri Sturluson's *Skaldskaparmál*, chapter 41. In one version, as exemplified, for instance, in the Eddic poem *Grímnismál* (stanza 31), Sigurd meets Brynhild and spends some time with her—three nights—in sexual innocence, "as if she were his mother." In other tellings of the story, it is a night, three nights, eight nights (as in the *Helreid Brynhildar,* stanza 12); in all, however, the naked sword Gram is laid between them, emphasizing the fact that there are no sexual relations, and so Sigurd has the right to claim that he is guiltless of the charge of seducing made later in the case of Brynhild, now Gunnar's wife. The Aslaug variant, of course, is different; there the Author allows Sigurd, in Gunnar's shape, to ride through the flickering flames, woo Brynhild, spend three nights with her, with the sword Gram between them for at least the first night, and still manage to impregnate her. Now, are we to suppose that Brynhild waits until she has given birth to Aslaug and so can turn the infant over to her *fóstri,* Heimir? Or is she making use of her powers of prophecy to foretell even the sex of the child?

The story of Aslaug is an old Norwegian tale picked up by the Author to enable him to write a sequel, the *Saga of Ragnar Lodbrók.* This theory has not been seriously shaken since Barend Sijmons's study of over a hundred years ago;

see bibliography, item 124. Such an explanation renders Sigurd's position rather equivocal, although in a way it does much to make Brynhild's vengeful and tormented outlook on life more credible than it would otherwise be.

107. *As has been said.* This seems to be still another passage from a lost poem on the familiar subject.

108. *burn him.* The usual culmination of a long-standing feud; see note 92 above.

109. *those men whom I had mentioned.* Perhaps those whom she had been told would be slain, in keeping with her function as a Valkyrie. Yet there appears to be something missing here; perhaps some version of the story had Brynhild surrounded by flames and guarded by some henchman of Odin against unwelcome suitors, or perhaps the Author has in mind some still different story.

110. *few.* None at all; see note 91 above.

111. *not torture dead men.* This is an extraordinary charge for Gunnar to be making, if it is directed toward Brynhild. In any event, there is no known story to substantiate it; very likely it is only an insult that he hurls at her in his extreme exasperation. For in her role as Valkyrie, Brynhild would bear the bodies of the chosen slain to Valhalla; she would be removing those whom Odin considered worth saving, and they would have an afterlife. She would not be concerning herself with the others, for her role was basically beneficial. From the mane of her steed (and that of the other Valkyries) would fall dew, which revivified the earth and brought harvest to men. To "torture dead men" would be, to say the least, highly unprofessional conduct. At the same time, there is much of the shrew in the later phases of Brynhild's characterization.

112. *chill of anger.* The Old Norse *hrollr* means a quaking or trembling. It could mean an ague of infectious nature, as some have suggested, but the more likely interpretation is that of a "nervous chill," a psychosomatic symptom of hysteria.

113. *dowry of slain warriors.* It will be recalled that in chapter 27 Brynhild said to Sigurd (while he was assuming Gunnar's shape): "Gunnar! . . .speak not of such things to me unless you are a better man than I think you are! For you must kill those who have tried to woo me, if you have the courage to do so." In view of the stringent conditions required for the conquest of Brynhild, it must be that those to whom she is referring were unsuccessful suitors, although there is nothing in either the Eddic poems or the Saga to account for them. The killing of unsucessful suitors who forfeit their lives because they cannot satisfy the requirements laid down to woo a lady would place Brynhild in the folklore category of the Unapproachable Female, the formidable woman who can be tamed only by the man who can overcome the aforementioned condition (the Taming of the Shrew motif). There is no other substantiation of this trait in Brynhild's complex character as here portrayed (warrior, wise woman, lover of Sigurd, vengeful and cruel human being), although there is a hint of it in the present scene, where most people (except Sigurd) are reluctant to interview her. I am inclined to regard this allusion to the slaying of suitors as either an interpretation by the Author (for reasons best known to himself) or a detail resulting from the confusion of one story with another (what the folklorists call contamination). See abstract of *The Nibelungenlied.*

114. *to charge up to them.* An account to be settled by the payment of wergild; see note 51 above. Here another version of the story has been introduced, referred to in the *Sigurdarkvida inn skamma* or Short Lay of Sigurd, stanzas 32–39. According to this version, Brynhild was living happily with her brother Atli until he was attacked by Gunnar and Sigurd and required to give his sister in marriage to Gunnar, something of a feat in view of the fact that Sigurd was Brynhild's hero because he had slain Fafnir. But Sigurd, of course, has deceived her by representing himself to be Gunnar.

This does not agree with the narrative in the Saga. Brynhild had obviously loved Sigurd from the beginning, even before he had first ridden through the "flickering flame" on Hindarfell (section 20) and discovered her, Brynhild the Valkyrie and the Bringer of Victory (Sigrdrifa). The whole matter emphasizes the difficulty of combining Brynhild the Valkyrie and Brynhild the daughter of Budli and sister of Atli.

115. *swollen were his sides.* This is a rather familiar trait among epic heroes: when enraged they become swollen and even, as in the case of the Irish hero Cuchulain, grossly distorted.

116. But these lines as quoted here are not in the Eddic poem, *Sigurdarkvida inn skamma*, and so appear to be another Völsung Fragment.

117. *king of Hunland.* Sigurd; see note 3 above; this is further evidence of the southern origin of Sigurd.

118. *brother-in-law and sister's son.* Sigurd and his infant son, Sigmund. The relationship of uncle and nephew (particularly the son of a sister) is very close in both Germanic and Celtic epic traditions and may well be explained by the possible matriarchal nature of both societies.

119. *all our oath-swearing.* We are told in Snorri Sturluson's *Skaldskaparmál,* chapter 41, that Gutthorm was a stepson of Gjuki, although at the beginning of chapter 25 of our Saga he is merely listed among the sons of Gjuki. But if he is only a stepson he cannot be bound strictly by the oaths of those who were nominally only his half-brothers, Gunnar and Högni. Besides, we are never told that he swore any oaths at all. According to the Eddic poem *Hyndluljód* ("Lay of Hyndla"), stanza 27, Gutthorm was not of Gjuki's race, which suggests that he was the son of Grimhild, but we are not told in the poem who his father was. (His name appears sometimes as Gotthorm.)

120. *skald.* It is hardly necessary at this point to define *skald,* the Norse designation for the professional bard. The verses given here, however, represent another Völsung Fragment, although there is a fairly close parallel in the Eddic *Brot af Sigurdarkvida* ("Fragment of a Sigurd Lay"), stanza 4.

121. *wood-fish.* Or forest-fish, a striking kenning for "snake."

122. *Gera.* The name of a huge wolf in the service of Odin; hence, any wolf, just as (see n. 57) the reference to Odin's raven can be interpreted in the same way to apply to any raven.

123. *sword-point.* Here is a miniature study in the formation of a kenning. The Old Norse *bloðrefill,* used here, breaks down into *bloð* ("blood") and *refill,* tentatively identified as "serpent" or "snake," and is not to be confused with *refill* ("tapestry," "hangings"). If this is indeed a compound of *blood* and *snake,* we have a bold kenning for "sword," for since a snake is dangerous only at its front

end, we then come up with "'sword-point.'' This reading, however, must be made with some caution.

124. *against her will.* In fact, through the drinking of one of Grimhild's medicated draughts: see chapter 32 below.

125. *Oddrun.* The love story of Gunnar and Oddrun is the subject of the Eddic poem *Oddrúnargrátr* ("Lament of Oddrun"). Oddrun joins the Saga rather furtively and then only by allusion. In the Eddic poem she is described as a sister of Atli, and therefore the sister of Brynhild. The love affair between Gunnar and her began after the death of Brynhild (as Brynhild herself has prophesied) and flourished until the two were spied upon by Atli's men, who in spite of bribes offered and received revealed the truth to Atli, but not to Gudrun. This story might account in part for the enmity of Atli toward the Gjukings, particularly toward Gunnar (whom he kills last; see chapter 37); another factor, which I think is the dominant motive, is his lust for gold as well as his envy of the Gjuking brothers because they possessed the Accursed Treasure. Still another consideration would be the incident referred to in note 114, which could have been sufficient to start a classic blood-feud between Atli and the Gjuking brothers.

126. *Jörmunrek.* The historical king of the Ostrogoths, Ermanric (or Eormanric or Hermanric), who died in 376, having been defeated by the Huns. He became a legendary figure of considerable importance and of bad reputation, for he was usually portrayed as a savage, tyrannical ruler who killed his sons and executed his wife in a brutal and ignominious manner. See chapters 41 and 42 below, as well as the introduction.

127. *slain with him.* The Saga does not furnish us with any direct account, but evidently there was a fight during or after the murder of Sigurd, in which warriors of both Völsungs and Gjukings fought each other, with consequent loss of life, as enumerated in the description of the funeral ceremonies.

128. *close on his heels.* The gate of the realm of Hel, goddess of death (see n. 50 above) closed so fast on one who entered it that it would catch anyone trying to follow through. Brynhild finds consolation in the fact that if she is cremated with Sigurd, the gate of Hel will not close so fast as usual. Yet Sigurd, of all people, should be eligible to be carried to Valhalla. The Author seems to have overlooked this important fact; on the other hand, it certainly adds to the human quality of the story to have this detail dramatized in this way.

129. *German.* The Old Norse *þyverskr* is generally taken to refer to the region that is now Germany, and since the Author goes on to specify the Northland in addition (which would mean lands inhabited by the Norse), the meaning "German" probably applied here. We then have still another suggestion of the early German origin of the Saga.

130. *leek.* See note 27 above.

131. *Hálf.* An otherwise obscure King. He has been tentatively identified with Álf, Hjördis's second husband and Sigurd's stepfather (see chap. 12), but this seems most unlikely.

132. *Hakon.* Nothing is known about this Hakon, but the name is a common one in Norse history and legend.

133. *Fjon.* The present Danish island of Fünen. Sigar is mentioned in the *Fornaldar sögur* ("Ancient Sagas"), 2:10, as the father of Siggeir, husband of Sigmund's twin sister, Signy (see chaps. 4-8 above). Snorri Sturluson's *Skaldskaparmál,* chapter 64, associates them in this way.

134. *as it is told.* In the Eddic poem *Gudrúnarkvida II,* stanza 20.

135. *blood of swine.* This is a controversial reading. If *sonar* is the Old Norse word here, it would be the genitive singular of "son," and there would be no need to supply *hennar* ("her"). The reference would then be to little Sigmund (Gudrun's son by Sigurd), who had been killed at the time of his father's murder, as Brynhild had ordered. Apart from the need to supply a word in the text, which is always a doubtful business, the general statement seems most unlikely. But if the reading is *sónar* (with long ó), the reference is to the boar sacrificed to Freyja at the winter solstice (cf. the boar's head at the Yuletide feast). Then the drink would contain the powers of earth and sea and sacrificial blood. This combination appears in the Eddic poem *Hyndluljód* ("Lay of Hyndla"), stanza 48, where the term *sónardreyra* ("swine's blood," boar's gore"), parallels the reading here in the Saga *(dreyra sónar).* In this Eddic poem just cited, the god Heimdall, son of Odin and nine sisters (!), is said to derive his strength from earth, sea, and the virtues of animals sacrificed.

136. *as it says here.* The lines, as noted, are from Eddic poem *Gudrúnarkvida II,* stanzas 23 and 24.

137. *lingfish.* The kenning for "snake"; see notes 47 and 121 above.

138. *land of the Haddings.* The world of the dead, which, according to the Danish chronicler Saxo Grammaticus (13th century), in Book 1 of his *Gesta Danorum* (trans. Oliver Elton [New York, 1905]), was visited by the Danish king Hadingus. It is another of the many medieval accounts of the voyage of a living human being to the Otherworld. In this passage from our Saga, it is not clear whether the snake or the uncut ear of grain comes from Haddingaland; a transporting of the comma merely adds to the confusion. See in particular Georges Dumezil, *La Saga de Hadingus* (Paris, 1953).

139. *four.* According to two of the paper-manuscripts, it is seven days, not four; in the Eddic source *Gudrúnarkvida II,* stanza 36, the period is a week.

140. *went to Hel.* This expression, which appears more than once in the latter part of the Saga, is a circumlocution for "died," and should not be read with any modern connotations.

141. *seldom.* Never; see notes 91 and 110 above.

142. *dais in the hall.* The platform (with poles at the corners) that held the royal seat, from which the king would hold court and dispense both judgments and largesse. The poles could be detached, and were carried by the king wherever he went, as a symbol of his office. It was considered a serious matter to lose them.

143. *said she.* Although it would seem that Kostbera is the speaker, it is not specifically stated in the manuscript, as is usually the case, and so I have supplied the stage directions.

144. *your goddesses.* Probably minor Norns who served as guardians of a warrior's personal destiny; see notes 27 and 40 above.

145. *have good fortune!* Under the tragic circumstances—and they are truly tragic, with the Gjukings hastening to their doom as if they could hardly wait for death—it would be inappropriate to translate *FariÞ vel ok hafiÞ góÞa tíma* as "Good-bye and have a good time." As a matter of fact, the Old Norse *tími* can be bent slightly in the direction of "luck" or "fortune."

146. *dark forest.* That is, a mysterious and secret murky forest. The reference here is to Markwood (or Myrkwood), the vast forest (including the present-day Black Forest of modern Germany) that served as a buffer between the Burgundians and the Huns at the time of their collision in 437. Since the Gjukings represent the Burgundians, and Atli represents the Huns, the historical allegory is only too obvious.

147. *Atli.* The speaker is identified for the sake of clarity.

148. *the eagle and the wolf.* The so-called Beasts of Battle—wolf, eagle, raven—appear in many Germanic battle-pieces, frequently enough to suggest that the burial of corpses slain in battle was not a matter of major consideration.

149. *said Atli.* Again, this is supplied for the sake of clearness; the speaker is not named in the manuscript.

150. *eleven left.* This suggests the customary number of thirty in a band.

151. *betrayed my sister.* Oddrun; see note 125 above.

152. *starve her to Hel.* This is at best an obscure statement. In the Eddic poem *Atlamál in Groenlenzku* ("The Greenlandish Ballad of Atli"), stanza 53, the charge is made that her husband Atli had caused the death of her mother (and of the Gjuki brothers), Grimhild. Yet the Eddic MS does not name the speaker; we have merely assumsed that it is Gudrun, beause she has occupied much of the stage this far in the poem. Following this accusation, there comes in the same stanza of the same poem the charge that Atli took Gudrun's niece and starved her to death, in prison. Otherwise we know nothing, and nowhere else is there any such account of Grimhild's death, to say nothing of even the existence of a niece. Here in the Saga the speech is given to Högni. It would appear that the garbling of the story has come about through unfamiliarity on the part of the Author with the original of his sources—it is not the first instance of deviations that cast some doubt on the theory that the Author had the Eddic poems before him when he composed the Saga. Of course, we can get around part of the difficulty by assuming a conative aspect for the verb—"he tried to kill her" rather than "he killed her"—but this we may have no right to do. Now if Högni is the speaker, as he is here, the kinswoman may be Gudrun herself, who, Högni charges, is being abused by Atli, but this is not likely, obvious though it is that the marriage of Atli and Gudrun has been anything but happy.

153. *twenty of King Atli's warriors.* This is not consistent with Atli's complaint in the preceding chapter that he had only eleven warriors left.

154. *allowed to live.* Here, and in a few passages below, it has been necessary to reconstruct the passages from the paper-manuscripts, because the parchment-manuscript Codex is in poor condition.

155. *He observed.* An entire line here has been reconstructed from the paper-manuscripts.

156. *and to my brothers.* Supplied from the paper-manuscripts.

157. *large and ugly adder.* Reputedly Atli's mother.

158. *block of wood.* There is the possibility of a more dramatic option here, because the word *stokkr* has been interpreted by at least one editor (Ranisch) as referring to the *setstokkr*, "pillars of the high seat"; see note 142 above. On the other hand, the usual meaning is "stick" or "block of wood," which in the present context may be more prosaic but probably more accurate, for I hardly think that even the young princes would be playing with a royal *setstokkr*; they were simply playing with a block of wood or a stick. In the Eddic poem *Atlamál*, stanza 72, Gudrun lays the boys on a block while she slits their throats.

159. *Niflung*, or Hniflung. This is the only appearance of this famous name in the Saga. The Niflungs ("Sons of the Mist") were probably at one time a mythological race who were the original owners of the treasure represented in the Saga by the hoard that Fafnir guarded, the so-called Accursed Treasure. The name was later applied in legend to the Burgundians (or Gjukings), and so it is in the German epic poem, the *Nibelungenlied*, which concerns these people. There has been a great deal of controversy about its importance in relation to that epic, but it is actually a point of only minor consideration in our Saga, and the very fact that it has been assigned in the Saga to one who appears to be a younger son of Högni is merely an indication, a foreshadowing, of what is to come about in the *southern* version of the story. He is named in the Eddic *Atlamál*, stanza 83, and mentioned in stanza 84 as a co-murderer of Atli, along with Gudrun. In a brief prose narrative in the *Poetic Edda*, *Dráp Niflunga* ("Slaying of the Niflungs"), the reference is only to the Gjuking brothers. There is no mention of Högni's son Niflung.

160. *mother-in-law sit weeping.* The only other allusion to Atli's mother is that in the Eddic poem *Oddrúnargrátr* ("Lament of Oddrun"), stanza 30, in which she is identified as the ugly adder that killed Gunnar at the end of chapter 37 of the Saga. What Gudrun did to make her mother-in-law weep, apart from the fact that she had married Atli, is not told, but the contrast between the weeping mother-in-law and the ugly adder is engaging. It will be remembered that at the conclusion of chapter 5, the report was current that the she-wolf who devoured nine of the ten sons of Völsung was the mother of King Siggeir and the mother-in-law of Signy.

161. *Erp.* This, according to the Eddic poem *Atlakvida*, stanza 40, was also the name of the older of the two boys, sons of Atli and Gudrun, whom she slew in revenge. There may be a carry-over, or contamination, in the appearance of this name for the youngest of the three sons Gudrun had by Jonak. But see note 5 to excerpt from the *Skaldskaparmál* below.

162. *Jörmunrek.* See note 126 above. This king actually plays a part in many stories not connected with Sigurd, the Gjukings, or the Völsungs. There is an undeniable tendency for medieval storytellers to connect their many heroes or protagonists, and the example here is obvious. Jömunrek is introduced to become the husband of Svanhild and to demonstrate his notorious reputation for cruel and rash actions. The execution of Svanhild and the abortive attempt at vengeance by her half-brothers, Hamdir and Sörli, are outlined in the Eddic poem *Gudrúnarhvöt* and *Hamdismál*. Once again let me call attention to the

masterly monograph by Caroline A. Brady, *The Legends of Ermanric* (Berkeley, Calif., 1943).

163. *involved in it*. The implication is that neither Jonak nor Gudrun wished, for political reasons, to offend Jörmunrek.

164. *they killed him*. It should be borne in mind that Erp is the youngest of three sons, not the usual two that we have met before in the Saga. This, according to folk-tales, places him in a special position, the favored of his parent(s), and an easy, obvious object of envy or jealousy on the part of the older brothers. (Consider the case of Cinderella.) His death, apparently a senseless murder, may be the vestigial remains of this old folk-motif.

165. *Hamdir stumbled*. In doing so, he evidently kicked up some dirt or pebbles and so ''harmed'' stones. The same thing is true of Sörli's misadventure a few lines below. If, however, we are to judge by the Eddic poem *Hamdismál*, stanza 14, Erp is only a half-brother, and so was therefore looked down upon by them, an attitude analogous to that of Gunnar and Högni toward Gutthorm in chapter 30 above.

166. *as it is told*. In the *Hamdismál*, stanza 27.

167. *with one eye*. Odin again, to end the line of the Völsung-Gjuking family. But what of Helgi? and what of Aslaug? Was Erp in reality a bastard?

It will be recalled from the introduction above that the appearance of Odin in support of the Völsungs was an effective device of the Author. Where did he get this detail? All but one of Odin's appearances belong to the first half of the Saga, for which there is no Eddic source. I have already postulated a lost *Sigmundarsaga*, which could include perhaps the career of young Sigurd until he went to meet Fafnir. There is no Eddic source of which we know, nor in the account by Snorri Sturluson, which follows immediately.

It has been suggested that the appearance of Odin is therefore a later detail—later, that is, than the Eddic poems or the Prose Edda. But see Caroline A. Brady, ''Odin and the Old Norse Jörmunrekr Legend,'' *Publications of the Modern Language Association* 55 (1940): 910–31. It may have been a contamination from some older version. Whoever gave the order to stone Hamdir and Sörli is referred to in the *Hamdismál*, stanza 25 (Dronke version) as *reginkunngi*, which would mean ''descended from the gods.'' Is this Jörmunrek? Or is it Odin? The Saga is the only one to identify this character as Odin specifically. Is it too much to suggest that the Author might have made this change himself? But I forget, he is not reputed to have any imagination, poetic or otherwise. At any rate, it makes a good dramatic finish.

PART TWO

Excerpts from the
Skaldskaparmál, the
Nornageststháttr, and the
Southern Branch of the
Saga—the *Nibelungenlied*
and the *Thidrekssaga*

From the *Skaldskaparmál*

Snorri Sturluson (1178–79 to 1241) is the most famous writer of early Iceland and one of the most important of medieval writers, as a skald, a historian, a critic, a teacher, and a student. His personal life was far from spotless: he was a corrupt magistrate, a treacherous politician, and a fiasco as a family man, ending up as he did, murdered by his son-in-law. He was suspected by many Icelanders of trying to betray the Republic of Iceland to the King of Norway (in this case Haakon IV), and the King in return apparently did not trust him.

Those matters, however, are for the biographer, and do not dim Snorri's solid achievements in letters. For most of his life he was involved with activities at Oddi, the center of Icelandic learning, and there he got inspiration from the Icelandic past—as historian, he wrote the *Heimskringla*, a chronicle of the kings of Norway and Iceland; as man of letters, he was responsible for the *Prose* (or *Younger) Edda*, which is a monument to his scholarship. We can see now that it is a kind of textbook for young poets. It consists of four parts: first, a prologue, in which he narrates briefly the history of Creation (as it is told in Genesis, through the Deluge, after which, he observes, the world as we know it began). It is a brilliant rationalization of Norse mythology from classical legend. The story of Troy is the true genesis. His gods are mortals descended from Trojan figures. It is not a question of belief or of disbelief: these facts are neither to be disbelieved nor to be tampered with; they have been the points of view of the Ancient Skalds, and it is up to you as would-be poets to accept them. The second part of the *Prose Edda*, the *Gylfaginning* (or "Beguiling of Gylfi") is a treatise on Norse mythology, as every budding poet should know it.

In the fourth part, the *Háttatál* or ''Enumeration of Meters,'' is a highly technical, virtually untranslatable tract on metrics, with copious examples from the older skalds as well as some of Snorri's own verses.

It is, of course, the third part that concerns us, the *Skaldskaparmál*, loosely translatable as ''The Poetry of Skalds.'' This, along with the other three parts, has survived in three manuscripts, Codex Regius (early fourteenth century); Codex Wormianus (fourteenth century), and Codex Upsaliensis, about 1300. The last-named of these may be a direct copy of Snorri Sturluson's original text; it definitely ascribes the work to him. The same thing is true of another parchment manuscript, Arnamagnean #748, which fixes Snorri Sturluson as the author.

Snorri's admirers in the present day—and they are many—have called attention to his fine and vigorous style: he never wrote a dull page. It is partly for this reason that I wish to include this selection below, for the reader to compare to chapter 14 of the Saga above. Snorri then proceeds to outline the rest of the story, and although some parts of the account are perhaps not his, it seems academic to separate them from the part we know to be his, for if they are not his, they were written by one of his best students! I should begin by quoting chapter 32 of the *Skaldskaparmál*:

''How should gold be paraphrased? Thus: by calling it Ægir's Fire, Needles of Glasir, Hair of Sif, Snood of Fulla, Tears of Freyja, Talk and Voice and Word of Giants, Drops of Draupnir, Rain and Hail of Draupnir, or of Freyja's Eyes, Otter's Ransom or Forced Payment of the Æsir, Seed of Fyris Field, Roof of Hölgi's Cairn, Fire of all Waters and of the Hand, or Stone and Reef or Gleam of the Hand.''

In subsequent chapters Snorri Sturluson proceeds to tell tales that explain these rather esoteric titles, and in the explanation of ''Otter's Ransom, or Forced Payment of the Æsir,'' he gives us his version of the *Völsungasaga*, which comprises chapters 39–41 inclusive of his treatise. His account, we can see, is rather cursory; it seems to be drawn partly from the Eddic poems (especially the *Reginsmál* and the *Fáfnismál*) and partly, perhaps, from other materials that had come his way. Yet it has certain special points of interest. We may regard it as the first account in Norse of the story of the Saga that was written down and survived, exclusive, of course, of some of the poems of the *Edda*. It makes no mention of Sigmund or Sinfjötli, although it recognizes Sigmund as Sigurd's father; this detail, however, is known to the Eddic poems. It takes no account of Odin's interest in the proceedings. It contributes nothing one way or another to the problem of the gap or lacuna in the *Sigrdrifumál* but near the end, almost as an afterthought, it speaks of Aslaug. This reference, as it happens, comes in a suspect chapter.

Chapter 164

This is the reason why gold is called Otter's Wergild or Otter's Ransom. Three Æsir were exploring the world, Odin and Loki and Hoenir. They came to a certain river and went along it to a certain waterfall, and beside that waterfall was an otter, which had taken a salmon from the water and was eating it, blinking his eyes while he did so. Loki picked up a stone and threw it at the otter, striking it in the head. Then Loki boasted about his catch that he had got at one blow, an otter and a salmon. And so they picked up the salmon and the otter and carried them along with them. They finally came to a farmhouse, entered it, and saw there a man who was called Hreidmar, the owner. He was a man of much substance and was skilled in black magic. The Æsir asked for lodgings overnight, adding that they had with them enough in the way of provisions, as they showed their day's catch. But when Hreidmar saw the otter, he called his sons, Fafnir and Regin, and told them that their brother Otr had been killed and who had done it.

Whereupon father and sons went to the Æsir, seized them and bound them, and told them about the otter, that he was a son of Hreidmar. On their part, the Æsir offered ransom or wergild for their lives, as much money as Hreidmar himself should decide, and it was agreed among them and bound with oaths, after which the otter was flayed. Hreidmar took the hide and demanded that they should fill it with red gold and then cover it altogether. That was the way it was to be, according to their agreement.

And so Odin sent Loki to Svartalfaheim, where he went to the dwarf named Andvari. Andvari was a fish while in water, and Loki caught him with his hands and, as ransom-fee for his life, imposed payment of all the gold that he owned, and that made a very great treasure. At that the dwarf swept under his hand a little gold ring. Loki saw that and ordered him to release the ring. The dwarf begged him not to take the ring away from him, saying that he who might be able to keep it could cause great increase in the treasure. Loki replied that Andvari would not have a penny, and took the ring and went away. The dwarf yelled after him that the ring would bring destruction to whoever had possession of it. Loki said that he thought that was all right, and that this condition should hold good, provided that he himself should give this information to whoever would be concerned with it.

Then Loki went back to Hreidmar and showed the gold to Odin, but when Odin saw that ring, he thought it fair, and so he took it from the treasure and paid the gold to Hreidmar.

Next he filled the otter-skin as well as he could, and set it up on its feet when it was full. Then Odin went up to it and covered the hide with gold and asked Hreidmar to go and look at it and see whether the skin was entirely covered. Hreidmar looked at it and pondered at length and saw a whisker sticking out and ordered that whisker to be covered, otherwise their agreement was null and void. So Odin then had to draw forth the ring to cover the whisker, saying that they were now free from their debt incurred by killing the otter.

But then, after Odin had taken his spear, and Loki his shoes, and they needed no longer to be afraid, Loki suddenly declared that the ring would mean death to whoever possessed it. And that statement held good later. Now it has been told why gold is called Otter's Wergild or Ransom, a Forced Payment by the Æsir, or Metal of Strife.

Chapter 40

What more is to be told about that gold? Hreidmar took it in payment for his son Otr, but Fafnir and Regin claimed some of the ransom for themselves. But Hreidmar would not give them a penny of that treasure. It became the evil intent of the brothers to kill their father for his gold. So Regin asked that Fafnir should share the gold with him, half and half. Fafnir replied that there was little chance for that to happen—sharing the gold with his brother, who had slain his father—and told Regin to get out, otherwise he would fare as Hreidmar had fared. By now Fafnir had taken the helmet that Hreidmar had possessed and set it on his head. It was called the Helmet of Terror, for every living creature that looked at it was filled with fright. Regin took the sword that was called Refill and fled away, while Fafnir went up on to the Gnitaheath and took on the shape of a dragon and lay down over the treasure.

Regin then went to King Hjálprek at Thjöd and became his smith. There he became fosterfather to Sigurd, son of Sigmund (son of Völsung) and of Hjördis, daughter of Eylimi. Sigurd was the most famous of all warrior-kings in respect to family and power and intellect. Regin told him where Fafnir was lying upon the treasure and urged him to hunt it out. Then Regin prepared a sword, which was named Gram; it was so sharp that when Sigurd brought it down to running water, it cut asunder a tuft of wool that drifted downstream against the edge of the sword. Next Sigurd split Regin's anvil to the stock with this sword. After that Sigurd and Regin went up on Gnitaheath, and Sigurd dug a pit in Fafnir's way and set himself in it.[2] So when Fafnir crawled to the water, he passed over the pit and Sigurd laid the sword into him, and that was his death.

But now Regin came forward and said that Sigurd had killed his brother. He demanded as satisfaction that he should have the heart of Fafnir, and then he went to sleep. And when Sigurd broiled the heart of Fafnir and thought that it must by now be fully cooked, he took it up in his fingers to see how tough it was, but when the juice ran out of the heart onto his fingers, he burned them, and so put them in his mouth. When that heart's blood came onto his tongue, he understood the language of birds, and knew what the nuthatches sitting in the trees were saying:

Fáfnismál,
stanza 32

"There sits Sigurd
Smeared with blood,
Fafnir's heart
Broiled with flame;
Wise would seem to me
This spoiler of rings,
If that heart-muscle
Gleaming he ate.

Fáfnismál,
stanza 33

"There lies Regin,
Taking counsel with himself
To trick that youth
That trusts him.
In anger he plots
Wrong accusations;
That smith of evil
Would avenge his brother."

Sigurd therefore stepped over to Regin and killed him; thence to his horse that was called Grani. He rode until he came to Fafnir's den. There he took up all the gold and loaded it into packs and laid them on Grani's back; then he mounted him and rode away. Now it has been told how, according to story, gold has been called Lair of the House of Fafnir or Metal of Gnitaheath or Grani's Burden.

Chapter 41

Sigurd then rode on until he found a house on a mountain. There was a woman asleep in it, and she had on a helmet and a byrnie. He raised his sword and stripped the byrnie from her. Then she awakened; her name was Hild, but she really was named Brynhild and was a Valkyrie. From there Sigurd rode off until he came to the king who was named Gjuki; his queen was called Grimhild. Their children were these: Gunnar, Högni, Gudrun. Gutthorm was the stepson of Gjuki. Sigurd stayed with them a long time. Then he married Gjuki's daughter, Gudrun, while Gunnar and Högni swore oaths of brotherhood with Sigurd. Then Sigurd and the sons of Gjuki went to seek a bride for Gunnar;[3] they visited Atli, the son of Budli, to sue for the hand of his sister Brynhild. She was living in a dwelling on Hindarfell, and around that dwelling were flickering flames. For she had made this solemn vow, to marry only that man who dared to ride through those flames.

Thus they rode along, Sigurd and the Gjukings (they were also called Niblungs) up the mountain, and Gunnar was supposed to ride through the flickering fire. He was on a steed called Goti, but

Goti did not dare leap through the fire. So the two of them, Sigurd and Gunnar, exchanged shapes as well as their names, because Grani would not go under any other rider than Sigurd. So when Sigurd (in the shape of Gunnar) mounted, Grani took him through the flickering fire. That evening he wedded Brynhild,[4] but when they came to bed, Sigurd (in the shape of Gunnar) drew the sword Gram from its sheath and laid it between them. And in the morning, when he rose and dressed himself, he gave Brynhild as a bridal gift the gold ring that he had taken on the Gnitaheath, which Loki had taken from Andvari, and took from Brynhild another ring as a remembrance.

Then Sigurd leaped on his horse and rode back to his companions; he and Gunnar changed back into their normal shapes, and afterward they returned to Gjuki's with Brynhild. Sigurd later had two children by Gudrun—Sigmund and Svanhild.

Once there came a time when Brynhild and Gudrun went down to the river to wash their hair. When the two women came to the river, however, Brynhild waded out from the bank, declaring that she did not wish to have touch her head that water which had run from the head of Gudrun, because she herself, Brynhild, had the braver husband. Gudrun immediately went into the river after her, declaring that she would wash her hair farther out, because she possessed a husband who no other man in the world could equal in valor, because he had slain Fafnir and Regin and afterward taken the heritage of both.

To that Brynhild answered: "That remark would be worth more if it had not been Gunnar who rode through the flickering fire, and Sigurd had dared!"

Gudrun laughed and said: "Do you think it was Gunnar who rode through the flickering flame? I am sure that he who went to bed with you is the one who gave me the gold ring, and that ring which you have on your finger—your so-called bridal gift—is called Andvaranaut, and I am sure it was not Gunnar who found it up on Gnitaheath!" Brynhild suddenly became silent, and went home.

After that Brynhild constantly urged Gunnar and Högni to kill Sigurd, but because they had sworn oaths to him, they persuaded their step-brother Gutthorm to do the deed. He thrust his sword into Sigurd while the latter was asleep, but when Sigurd felt the wound, he threw the sword Gram after Gutthorm and cut the man in two at the middle. So perished Sigurd and his three-year-old son Sigmund, whom they also killed.

Then Brynhild stabbed herself with a sword, and she was burned together with Sigurd. Gunnar and Högni got the heritage of Fafnir and Andvaranaut, and they ruled the land jointly.

Chapter 42

King Atli Budlison, brother of Brynhild, then married Gudrun, who was the widow of Sigurd, and they had two sons. King Atli then invited Gunnar and Högni to his stronghold, and they accepted. Before they left home, however, they hid the gold of the Fafnir heritage in the River Rhine, and that gold has never since been found. But King Atli had a great army ready, and they fought with Gunnar and Högni, who finally were taken prisoner. King Atli had the heart cut out of Högni while he was still alive. That was his death. He then had Gunnar cast into a pit of serpents, where a harp was secretly brought to him, and he struck it with his toes, because his hands were bound, so that all the serpents fell asleep save one, who glided up and struck Gunnar through the cartilage of his breast-bone so far that she got her head into the hole and clung to his liver until he died. Gunnar and Högni are called Niflungs or Gjukings; therefore gold is called the Niflung Treasure or Heritage.

Shortly thereafter Gudrun killed her two sons, and had gold and silver goblets made from their skulls, and then the funeral-feast of the Niflungs took place. At this feast Gudrun poured mead for King Atli into the goblets, which was mixed with the boys' blood, and she had their hearts broiled and given to the King to eat. When that was done, she told him in many ugly words what she had done. There was no lack of strong drink, so that most of the people fell asleep where they were sitting. That night Gudrun went to where the king was asleep, and with her a son of Högni. They both struck at the king, and that was the end of him. Then they set fire to the building and burned to death all the people who were in it. Then Gudrun went to the sea and jumped in, meaning to end her own life, but she was driven away over the sea by great waves. She came to the land where King Jonak ruled. When he saw her, he took her to himself and married her. They had three sons, who were named Sörli, Hamdir, and Erp.[5] They were all dark-haired as ravens, like Gunnar and Högni and the other Niflungs.[6]

Then Svanhild, daughter of Sigurd when a young man, grew up; she was most beautiful of all women. King Jörmunrek the Mighty heard of her. He sent his son Randver to ask for her hand. When Randver came to Jonak, Svanhild's hand was awarded to Jörmunrek, and Randver went to take her back to his father. But Bikki then said it would be more fitting that Randver should marry Svanhild, for he and she were both young, while Jörmunrek was old. This remark amused the young people. Bikki told the story to Jörmunrek, whereupon Jörmunrek had his son seized and led to the gallows. Randver took his hawk and plucked off all its feathers and sent it to his father. Then he was hanged. When King Jörmunrek saw the hawk, it occurred to him that just as the hawk was powerless to fly without its feathers, so was his kingdom disabled and unable to move, for he was now old and without a son.[7]

Soon after, King Jörmunrek came riding out of the forest from the hunt, along with his troop, and Queen Svanhild was bleaching her hair. They rode upon her at once and trod her to death under the feet of their horses.

When Gudrun heard this news, she urged on her sons to avenge Svanhild. When they were getting ready for their adventure, she brought them byrnies and helmets so strong that iron could not bite into them. She also laid these instructions on them: that when they came to King Jörmunrek, they should attack him at night while he was asleep. Sörli and Hamdir should cut off his arms and legs, and Erp his head.

But when they had started on their journey, they asked Erp what help in this adventure they might expect from him, if they should ever meet with King Jörmunrek. He answered that they should expect as much as arm helps leg or hand foot. They were so angry at their mother, because she had sent them forth with words of hatred, that they decided to do that which would hurt her most, and so they killed Erp, because she loved him best.[8] A little later, as Sörli was walking along, one of his feet slipped; he steadied himself with his arm. Then he remarked: ''Now the arm supported the leg! Better now if Erp were alive!'' When they came to King Jörmunrek at night, while he was asleep, they hewed off his arms and his legs. He awoke and yelled to his men, bidding them get up and help him. Then Hamdir spoke: ''His head would now be off, if Erp were alive!''

The retainers arose and attacked them, but neither was wounded by weapons. King Jörmunrek called out that they should fight with stones.[9] And so it was done. There they fell, Hamdir and Sörli. Then the family and descendants of Gjuki were all dead. [10]

Following Sigurd as a young man, there lived his daughter, named Aslaug, who was brought up by Heimir in Hlymdale, and great families were descended from her. It is said also that Sigmund Völsungsson was so powerful that he could drink poison and it would do him no harm, and that Sinfjötli and Sigurd, his sons, were so thick-skinned that no poison could reach them from without. Therefore Bragi the skald[11] spoke thus:

> Then the Völsungs' drink's
> Writhing eel hung wound on old Lit's
> Seaman's wrestling-challenger's [Thor's] fish-hook. [12]

Many a skald has taken words and different stories from these sayings.

Notes on Excerpt from the *Skaldskaparmál*

1. *Hoenir*, See note 48 to the Saga.
2. *set himself in it*. There is no Odin to advise him, as in the Saga.
3. *seek a bride for Gunnar*. Nothing is said of the machinations of Grimhild, in the case of either Sigurd or of Gunnar.
4. *he wedded Brynhild*. Snorri uses the phrase ''drank the bridal draught'' with Brynhild, though not in the presence of witnesses. In the Saga it says that she seemed glad to see him.'' If Snorri's assertion is to be taken at face value, it would seem to infer that Sigurd was guilty of bigamy, in his own consciousness at least. This would make the subsequent behavior of Brynhild far more credible. The very least to be said is that Sigurd's conduct here is strange, in view of the fact that he has already been legally married to Gudrun.

5. *Erp.* I call attention once again to note 164 of the Saga chapter 39 in which it is specifically said that Jonak and Gudrun had three sons. Yet in the Eddic poem *Hamdismál,* stanza 14, Erp is definitely called their half-brother, and, as already pointed out, this makes a difference in their attitudes toward him—he is an outsider, like Gutthorm. The Eddic poem therefore makes much clearer the motivation in the killing of Erp. Both Hamdir and Sörli are resentful at having to risk their lives in revenge for Svanhild, and they are angry especially at Gudrun for her "urging on," and so they vent their rage in a way that would hurt Gudrun most; namely, by killing Erp, who is assuredly Gudrun's son even if the others are not. The Author of the Saga, on the other hand, has no motive to offer; it is a senseless killing. In the *Hamdismál,* the two older sons refer to Erp as a bastard (*hornungr*); there is no further helpful information. I think we should follow the folkloristic line here: if there are three children (even by one mother), the first two are more or less evil, and the third is the darling (as with Cinderella). On the other hand, we learn from stanza 8 of the *Hamdismál* that Erp was also the name of the older of Gudrun's two sons by Atli, killed in chapter 38 of the Saga. Was her transferring of this name to her youngest (?) son by Jonak a reaction to a guilt complex? The matter is too bizarre to await any ready answer.

6. *Niflung.* See note 159 of the Saga above. Snorri Sturluson, writing a hundred to a hundred and twenty years earlier, does not know any son of Högni named (H)Niflung; he applies the name to the whole family of the Gjukings. Note also that, as epic representatives of the Huns, they are black-haired, not Nordic blonds.

7. *without a son.* The point is made in chapter 40 of the Saga that the significance of the plucked hawk is interpreted by Jörmunrek in terms of honor, whereas here it is interpreted in terms of realism: he realizes that he is now an old man without the strength to defend himself or his kingdom and is without a son who could do both. In either case, I suppose, we have a motive for the death (by or not by suicide) of the historical King Ermanric. See again Caroline A. Brady, *The Legends of Ermanric* (Berkeley, Calif., 1943).

8. *she loved him best.* See note 5, above.

9. *fight with stones.* Snorri Sturluson says nothing about Gudrun's injunction to the young man about "harming" stones. In chapter 42 we have the Saga setting forth: not to harm stones or other "large things," for it would go hard with them if they did.

10. *were dead.* All except Aslaug, of course, and for all we know, Helgi too.

11. *Bragi.* Bragi inn Gamli, or Bragi the Old, probably the most distinguished of the ancient skalds. It is also the name of the god of poetry in Asgard (one of the later additions), and if, as Snorri Sturluson suggests in his prologue, the gods of Asgard were once mortals or descended from mortals in a euhemeristic pattern, then Bragi the Old may be the actual prototype of Bragi the god. He flourished about 750. He is a favorite of Snorri's.

12. The poem quoted is part of a stanza dealing with Midgardsorm, the great serpent that encircles the entire earth. This portion tends to demean the serpent's strength and size, but the rest of the stanza does not. He is being opposed by the great god Thór ("the wrestling-challenger"), who has hooked him, assisted by an old giant ("old Lit"). There is a good brief analysis of these

verses in Peter Hallberg's *Old Icelandic Poetry,* (trans. Schach and Lindgrenson, no. 50 in the bibliography), pp. 109—10.

Needless to say, the reference to the Völsungs' drink is to the attribute of Völsung's son Sigmund that he could drink poison and it would not hurt him, and that both Sinfjötli and Sigurd were resistant to poison on the outside. In other words, the serpent is a venomous serpent spewing poison.

From the *Nornageststháttr*

There are two surviving Old Icelandic sagas concerned with King Olaf Tryggvasson, who ruled in Denmark from 995 to 1000 and was the official bringer of Christianity to the Norse world. This fact, in addition to the story of his tragic suicide in a naval battle with the English in 1000, no doubt accounts for the idealistic, pietistic concept of him as the protagonist of the two sagas, a shorter one and a longer one. We are concerned here with the longer one, which comes down to us in three surviving manuscripts, not far apart in date (1350-1450), and about a generation or so after the date of the *Völsungasaga*. There is very little variation among the three manuscripts, but I have chosen the one in the large repository of Old Icelandic literature, the *Flateyjarbok*, or Book of Flat Island (off the west coast of Iceland). This manuscript dates from about 1390.

The chief interest of the *Saga of Olaf Tryggvasson* for readers of the *Völsungasaga* lies in the fact that it contains a most interesting *tháttr,* which can be defined as a story within a story, an episode of digressive nature. It is a fairly common device in medieval narrative, for although they may not be called *thaettir,* the so-called digressions of *Beowulf*—Sigmund-Sinfjötli, Heremod, the so-called Finnsburg Episode, the brief account of the death of Hygelac among the Franks and Frisians—all these are analogous. This whole problem has been well explored by the Chadwicks in their *Beginnings of Literature* (see bibliography), and a certain kind of formula has been set up by Joseph C. Harris in his "Genre and Narrative Structure in some *Íslendiga Þaettir*," *Scandinavian Studies* 44(1972):1-27, although he does not consider the *Nornageststháttr,* and if he had, he would have found that this particular *tháttr* did not exactly fit his formula.

In brief, the *Nornageststháttr* tells of the arrival of a stranger, punningly called Gest, at the court of King Olaf. He is mysterious, for on the first night of his stay with the King, an elf is seen hovering over his bed in the middle of the night, observing: "An empty house, and a very strong lock on the door! They say that this king is the wisest of men, but . . . if he were so wise, would he sleep so soundly?" Under such circumstances, it is no surprise that Gest proves to be a fascinating visitor, and his stories keep all who hear them vastly entertained. And yet these various stories could not have been experienced by any one mortal, for, like the rulers visited by Widsith in the Old English poem of that name, Gest's "experiences" cover centuries, from Sigurd (whose historical antecedents, such as they are, run from the fifth century, and who is at least much fictional as real), to the sons of Ragnar Lodbrók in the ninth. One gets the impression that Gest has been everywhere and known everybody at all times. He himself admits to being three hundred years old, a favorite round number for a long, long time in medieval fiction. One is reminded of the beautiful ending in the Breton *lai, Guingamor,* where, in the delights of love, three centuries pass in the twinkling of an eye.

Moreover, we have in the final chapter another version of the old folktale best known through the Greek tale of Meleager, the length of whose life depended upon a burning brand. In Gest's case it is a burning candle, and the decree comes from the Norns at the time of his birth; hence his name.

Only that part of the *tháttr* bearing upon Sigurd and the burning candle has been included here. The earlier chapters are summarized within parentheses.

Chapter 1

(Gest, having arrived unexpectedly at the court of King Olaf, is granted lodging for an indefinite period. It is a friendly, gentle, and companionable kind of court. Following the incident of the elf in the night already mentioned, Gest explains that he is a Dane. He is strong and capable-looking, although "advanced in years."

King Olaf observes that he will not remain long with him in an unbaptized state. Gest says that he has already been prime-signed.[1] He accepts these conditions and stays, admired and respected by everyone for his talents in music and story-telling.)

Chapter 2

(At Yuletide, one of the King's followers, Ulf, returns to spend the holidays with Olaf. He brings with him some gifts, including the ring Hnitud, which wins the admiration of all except Gest. On being questioned, he asserts that he has certainly seen better gold than is in Hnitud. The men wager four marks against Gest's knife and bet that this cannot be so.)

Chapter 3

(Next morning, when the King hears of the wager, he tries to dissuade the men, but both they and Gest are determined to hold the wager. While the others have gone out for a drink, the King questions Gest, who produces a saddle-buckle that far outshines Hnitud. Although he has won the bet, Gest is not at all interested in winning the money, for, he says, one should learn that there is always a chance that one may meet someone who knows more than you do. When asked for details about the origin of the saddle-buckle, Gest suggests that if they want to hear that, they will want to hear the rest of the story. "It may be," said the king, "that you are absolutely right!")

(*At this juncture, from our point of view, comes the relevant portion of the tháttr.*)

Chapter 4

"Then I will tell you how once I went south to Frankland.[2] I wanted to see for myself the king's habits and the great excellence that flowed from Sigurd Sigmundarson in terms of bodily beauty and manhood. Nothing notable happened before I came to Frankland and met with King Hjálprek, who had a great troop with him. There was Sigurd Sigmundarson (son of Völsung) and Hjördis, Eylimi's daughter. Sigmund had fallen in battle against the sons of Hunding, and Hjördis had married Álf, son of Hjálprek. There Sigurd grew up in his youth, and all the sons of King Sigmund; they were greater than all other men in strength and stature, Sinfjötli and Helgi, who slew King Hunding and therefore was called Hundingsbane; the third was called Hámund.

"Yet of all these brothers Sigurd was the bravest, and it is well known that Sigurd was the most noble of all warrior-kings and the best in his own right in ancient times. Now there had come to King Hjálprek one Regin, son of Hreidmar; he was more skillful in most things than any man, but he was a dwarf in stature; a wise man, grim and versed in black magic. Regin taught Sigurd many things and was much devoted to him. He told him about his ancestors and the wonderful circumstances of his birth and bringing up. And when I had been there but a short time, I became manservant to Sigurd, along with many others. All of us were greatly devoted to him because he was friendly and unassuming and generous toward us.

Chapter 5

"It happened one day, when we were approaching the house of Regin and were well received there, that Regin began to speak these verses:

Reginsmál,
stanza 13

'Come hither to our hall
Is the son of Sigmund,
The quick and resolute.
More strength has he
Than I, an old man,
Against the rough attacks
Of the raging wolf!

Reginsmál,   'Yet will I cherish this warrior
stanza 14   Bold among the people,
                           Now that the heir of Yngvi[3]
                           Has come among us.
                           May this prince under the sun
                           Be mightiest, in all lands famous
                           For his praiseworthy deeds!'

"At that time Sigurd was always with Regin, who told him much about Fafnir—how he was dwelling upon Gnitaheath in the shape of a dragon and that he was of wonderfully great size. Regin then made a sword for Sigurd which was called Gram. That was so sharp-edged that when he thrust it into the River Rhine, a strand of wool came floating downstream, and the sword cut the tuft asunder. After that Regin egged on Sigurd to kill Fafnir, Regin's brother, and spoke these verses to Sigurd:

Reginsmál,   'Loud would laugh
stanza 15   The sons of Hunding,
                           Those who from Eylimi
                           Bereft his life,
                           If he should tempt me
                           More to seek red rings of gold
                           Than avenge his father!'

"Afterwards Sigurd prepared for his adventure, with plans to make war on the sons of Hunding, and King Hjálprek brought him a great army with some ships of war. In this expedition there was with Sigurd his brother Hámund and the dwarf Regin. I was there also, and they then called me Nornagest.[4] King Hjálprek was known to me, because he had been in Denmark with Sigmund Völsungsson. Then Sigmund married Borghild, but they separated when Borghild killed Sinfjötli, son of Sigmund, with poison.

"Later Sigmund went south into Frankland and married Hjördis, daughter of Eylimi, whom the sons of Hunding slew, so that Sigurd had to avenge both his father and his mother's father. Helgi Sigmundarson, who was called Hundingsbane,[5] was the brother of Sigurd, who later was called Fafnisbane. Helgi, the brother of Sigurd, had slain Hunding the king, and his three sons:

Eyjulf, Hervard, and Hjörvard. But Lyngvi had escaped, and his
two brothers, Álf and Heming. These were famous men for all
their exploits, but Lyngvi was foremost among the brothers. They
were greatly skilled in magic: they had cowed many petty kings
and slain many warriors and burned many towns and done the
greatest havoc in both Spainland and Frankland, but the Imperial
Power[6] had not yet come thither over the mountains. The sons of
Hunding had taken over the land that belonged to Sigurd in
Frankland, who had large forces there.

Chapter 6

"Now it is to be told that Sigurd prepared for the battle against
the sons of Hunding. He had a very large, well-equipped army.
Regin had had much to do with the planning. He had a sword that
was named Ridil, that he himself had forged and smithed. Sigurd
asked Regin to lend him his sword. He did so, insisting, however,
that Sigurd should kill Fafnir when he had come away from this
battle. This Sigurd promised to do for him.

"Then we sailed south along the land, when there came upon
us a great storm brought about by witchcraft; many blamed it on
the sons of Hunding. As we sailed along, hugging the shore, we
saw a man on a sort of rocky headland jutting out between two
cliffs. He was old and wore a green coat and dark-blue breeches,
with high boots on his legs, and he held a spear in his hand. This
man sang out to us, saying:

Reginsmál,	'Who ride here the steeds of Raefil,[7]
stanza 18	The high waves and the ocean
	Noisily dashing? Your sails
	Are soaked by the sea,
	Nor can your weaponed ships
	Stand up against the wind!'

"Regin spoke in reply:

Reginsmál,	'Here are we with Sigurd
stanza 17:	Come over the sea,
	A favoring wind gives us
	To our own deaths;

Soon will fall the breakers
Higher than our prows!
Will dash our sea-rollers!
But who is asking about us?'

"The man in the cloak replied:

Reginsmál,   'Hnikar[8] they did call me
stanza 18:   When I gladdened Huginn,[9]
                   Young Völsung! . . .'

"Then we steered toward land, and the storm immediately
weakened, and the youth Sigurd invited the man to come into the
ship. He did so, and the storm ended and a fair breeze sprang up.
The fellow sat himself down and was very agreeable. He asked if
Sigurd would accept some advice from him. Sigurd said he would
be glad to; he said that he thought sure that the stranger would be
full of good advice for anyone who wished to profit from it, and
addressing the man in the dark cloak, he spoke:

Reginsmál,   'Tell me this, O Hnikar,
stanza 19:   You know everything good
                   Both of gods and of men;
                   Which signs are the best
                   When there is to be a fight,
                   And best for the sweep of swords?'

"Hnikar replied:

Reginsmál,   'Many are the good signs,
stanza 20:   If men care to know them,
                   Sound at the swinging of swords,
                   Faithful the guidance, I think,
                   When a warrior finds at his side
                   A raven for companion.

Reginsmál,   'This is another; if you have come out
stanza 21:   Ready to go to adventure,
                   You will see them before you,
                   Standing in your path,
                   Two warriors proud of their fame.

Reginsmál,   'This is a third: if you hear
stanza 22:   The howling of a wolf
                   Under an ash-tree,

It augurs well for you,
If fortune makes you to see,
First to behold the warriors.

Reginsmál,   'No warrior will fight
stanza 23:   When he must face
                     The moon's shining sister.[10]
                     Victory they will have
                     Who are able to see how,
                     Active in sword-play,
                     To draw up their force in wedges.

Reginsmál,   'It is a grievous mischief
stanza 24:   If you stumble along;[11]
                     When it is fighting weather
                     Guileful spirits will stand
                     On either side of you,
                     Will see to it that you are wounded.'

"And after this we sailed along the coast of Holstein and to the east of Friesland,[12] and so to land. The sons of Hunding heard at once of our expedition and gathered their forces.[13] Soon there was an army, and when we came upon them, a hard battle began. Lyngvi was the bravest of all the brothers in all kinds of feats of battle, although they all did well. Sigurd attacked so hard that everything gave way before him, for the sword Gram became too likely to wound. No one, in short, could reproach the courage of Sigurd. So when he and Lyngvi met, they exchanged many blows and fought most daringly. Then came a lull in the battle, while men turned to watch this single combat. A long time passed, but neither of them seemed able to wound the other, so skilled was each in the art of battle. Then the brothers of Lyngvi attacked and killed many men, while the rest of them fled. Soon Hámund, Sigurd's brother, turned on them, and I with him, so that another battle soon began.

"At last the combat between Sigurd and Lyngvi ended— Sigurd took him prisoner, and he was placed in irons. When Sigurd came up to me, things changed very quickly. The sons of Hunding fell, and all their host; in fact, the night was growing dark indeed. When it grew light in the morning, Hnikar had vanished and was never seen again. Men thought that he must have been Odin.

"It was then discussed, what kind of death Lyngvi should die. Regin said that in his opinion the "blood-eagle" should be cut on his back.[14] Regin took the sword from me and carved the back of Lyngvi, so that the ribs were cut away from the spine, and his lungs were then drawn out. So died Lyngvi, with great courage.

"Then Regin said:

Reginsmál, stanza 26:	'Now with the bloody eagle Is the slayer of Sigmund Slashed on the back. Few were there fiercer Who reddened the earth With the strength of a prince And gladdened the ravens!'[15]

"We got great booty from that battle. Sigurd's men took it all, because he himself did not want it. There were great riches in the battle-clothes and weapons.

"Afterwards Sigurd slew Fafnir and after him Regin, because the latter was about to betray him. Sigurd then took Fafnir's gold and rode up to Hindarheath[16] and found Brynhild there, and things went as they are told in the Saga of Sigurd Fafnisbane.[17]

Chapter 7

"Later Sigurd wedded Gudrun, daughter of Gjuki.[18] He stayed for a time with the Gjukings, his new kinsmen.

"I was with Sigurd up north in Denmark. I was also with him when King Sigurd Hring sent the sons of Gandalf,[19] his brothers-in-law, to meet with the Gjukings, Gunnar and Högni, and demand that they pay him tribute or suffer otherwise the harrying of their land. They decided, however, to defend themselves and their realm. Then Gandalf's men challenged the Gjukings to a pitched battle at the frontier, and then they returned home. And so the Gjukings asked Sigurd Fafnisbane to battle with them on the Gjukings' side, and he said that he would. I was following Sigurd at the time. We sailed north to Holstein and landed at a place called Jánamóda,[20] and at a short distance from the harbor, hazelwood poles were set up,[21] to show where the pitched battle was to take place.

"There we saw many ships sailing down from the north. The sons of Gandalf were in command. The two sides attacked each other. Sigurd Hring was not there, because he had to defend his own land, Sweden, against the invasions of the Kurir[22] and the Kvaenir.[23] Sigurd was by then very old. When the bands came together, there was a very great battle and slaughter of men. The sons of Gandalf fought very hard, because they were both bigger and stronger than other men. In their band was an exceptionally strong man, who killed men and horses, so that nobody could withstand him, for he was more like a giant than a man. Gunnar told Sigurd to attack this scoundrel, because, he said, otherwise they would never win. So Sigurd rode out to meet this big fellow, and some men with him, but most of the others were far from eager.

"We soon came up to this mighty man," continued Gest, "and Sigurd asked him his name and where he came from. He said his name was Starkad Stórverksson,[24] out of Fenhring in Norway.[25] Sigurd seemed to think he had heard about him, chiefly bad things; 'such men are not to be spared for their wickedness.'

"Starkad said: 'Who is this man so big of words?'

"Sigurd told him.

"Starkad said: 'Are you called Fafnisbane?'

" 'So I am,' replied Sigurd.

"Starkad tried to escape, but Sigurd hurried after him and raised in the air the sword Gram, and struck him with its hilt on the jaw so that two of Starkad's molars fell out. It was a wicked blow!

Then Sigurd told the cur to drag himself off. Starkad hurried away, and I picked up one of his teeth and carried it with me. It is now being used as the handle of a bell-rope at Lund in Denmark[26] and weighs seven ounces. Men consider it a curiosity, a real wonder to look at there.

"So after Starkad had fled, the sons of Gandalf did likewise. We took great booty there, and Sigurd and the princes went home to their realm and stayed there for a while.

Chapter 8

"Shortly thereafter we heard that Starkad had committed a foul murder, killing King Ali in his bath.[27]

"It happened that one day Sigurd Fafnisbane was riding to some kind of meeting. He rode into a stagnant pool, and his steed Grani leaped up so hard that the saddle-girth broke apart, and this buckle fell to the ground. When I saw it shining there in the mud-flat, I picked it up and carried it over to Sigurd, and he gave it to me. You were looking at that same gold just a little while ago. Then Sigurd leaped from his horse's back and I rubbed down Grani and washed the mud off him, and took a hair from his tail to show his great size."

Then Gest showed this lock from Grani's tail, and it was seven ells long. King Olaf said: "I think a lot of your stories." All present praised his tales and his talents.

Gest spent the time till evening telling many entertaining tales. Then the men went to sleep, and the next morning King Olaf had Gest called, wishing to talk with him at greater length. The King said:

"I cannot quite make out your age; how can it be believed that you could see a man so old, or that you have been where such events took place? You will have to tell us other stories, so that we can be truly informed."

Gest answered: "It seemed to me that you might wish to hear other stories of mine, if I told you about that gold and what happened to it."

"You must certainly tell us about it!" exclaimed the King.

Chapter 9

"I wish to tell you now," said Gest, "that I went north to Denmark and settled there on my father's land, because he had just died, and a little later I heard of the death of Sigurd and then of the Gjukings, and I thought it was very important news."

The King asked: "What caused Sigurd's death?"[28]

"It is the saying of most men," answered Gest, "that Gutthorm Gjukason ran him through with a sword while he was asleep in bed with Gudrun. The Germans,[29] however, say that Sigurd was killed out in the forest. In the *Gudrúnarræðu*[30] it is said that Sigurd and the sons of Gjuki had been riding to some gathering, and they killed him. There is agreement at least on this point: that they struck him while he was down and unaware, and that they betrayed his trust in them.''

One of the group of retainers asked: ''How did Brynhild behave then?''

Gest answered: ''Then Brynhild slew seven of her thralls and five handmaidens and ran herself through with a sword, asking that she be carried to the pyre, where she might be burned to death. And so it was done: a pyre was built for her and another for Sigurd, but he was burned before Brynhild. She was carried to her pryre in a wain hung with purple velvet and glowing all over with gold, and so she was burned.''

The men asked Gest whether Brynhild had composed anything at her death. He said it was true that she had. They asked him to recite it if he could.

Then said Gest: ''When Brynhild was being driven to the pyre on her way to Hel, she was brought near some cliffs where a giantess was living. She was standing outside the gates of Hel, wearing a skin-kirtle that was colored black. She held in her hand a long wooden wand and spoke: 'I am going to burn you with this, Brynhild! And it were better for you if you had been burned while you were still living, for you had Sigurd Fafnisbane killed—that so famous man!—and ever after I was partial to him. And therefore I will make verses in a song of reproach, so that you will be hated by all who hear such things said about you.'

''So they chanted there, one to the other, Brynhild and the giantess. The giantess spoke first:

Helreid Brynhildar, stanza 1	'You shall not go through My courts pillared with stone; More seemly for thee To stretch out the tapestry Rather than to visit thus The husband of another!
Helreid Brynhildar, stanza 2:	'What will you have From the Land of Slaughter Here in my abode,

Fickle-minded brain?
Many wolves have you made
Partakers of flesh—
If you wish to know—
Life-blood of heroes.'

"Then said Brynhild:

Helreid Brynhildar,
stanza 3:

'Chide me not, thou woman!
From your rocky dwelling,
Though I was of yore
In Viking battles.
Of us two I shall seem higher
To those who know my nature!'

"The giantess replied:

Helreid Brynhildar,
stanza 4

'Thou, Brynhild, art
Daughter of Budli,
The worst in evil
Born into this world!
Thou didst destroy the sons of Gjuki
And brought low
Their goodly dwellings!'

"Then Brynhild spoke:

Helreid Brynhildar,
stanza 5

'I will tell you
The truth in anger,
If you would listen,
How the heirs of Gjuki
Left me joyless
As well as perjured.

Helreid Brynhildar,
stanza 7

'The king, full of courage,
Let me, sister of Atli,
Dwell out of harm beneath an oak—
If you would care to listen—
When I swore oaths
To that king so young,

Helreid Brynhildar,
stanza 8

'I let that old fellow,
Brother of the giantess
(Leader of the Goths[31]),
Hjálmgunnar[32] thereupon
Speed on his way to Hel;

Victory I gave to the brother of Aud;
For that was Odin
Very fearsome to me.

Helreid Brynhildar,
stanza 9:

'He locked me in with shields
In Skatalund, both red and white,
There indeed he put me to sleep,
Then bade him awake me
From my slumber
Who never in the land
Knew the fashion of fear.

Helreid Brynhildar,
stanza 10

'About my hall he set,
High-leaping from the south,
Fiery flames like howling dogs;
There he bade a thane
Ride over these
When he bore to me
The treasure of Fafnir.

Helreid Brynhildar,
stanza 11:

'Grani he rode,
The good giver of gold,
Where my foster father
Ruled his retainers;
Alone he seemed to all
Better, that Viking of the Danes,
In all his glorious powers.

Helreid Brynhildar,
stanza 12

'We two slept beneath
Together in one bed,
As if he were born my brother.
Neither laid hand upon the other.
For eight nights long
We lay together.

Helreid Brynhildar,
stanza 13

'For this Gudrun reviled me,
The daughter of Gjuki,
That I had slept in the arms of Sigurd;
Then was I aware
Of the thing I would not,
That they two hid from me
The fact of their marriage

Helreid Brynhildar,
stanza 14

'All too long[33] have I struggled
Against adversity; women and men
Strive to escape alive,

Never shall we two
Tear each other apart.
Now sink down, thou giantess!'

"Then that giantess shrieked a terrible shriek and leaped back
into the cliff."

The retainers of the King said: "That was a good story. Now
tell us some more!"

The king demurred, however: "That is not necessary; you
need not tell us more about such things."

But then he added: "Were you ever with the sons of
Lodbrók?"[34]

Gest replied: "I was with them for a short time. I came to them
while they were making an expedition south to Mindarfell and
destroyed Vifilsborg.[35] There was fear everywhere, because they
won victory wherever they went, and so they decided to go right
on to Rome. There came a day, however, when a stranger ap-
peared before King Björn Járnsida and greeted him. The king
received him in friendly fashion and asked him whence he had
come. He told the King he was from the south, from Rome.

"The King asked: 'How far is it from here?'

"He answered (his name was Sónes): 'You can see here, O
King, the shoes that I am wearing on my feet'—he took the iron-
bound shoes from his feet, which shoes were very thick on top but
much torn up on the bottom—'so far is the journey from here to
Rome, as you can now see from my shoes, how much they have
suffered!'

"The King said: 'That is indeed a wonderfully long journey
for us to go, and so we will turn around and not make an attack
upon Rome.'

"And so they did, for they went no farther, but it seemed to
each of them a remarkable thing that they should so quickly
change their plans from the words of one man, when all their
plans had been laid. At any rate, the sons of Lodbrók went back
north and harried the south no more."

King Olaf observed: "It is easy to see that the holy men in
Rome did not want them to come there, so it must have been a
spirit sent by God that caused them to change their previous
plans so quickly and not deal destruction in Rome, the holiest
city of Jesus Christ!"

Chapter 10

Next the King asked Gest: ''When you have come among
kings, who seemed to you to be the best?''

Gest replied: ''I enjoyed most being with Sigurd and the Gjuk-
ings and the sons of Lodbrók were most independent in allowing
one to live as one liked, and with Eirek at Uppsala[37] there was the
greatest happiness, but King Harold Fairhair[38] was most exacting
in the duties of his retainers among all the kings whom I have
named. I was also with King Hlödver[39] in the land of the
Saxons,[40] and it was there that I was prime-signed, because there I
could not be otherwise, for Christianity was well observed there,
and that, it seemed to me, was the best place of all.''

The King said: ''You are full of information about those things
which we wish to ask!''

Indeed, the King questioned Gest at length, and Gest told him
everything clearly, and finally said: ''Now I must tell you why I
am called Nornagest.''[41] The King said he would like to hear.

Chapter 11

Gest explained: ''It happened that I was brought up at my
father's, in the place named Grœning—my father was wealthy
and kept a magnificent home. Wise women were going about the
country at that time; they were called 'spae-wives' or proph-
etesses, and they foretold the lives of men. For that reason
many men invited them to their homes and made feasts for them
and gave them gifts when they left. My father also did this, and
they came to him with a large following to prophesy. I lay there in
the cradle while they were supposed to talk about my fate. There
were two candles burning above me. Then they spoke to me and
said that I would become a very lucky man and become greater
than my ancestors or some of the chieftains in the land, and they
said that everything would come to pass, just as it has done. The
youngest Norn, however, thought little of the attention paid to
her, compared to that paid to the other two, and was annoyed
because they did not consult her about the prophecies. For it ap-

peared that they were of higher rank. There was also a great crowd of roughnecks present, who pushed her off the seat, so that she fell to the ground. She was greatly vexed at this and called out loudly and angrily, telling them to stop saying such favorable words about me:

" 'Therefore,'' she said, 'I shape it that he shall not live longer than that candle burns—the one lighted beside the boy!'

"So the oldest spae-wife took the candle and put it out, telling my mother to take care of it and not to light it again until the last day of my life. Then the prophetesses went away, binding up the young Norn and taking her with them, and my father gave them good gifts when they left. When I was a full-grown man, my mother brought me the candle and placed it in my care. I have it with me now.''

King Olaf said: "Why did you come here to me?''

"This idea came into my mind,'' replied Gest. "I thought I might get some good luck from you, because you have been much praised to me by good and wise men.''

The king said: "Are you willing to receive holy baptism now?

Gest answered him: "That I would like to do, since you advise it.''

And so it was done, and the King took Gest into his beloved favor and made him his retainer. Gest became a true believer and followed well the King's way of life, and at the same time remained popular with all other men.

Chapter 12

One day the King asked Gest: "How long do you wish to live, if you could make the decision?''

"A short time from now,'' answered Gest, "if God wills it.''

The King asked: "What will happen if you take that candle about which you were telling me?''

Gest took the candle out of his harp-case. The King ordered that it be lit, and so it was done, and when the candle was burning brightly, it began to melt away.

The King asked: "Gest! How old a man are you?''

He answered: "Now I am three hundred years old."

"You are very old indeed!" remarked the King.

So Gest then lay down, asking to be anointed. The King bade them do that. When it was done, there was little left to the candle. They saw that Gest was near his end, which came even as the candle burned itself out, and thus Gest died, and his passing seemed marvelous to all. The King had put great store on his tales, and believed that the story of his life, as he had told it, was altogether true.

Notes to the *Nornageststháttr*

1. *prime-signed*. Had had the *prima signatio*, or Sign of the Cross, made over him, as a preliminary to baptism. Even though he had not been actually baptized, a person who had been "prime-signed" was admitted to a certain part of the Mass and had certain social privileges in the Christian community, such as free social relations with both Christians and heathens.

2. *Frankland*. Not necessarily just the land of the Franks, but a large area west of the Rhine; see the *Völsungasaga*, note 68 above. It may be presumed that a knowledge of geography on the part of the author of the *Nornageststháttr* is scarcely more expert than that of the Author of the Saga.

3. *heir of Yngvi*. To call Sigurd the son of Yngvi is absurd, for Yngvi was one of the sons of the Danish king Halfdan the Old, and by tradition an ancestor of Helgi. The mistake is in the *Reginsmál*, which seems to belong pretty much to the Helgi Hundingsbane cycle.

4. *Nornagest*. The explanation of this name, literally, "guest of the Norns" (or Prophetesses), is in the last two chapters of this selection.

5. *Hundingsbane*. See chapter 9 of the *Völsungasaga* above.

6. *Imperial Power*. It is not clear whether or not this is a reference to the establishment of the Holy Roman Empire under Charlemagne in 800 or to the accession to the throne of Otho I of Germany in 962. I prefer the first theory, making this distinctly a ninth-century allusion.

7. *steeds of Raefil*. Raefil was a legendary sea-king; the "steeds of Raefil" would therefore be a bold kenning for "ships."

8. *Hnikar*. One of the many "other" names for Odin; see the *Völsungasaga* above, note 56. We can see from this passage (with its fuller quotation from the *Reginsmál*), how much help Odin really gives on this particular occasion.

9. *Huginn*. See *Völsungasaga*, note 57. As explained there, this is the name of one of Odin's favorite ravens; hence any raven, especially a raven representing the Beasts of Battle.

10. *moon's shining sister*. The sun. According to the Eddic poem *Vafthruthnismál* ("Ballad of Vafthruthnir"), stanza 23, the sun and moon are brother and sister, and in the *Prose Edda* by Snorri Sturluson, chapters 11 and 12, their story is told in greater detail.

11. *stumble along*. It is proverbial in Old Norse folklore that to stumble brings bad luck, as illustrated once and for all in the last chapter of the *Völsungasaga*.

12. *Friesland*. The Frisians in early times occupied the coast all the way from the present-day boundary of Belgium and the Netherlands to the mouth of the River Weser.

13. *gathered their forces*. By summoning all men "who wish to come to him and serve him," rather than by outright conscription.

14. *the "blood-eagle" . . . on his back*. This particularly barbarous form of execution was reserved for the slayer of one's father. The ribs were carved in the shape of an eagle, and the lungs were then drawn out through the openings.

15. *gladdened the ravens*. Another reference to the so-called Beasts of Battle motif.

16. *Hindarheath*. The usual name in the Saga is Hindarfell, but the same place is probably intended here.

17. *Sigurd Fafnisbane*. It is, of course, impossible to tell whether the reference here is to our *Völsungasaga* or to some earlier version.

18. *Gjuki*. As pointed out in the introduction, Gjuki is probably the Gibica of the *Lex Burgundionum* of about 500, and is most probably based on a historical character. He is mentioned in the Old English poem *Widsith* (1.19) as ruling the Burgundians.

19. *Sigurd Hring . . . sons of Gandalf*. Sigurd Hring, or Ring, was a half-legendary king of Denmark and Sweden, reputedly the father of Ragnar Lodbrók and victor over King Haraid Hilditönn ("Battle-Tooth") at the decisive Battle of Bravell (cf. n. 35 to the *Völsungasaga*). It is he rather than Sigurd Fafnisbane who is named in the Frankish chronicles under the year 812. The Battle of Bravell took place about 750, and secured the independence of Sweden from Denmark. Note that if he was given the name of Sigurd by that date, it is evident that Sigurd was a heroic name in the Scandinavia of the eighth century, which points to a progress from the Frankish-Burgundian area northward across the Baltic rather than through the Celtic or Saxon regions of France or Britain. To this point should be added the fact that Gest speaks of going from Frankland north to his father's home in Denmark, and not across the sea. As for *Gandalf*, he was a Norwegian chieftain in constant conflict with King Harold Fairhair of Norway in the ninth century.

20. *Járnamóda*. This locality is unknown, but the first element of the name, *Járna-*, is given to some forests in present-day Holstein.

21. *hazelwood poles*. To set up the boundaries of the field in this so-called "pitched" battle.

22. *Kurir*. The inhabitants of what is now Courland, probably the ancestors of the Lithuanians, a Baltic rather than Germanic people.

23. *Kvaenir*. Finnish inhabitants of northern Sweden.

24. *Starkad Stórverksson*. Judging by his patronymic, Starkad can hardly be, as in the Eddic poem *Helgakvida Hundingsbana II* (prose selection iii), the third son of Granmar, who opposed Sigmund and Sinfjötli in chapter 9 of the Saga. Rather, he is an ancient Norse hero and a once great one, who suffered, in the course of time, a not too unusual fate, as did Arthur and Charlemagne, either in respect to his morals or his character—the process known as epic degeneration. Sometimes, as in Starkad's case, it is a matter of criminality; more often it is a growing weakness and inefficiency. See Marlene Ciklamini, "The Problem of Starkathr," *Scandinavian Studies* 43 (1971): 169–88; she does not emphasize in any way his appearance here.

25. *Fenhring*. Not far from present-day Bergen, Norway.

26. *Lund*. This present-day Swedish city was in ancient times the ecclesiastical center of Denmark.

27. *King Ali in his bath*. This story is told in Saxo Grammaticus's *Historia Danorum,*, p. 314. This version has it that twelve of the Danish King Ali (Olo)'s retainers conspired to murder the King and persuaded Starkad to do the deed. Overcome with remorse (for he and the King had been friends), he killed most of the conspirators. But according to the *Egils saga ok Asmundar* ("Saga of Egil and Asmund") of the fourteenth century, it was another warrior, Armath, who was slain instead of Ali. Armath is the *Heremod of Beowulf* (ll. 901–15), who is presented in contrast to Sigemund as a cruel, tyrannical leader.

28. *caused Sigurd's death?* Note that Sigurd has been described as "very old," which hardly tallies with the account in the Saga. More than once in the *Nornageststháttr* the reference is to "the young Sigurd", or "Sigurd in his youth," yet we do not hear of his murder until he is very old (*gamall mjök*), which illustrates the complete timelessness of Nornagest's account.

29. *Germans*. A direct reference to the *southern* branch of the Saga, as told in the *Nibelungenlied*, Aventiure 16, in particular stanzas 985–95. See summary of that poem below.

30. *Gudrúnarraedu*, or "Rule of Gudrun." This is not in the existing canon of Eddic poems; it may refer to a lost Eddic poem; it may refer to a lost poem not associated with the Edda; it may be another name for the Eddic *Gudrúnarkvida II*, which in stanza 5 tells how Sigurd's steed Grani came home riderless from a meeting of the Thing.

31. *Leader of the Goths* The Flateyjarbók MS has here *gýgjar bróður* ("brother of the giantess"), but the others give the reading translated as above. The reference should then be to the Eddic *Sigrdrifumál*, stanza 3, in which it is Hjálmgunnar who was killed against Odin's orders. Since we know nothing further about Hjálmgunnar, the allusion here is utterly obscure. In any event we know even less about the brother of this giantess.

32. *Hjálmgunnar*. See preceding note.

33. *All too long*, etc. The idea here is that men and women will be together in some future life, which is utterly against Norse traditions and suggests a Christian provenance for this stanza, if not for the whole poem, since the giantess has adopted a moralistic stance.

34. *Sons of Lodbrók.* Lodbrók is, as we have seen, the half-legendary King Ragnar Lodbrók ("Ragnar Shaggypants"), so called because he wore a pair of ragged breeches when he went to fight a dragon. He is celebrated in the Saga already referred to (introduction above), which follows the *Völsungasaga* in the same MS (Codex Regius 1824 b4°) and may well be by the same author. He is mentioned in Saxo Grammaticus's *Historia Danorum*, but despite the connection through Aslaug in the doubtful chapter 43 of the *Völsungasaga*, which is generally taken now to be chapter 1 of the *Saga of Ragnar Lodbrók*, there should be no connection between the two sagas. In addition to the Saga and the reference in Saxo Grammaticus, there is also a *tháttr* celebrating the exploits of his sons. He is said to have invaded Northumbria, where he was defeated and killed by King Aella, who threw him into a snakepit, where "he died laughing." His death was avenged by his sons, who invaded Northumbria in 866 and subjected Aella to the "eagle" torture (see n. 14 above). Very little is known about Ragnar historically.

As to his sons, however, there is quite a bit known, and it is important, for it marks one of the high spots in the Norse expansionism of the ninth and tenth centuries. Their part in the Norse invasion of Northumbria is evident, but they made deep inroads on the Continent, perhaps as far from their bases as any Norsemen except those who went into Russia through the Volga Basin. The most famous of these sons, named Björn Ironside in the text, made expeditions between 859 and 862 into Spain, northern Africa, the south of France, and Italy, where he actually occupied Pisa and Luna and certainly had designs on Rome. That they were turned aside in the manner told in the text is altogether plausible, although I think it was clearly a case of military overextension.

35. *Mindarfell . . . Vifilsborg.* Mindarfell is tentatively identified as in the region of the French Alps; Vifilsborg is identified with more assurance as the modern Avenches in Canton Vaud, Switzerland.

36. *Rome.* This city appears to have been the particular objective of the expedition of 860.

37. *Uppsala.* The seat of King Eric of Sweden, contemporary of King Harold Fairhair of Norway in the ninth century (see note 38 below). This capital was a few miles from the present Swedish city.

38. *Harold Fairhair*, perhaps the best known of the older Kings of Norway (ca. 850–ca. 933); it was during his reign that Iceland was colonized by the Norse.

39. *King Hlödver.* Louis I, King of the Franks and Charlemagne's successor as Holy Roman Emperor (814–840).

40. *land of the Saxons.* Most of northwest Germany and the Netherlands; in terms of the Holy Roman Empire, most of the German portion.

41. *Nornagest.* Guest of the Norns. He could live only as long as their candle bestowed on his family could remain unburnt.

The Southern Branch of the Saga:
A Brief Consideration of the
Nibelungenlied and the
Thidrekssaga

These two works are the most important surviving exemplars of the Saga in its *southern* version, and I am therefore including the following summaries of the two. They should be considered only after the reader has completed the reading of the *Völsungasaga*. Then he or she should consider the following questions in the reading of these abstracts:

Always keeping the *Völsungasaga* in mind:

1. What is the importance of Sigurd?
2. What is the importance of Sigmund?
3. What is the importance of Brynhild?
4. What is the importance of the Gjukings, or, as they are called in these two works, the Burgundians or the Niflungs?
5. What differences in detail can be seen in reference to (a) the birth and bringing up of Sigurd (Siegfried); (b) Sigurd and the dragon; (c) the relations of Sigurd and Brynhild; (d) the relations of Sigurd and the Gjukings (Burgundians/Niflungs); (e) the quarrel of the queens; (f) the grievance, real or imaginary, felt by Brynhild; (g) the grievances experienced by Gudrun (Kriemhild, Grimhild); (h) the revenge of Gudrun (Kriemhild, Grimhild); (i) the details in the fighting between Atli (Attila, Etzel, the Huns) and the Gjukings (Burgundians/Niflungs); (j) the murder of Sigurd (Siegfried) and the reactions of all thereto; (k) the death of Brynhild; (l) the death of Sigmund; (m) the conclusion.

An essential consideration is, of course, the genesis of each of the three works. The *Völsungasaga,* as we have seen, must have had its predecessors—perhaps an earlier saga or two, and in any case a *Sigmundarsaga,* along with an indefinte number of unknown ballads or songs, and it is heavily indebted to many Eddic poems, which are distinctive products of the Norwegian-Icelandic axis, going in some cases back to the ninth century and including such outlying regions as the Faroes and the Hebrides. The other two are products of the so-called chivalric age (a term that today needs some reconstruction and reevaluation), but in any event they are composed under the combined French tradition of the twelfth century and the contemporary German tradition of the Minnesinger, of Chrestien de Troyes on the one hand and Gottfried von Strassburg or Walther von der Vogelweide on the other, with their tensions between love and honor to complicate matters. These ideas are pretty far removed from the bleak Icelandic settlement or even the court of the romance-loving King Haakon IV ("the Old"). Yet all three works, as far as we can tell, belong to the thirteenth century.

Let us begin, then, with the *Nibelungenlied.* There has been general agreement that this long epic poem was composed by one of that indeterminate class of writers known as "minstrel poets," between 1200 and 1205, in southern Germany or Bavaria or along the reaches of the Upper Danube. The author's main sources appear to have been many; most of them, unfortunately lost. These would comprise (a) a group of lost lays on the fall of the Burgundians, going back to that original fifth century; (b) a group of lost lays dealing with young Siegfried (barely touched upon in the epic), dating from the sixth century in Frankish territory; (c) probably a lost Bavarian lay of the eight century on the same general subject (a fine example of Chadwick's lay-theory of the beginnings of an epic), which may or may not have influenced the composition of Eddic poems on the story; (d) two lost lays on Sigurd and Brynhild from the twelfth century; and (e) in the preceding generation, a full epic known as *Diu Not (der Nibelungen)* from about 1160–80. With these various sources, but more particularly considering *Diu Not,* it might be expected that more than half of the *Nibelungenlied* has to do with the revenge of Siegfried's wife, Kriemhild, for the murder of her husband. In actuality, we have a poem of 39 *divisions*—I call them "chapters" below—of which only 16, or only some 40 percent, have to do with Siegfried in person, although his ghost lies over the whole poem to the very end.

Chapter 1: Kriemhild, a Burgundian princess, is a paragon of beauty and charm in the eyes of all beholders, including her brothers, King Gunther of Worms, Gernot, and Giselher. Their father is Dancwart, Sr., and their mother is Uote. Their chief vassals are Hagen and Dancwart, Jr. It is a medieval court, with great attention to fine clothes, shining armor, minstrelsy, feasting, tournaments, and other equestrian games known as bohorts. Kriemhild complains that she has dreamed of her pet falcon, which two eagles tore to pieces. Her mother Uote interprets this to mean that she will lose someone dear to her. Kriemhild proposes that she will never marry.

Chapter 2: We are next introduced to Siegfried, a surpassing young man, the son of Siegmund and Sieglind, another paragon of excellence, although we are told nothing of his boyhood or his bringing up. He is being knighted by his father amid great pomp and circumstance—crowds of loyal and devoted people, feasting, entertainment, and hopes for the future. (He is from Xanten and is in line for the crown of the Netherlands. Yet at the moment he is not interested in that.)

Chapter 3: Siegfried hears of Kriemhild's beauty and her eligibility as his wife. He therefore goes to Worms; his behavior, for one so well brought up, is aggressive and haughty. He has heard of the beauty of Kriemhild and is determined to marry her; not only that, he is resolved to conquer Burgundy. As for his marriage to Kriemhild, that seems acceptable enough, despite the worries of his parents, especially of his aged father, Siegmund. Siegmund, however, ultimately approves. But what of Hagen? (There is still great attention to dress, armor, entertainment.) His parents and his retinue have arrived in Worms. Gunther receives the visitors with some curiosity. Hagen is sent for, and gives his opinion: Siegfried is an impressive hero, who has slain Princes Schielbung and Nibelung, guardians of the Treasure, and seven hundred other Nibelungs with his sword Balmung. He once slew a dragon, and from bathing in that dragon's blood, he has a skin so tough that no steel can penetrate it. From the dwarf Alberich, who hoped to avenge his master (the dragon), Siegfried has received a *Tarnkappe*, a cloak of invisibility; he now has Alberich's loyalty. So all in all, Hagen vouches for Siegfried and his lineage.

Now, when Siegfried announces his intent to take over Burgundy, he is haughty and conceited—some traces of his upbringing are hinted at in this way, but no more. Ortwin proposes conciliatory procedure. The tension is lessened, following the traditions of the Minnesinger, because Siegfried is rendered more tractable when Kriemhild appears and he falls in love with her. Still, a year has to pass by before he sees her.

Chapter 4: When it is reported that Gunther's kingdom is about to be invaded by King Liudegar of the Saxons and King Liudegast of the Danes, Siegfried offers his services to Gunther. Aided by the Burgundian princes, he defeats both of his opponents, taking Liudegast prisoner and sending him back to Gunther. In this battle Volker, Ortwin, and Hagen perform prodigies of valor. Liudegar recognizes Siegfried and orders his Danes to quit. The fighting parties return to their respective kingdoms. The Burgundians have gained greatly in reputation. All this pleases Kriemhild. There are more sports, tourneys, bohorts, and general entertainments, in which Siegfried is especially honored. Kriemhild helps to make special garments for the occasion.

Chapter 5: At the festivities, gold is dispensed; there are five thousand knights present. It is a very "chivalric" scene when Kriemhild makes her appearance, with all kinds of royal pageantry. Siegfried, when consulted by Gunther, sanctions the arrangements with the Danes and Saxons, provided there be no more hostilities. Gunther once more dispenses treasure. Siegfried can now see Kriemhild every day.

Chapter 6: Meanwhile Gunther decides to take for himself a wife, the athletic Brunhild in Iceland, known for her prowess in lifting and throwing. If any one woos her, he must either compete successfully against her or lose his life (the Unapproachable Female or Taming of the Shrew motif). Gunther is nevertheless willing to take his chances, though depending on Siegfried's help. Siegfried, for his part, wants only Kriemhild and agrees to help Gunther only if he can marry Kriemhild when they get back from

Iceland. He takes along his cloak of invisibility, which has the further invaluable property of giving the wearer twelve times his usual strength. Kriemhild and her maidens prepare clothes for the four knights—Siegfried, Gunther, Hagen, and Dancwart. It takes seven weeks before these are ready. The four of them set out for Iceland, which they reach in twelve days.

Chapter 7: Gunther is entranced by Brunhild. Hagen, however, is as usual suspicious, and most reluctant to doff his armor and weapons, as is the custom of the castle. In this chapter there is something of the comic about Brunhild. How much does she know? She has been told that one of the four visiting knights *looks* like Siegfried. Was there ever anything between them? A field is laid out for the contests, with seven hundred knights as witnesses. It takes three men even to lift Brunhild's spear. Hagen waxes sardonic when he sees the boulder that Brunhild is to lift and cast, let alone the spear that she is to hurl. Taking advantage of his cloak of invisibility, Siegfried knocks down Brunhild with a return throw of her spear (with the blunt end, of course). Brunhild casts the boulder twenty-three yards and then leaps even farther! But Siegfried betters both marks; Gunther is therefore acclaimed as victor, to Hagen's great disgust at the treachery. They lie about Siegfried's presence, and Brunhild seems to accept it, summoning her warriors to go with her to Burgundy. Siegfried hurries home "for reinforcements," since there are only four of them present.

Chapter 8: Still wearing his magic cloak, Siegfried secretly sculls away from Iceland, stopping at the land of the Nibelungs (not Burgundy), first having to persuade and overcome the warden of the Treasure, Alberich the dwarf, who does not appear to recognize Siegfried and attacks. After gaining recognition from Alberich, he commands him to procure men to serve in Siegfried's retinue. They come, splendidly accoutered, three thousand instead of the thousand requested. All return to Iceland. Brunhild welcomes them all, but takes a particular interest in Siegfried, amid general feasting and dispensing of gold; Brunhild manages to fill twenty trunks with silken garments and gold, and she appoints a "governor" for her kingdom, her maternal uncle. The expedition sets out for Worms.

Chapter 9: Siegfried is deputized to go in advance to Worms and report the outcome of the expedition to Queen Uote. (Siegmund, as he appears in this work, seems to be both senile and ineffective.) Preparations are made at Worms for the arrival of Gunther, Brunhild, and their retinues; they are to ride out to the bank of the river near the city. Again, there is much attention to the dress of the women and the armor of the men—another opportunity for medieval pageantry. In the group are no less than a hundred and forty ladies.

Chapter 10: First there is a grand reception for Gunther and Brunhild, terminating in an enormous bohort; there is much kissing and fondling, jousting and feasting. Brunhild is crowned Queen of Burgundy. Siegfried, however, is in an irritated mood, asking constantly for Kriemhild. His wish is granted. Brunhild, however, weeps to see Kriemhild sitting as a prospective bride to a vassal, as she regards Siegfried, because she once saw him holding Gunther's steed while the latter mounted him. That night she refuses to have anything to do with Gunther and hangs him up, burlesque-fashion, on the bedpost, not releasing him until dawn. Gunther, not unnaturally, is dejected. The next morning he tells Siegfried all about it. Siegfried decides to substitute himself for Gunther; using his magic cloak of invisibility, he succeeds in subduing her after a tough tussle. She, believing it to have been Gunther, apologizes to him. Siegfried departs, first having taken from Brunhild a ring and her girdle. With the loss of her maidenhead, Brunhild has now lost also her Amazonian strength. The wedding festivities continue for two weeks.

Chapter 11: When Siegfried and Kriemhild are to leave for Xanten, Kriemhild expresses the wish that her brothers should share half of Siegfried's kingdom. This does not sit well with Siegfried. Siegfried and the brothers then offer to share their possessions and retinue, but Hagen is resentful, saying that he will be liegeman only to Gunther. Old Siegmund is delighted. Xanten outdoes Worms in the splendor of the reception of Siegfried and Kriemhild. Old Siegmund hands over his crown to Siegfried. In ten years, Siegfried and Kriemhild have a son, Gunther. Siegfried's mother, Sieglind, dies. Meanwhile Brunhild has a son by Gunther, whom she names Siegfried.

Chapter 12: But for some reason, never made quite clear in the poem, Brunhild remains jealous. How can Kriemhild hold her head so high when, Brunhild is convinced, Siegfried is only a vassal? She persuades Gunther to invite them to Worms; instead they get a counter-invitation to Xanten.

Chapter 13: A more or less pictorial *Aventiure*. Siegfried and Kriemhild come to visit Gunther and Brunhild, leaving their little son behind; he is never to see his parents again. There is a great deal of bohorting and festivity.

Chapter 14: Brunhild and Kriemhild begin to quarrel. Kriemhild starts it off by raising the question who shall first enter the cathedral. Brunhild insists that she should enter first, calling Kriemhild only a liegewoman; but when they confront each other on the way to the cathedral, Kriemhild and her retinue sweep in first. Before doing that, however, she calls Brunhild a paramour only. On their way out, they confront each other again and Brunhild demands proof of the charge. This time Kriemhild shows Brunhild the ring that the invisible Siegfried had taken from her on her second "wedding" night. Brunhild is for the moment silenced, but when Siegfried hears of the matter, he begins to swear that he is innocent, only to be shut off by Gunther, for obvious reasons. Hagen, finding Brunhild in tears, swears that Siegfried shall pay for all this. Ortwin agrees. There is talk of killing Siegfried.

Chapter 15: At Hagen's instigation, thirty-two men come before Gunther and inform him that Liudegar and Liudegast are preparing to resume hostilities. Kriemhild, saying farewell to Hagen, admits that Siegfried has beaten her soundly for her insult to Brunhild. Women are to be kept in their place! She explains that Siegfried has indeed a vulnerable spot—when he was acquiring his horny hide by bathing in the dragon's blood, a leaf fell on his back, keeping the blood away from that spot on his body. Hagen induces Kriemhild to mark that spot on Siegfried's wartunic. When the warriors have started off, word is received that the threatened war with Liudegar and Liudegast has been aborted.

Chapter 16: To celebrate the calling off of the war, a royal hunt is proclaimed. Kriemhild complains of a dream that Siegfried is dead among flowers. In the hunt, Siegfried gets an incredible bag, including a bear, which he attaches to his saddle and releases unharmed in the royal kitchen, to the great fright of the cooks and servants. The wine is not yet ready to serve, but Hagen remembers where there is a brook nearby. While Siegfried is drinking at the brook, Hagen spears him through the vulnerable spot in his back. Siegfried makes an embittered dying speech; Hagen is unrepentant; Gunther deplores the whole business. All agree, however, to hush up Hagen's guilt, and Hagen himself is unmoved.

Chapter 17: On Hagen's orders, Siegfried's body is carried to his apartment and laid across the threshold of the front door. Here a chamberlain discovers it, but Kriemhild is fully aware of all the circumstances. There is great lamentation and commotion. Old Siegmund is informed; his hundred men plus a thousand more—eleven hundred in all—rush out, forgetting to put on any clothes (!). Kriemhild manages to keep them from killing Gunther and his whole troop. When the company, to whom must be added Gunther, Hagen, et al., come to view the body, the corpse of Siegfried begins to bleed in the immediate presence of Hagen, indicating that he was the murderer. Kriemhild nevertheless restrains every one; and her brothers join her. Mass is sung. The Burgundians refuse to join the funeral-feast and suffer three days' deprivation. Everyone, rich or poor, contributes something to Siegfried's funeral. He is finally buried with great pomp.

Chapter 18: The aged Siegmund and Kriemhild decide to retire to Xanten, although Kriemhild's kinsmen attempt to detain her. And she is inclined to stay, although she knows that she will not have her proper due there as a reigning queen. Her knights object, but she remains obstinate. Gernot and Giselher are most sympathetic. But, says the author, "I cannot tell you how they fared at this time." Meanwhile, Brunhild sits enthroned in her pride.

Chapter 19: Kriemhild now has a new home in Worms, where she dwells and constantly visits Siegfried's grave. Even her mother can give her no comfort. For three and a half years she stays there, never speaking to her brother Gunther. Meanwhile Hagen is restless for the Nibelung treasure. Kriemhild is certain that Hagen did the murder, and so she makes friends with everybody except Hagen. She finally consents to have the

Nibelung treasure brought to Worms; after all, it was her nuptial dowry! It requires eight thousand men to bring it from Alberich's keeping in the hill, across the Rhine and into Worms, and it calls for a dozen wagons making trips three times a day four days and four nights to complete the task. Hagen does not think that such a treasure should be left in the control of a woman, but Kriemhild receives it. Gernot proposes that it should be sunk in the River Rhine, and this is done while Gunther is absent. Kriemhild goes on living in anguish for thirteen years.

Chapter 20: Helche, the wife of King Etzel of the Huns, dies. He now seeks Kriemhild's hand in marriage, although admitting that he is a heathen, in the sense that he has never been baptized. Rüdiger of Pöchlarn is entrusted with the diplomatic end of the negotiations. He and his retainers ride out from Hungary, stopping in Vienna for equipment and shelter. Then they go through Bavaria and finally come to Worms, where they are welcomed by Gunther and Hagen. Rüdiger makes known his mission. Gunther is delighted, but Hagen strongly objects. Kriemhild at first rejects the proposal but finally agrees to think it over. Gunther and the others, except for Hagen, press her to accept, and she finally does so. It takes four and a half days to get properly prepared for the journey. She takes thirty thousand marks of the Treasure with her, leaving the rest in the Rhine. They leave in royal style. Gunther escorts them but a short distance from Worms; Hagen does not even go that far. The rest of the enormous band go on to the Danube.

Chapter 21: In Bavaria, the Bishop of Passau rides with them. They spend some time with Rüdiger and his wife in Pöchlarn, and when they arrive there is great entertainment; when they leave, there is much gift-giving.

Chapter 22: Christians, heathens, Poles, Russians, and Wallachians go to make up the army which Etzel takes to his borders to greet his new queen. There is much kissing and many tournaments. They finally reach Vienna and are married at Whitsun. The wedding festivities continue for seventeen days. It is pointed out that Helche, Etzel's first wife, never wielded the power that Kriemhild did on the first day of her marriage.

Chapter 23: Kriemhild and Etzel live together for seven years and have one son, Ortlieb. Kriemhild broods constantly and at the same time becomes more and more self-willed. She wishes particularly to get Hagen into Hungary, so that she can then dispose of him and thus avenge Siegfried. So one night, in bed with Etzel, she persuades him to invite the whole court of the Burgundians to Hungary. She sends messengers north with the invitation. These are enjoined, however, not to let anyone know that Kriemhild has been sad. At home Kriemhild dreams that she is walking with her brother Gunther and kisses him. She regrets having married a heathen, and she feels very vengeful toward Hagen. But in any case, the invitation is to apply to the coming summer.

Chapter 24: On their way the Hunnish messengers are entertained by Rüdiger. When they get to Worms, they are received most cordially by Gunther. All accept with pleasure the invitation to go to Hungary except Queen Uote and Hagen, who feels more suspicious—and guilty—than ever. He decides at first to stay in Worms but finally decides it is his duty to go, although he warns that if they should go, they should take along as escort at least a thousand warriors. The envoys are not permitted to see Brunhild. Word of the Burgundians' coming reaches Hungary.

Chapter 25: The Burgundians finally set off for Hungary. Queen Uote has dreadful premonitory dreams. Query: What has happened to Siegmund? Her vassal, Rumold, asks Gunther what to do if anything should happen. Gunther rather unhelpfully replies that all should be careful, but he hopes for the best. They depart amid forebodings among all the women. Ultimately they reach the Danube, but no ferries are in sight anywhere. Hagen offers to go look for a boatman. He comes across three water-fairies, or nixies. When they see him, they flee, but Hagen takes up their clothes. To get these back one of the nymphs, Hageborg, offers to tell him how their visit to Hungary is going to turn out (for nixies are said to have second sight). She tells Hagen that they can ride on safely into Hungary. Hagen returns their clothing. Another of the nixies, Sieglind, tells him, however, that her ''cousin'' lied to him in order to get back her clothes—and that he had better turn back now while he still has a chance, otherwise the Burgundians will all die. The nixies agree that the only one to survive will be the king's chaplain. When Hagen insists on going ahead, they tell him that the Nibelungs (from this point on in the poem the Burgundians are so called) will first have to travel through the domain of a margrave named Else. Furthermore, they warn him of the ferryman, who is a ferocious customer. Ultimately this ferryman shows up, and he is indeed a very churlish fellow. When Hagen lies to him by saying that he is a liegeman of Else's, he is furious. He attacks Hagen, and in the ensuing fight Hagen quickly dispatches him with the sword Balmung.

Meanwhile the boat is drifting, and Hagen breaks an oar but mends it with a shield-sling. The Nibelungs, waiting on shore, ask Hagen what has happened, and Hagen lies about the ferryman. Some of the Nibelungs get their horses across (and themselves) by swimming. The boat, once it is serviceable, takes all their gold and most of the thousand men. Hagen at one point tries to drown the king's chaplain, but the Lord saves him: he makes the original shore and thence goes back to Burgundy.

Chapter 26: Volker offers to guide them through the territory of Gelpfrat, but Hagen grimly tells all that they will never get back to Burgundy, and finally reports what the nixies had told him, explaining that that was why he tried to drown the king's chaplain. "So get ready, and be ready at all times!" They meet Gelpfrat, and it comes to battle between Hagen and him, and it takes the help of the elder Dancwart to dispose of Gelpfrat. They eventually come to rest with Rüdiger in Passau.

Chapter 27: Here at Passau the Nibelungs show their good breeding. There is an inexhaustible supply of good-looking women around. Margrave Rüdiger's daughter, the young Margravine, greets all the guests with a welcoming kiss, but it takes an effort for her to do this to Hagen. Instead, she is much taken with young Giselher, who wishes in turn to marry her. The lady is granted him. The Nibelungs remain until the fourth morning. On their departure, they all get gifts, but Hagen rather crudely requests the shield of Nuoding, the slain brother of his hostess Gotelinde. Although this hurts Rüdiger and his wife, they comply. Meanwhile, we are told, Kriemhild is anxiously awaiting them all at home in Hungary.

Chapter 28: Dietrich of Bern (sometimes called Dietrich of Verona) and his trusted warrior, old Hildebrand, assisted by

Wolfhart, greet the Nibelungs when they arrive in Hungary. Dietrich himself is friendly but reminds all that Kriemhild is still weeping for Siegfried. Hagen says that it all happened a long time ago, and that Kriemhild should know better by now. Indeed, Hagen suggests that they are more interested in Kriemhild's ultimate designs. Volker reminds them all that Kriemhild's grief cannot be helped—let them ride on and see how things go with them when they get to Etzel's stronghold. When they arrive, Kriemhild immediately shows hostility to Hagen, "so that he laced his helmet tighter." She asks about the Nibelung Treasure. Hagen answers that it has been sunk in the River Rhine. Kriemhild lays down the rule: none can go armed into Etzel's hall, for all weapons are to be parked at the door, so to speak. Hagen, as a matter of principle to a warrior, of course refuses. To Kriemhild's considerable confusion, Dietrich backs up Hagen. Etzel sees them in conversation and asks who this fierce newcomer may be; one of Kriemhild's retainers says his father was Aldrian. Etzel remembers Aldrian well and remarks what fine young men Aldrian and Walter of Spain were.

Chapter 29: Hagen and Volker go outside to converse in front of Kriemhild's hall. She sees them and becomes downcast, telling all who will listen that it is Hagen who has been the cause of all her trouble. She asks for somebody to kill him. Sixty warriors volunteer their services. She tells them that they are not enough, whereupon their number swells to 480. Neither Hagen nor Volker will rise when Kriemhild comes out of her hall toward them. She recognizes Hagen's sword, Balmung, as that which once belonged to Siegfried. Even when she comes nearer, neither of them rises, although Hagen accepts full responsibility for the death of Siegfried. Kriemhild's retainers begin to murmur; Hagen and Volker then rise to go to their men, who are officially greeted in a speech by Etzel. The feasting begins.

Chapter 30: After the feast, the various leaders retire to their quarters. When the populace begins to crowd the Nibelungs, Volker scolds them. "Make way!" Their quarters are infallibly luxurious. Hagen and Volker nevertheless keep constant watch; Volker finally plays the rest of them to sleep with his fiddle. Kriemhild's men consider attacking, but are dissuaded by the menacing sight of the two champions, Hagen and Volker.

Chapter 31: Morning comes. The Nibelungs go to Mass. What clothes! What shining armor! Etzel and Kriemhild arrive. (Etzel should have been informed of the scene the previous night!) After Mass is over, Kriemhild and seven thousand knights engage with the Nibelungs in a bohort, Kriemhild watches intently, hoping that in some way the Nibelungs will come to harm. Hagen and Volker want better competition. The Huns are enraged at Volker when they see that one of their men has fallen, and begin to rush the Nibelungs. Etzel, however, calms them, reminding them that this was an accident. Dietrich and Hildebrand are implored by Kriemhild to take a hand, but they refuse. Etzel asks the Nibelungs when they return to take his young son Ortlieb with them, for he will be a credit to his mother. Hagen remarks dourly that the boy has an ill-fated look.

Chapter 32: Bloedelin goes to the support of Kriemhild and challenges Hagen, only to have his head knocked off for his trouble. There is immediate heavy retaliation, and only Dancwart survives the fray, performing prodigies, while nine thousand lie dead around him.

Chapter 33: Dancwart's brother Hagen is now drawn into the fight. Young Ortlieb is beheaded, so that his head falls into the lap of his mother, Kriemhild. So is his tutor. Hagen then goes on a rampage. Volker also "made rough music" with his "fiddle-bow" on the heads of his opponents—a commonplace of old Germanic poetry, even in *Beowulf*. Among the others who rage are the Burgundian princes Gernot and Gunther. As for Kriemhild and Etzel, they are badly frightened. Dietrich, on the other hand, coolly attempts to get his men out of the hall. Volker continues to ramp around, killing everyone who gets in his way. For the moment, the Huns are defeated.

Chapter 34: Giselher reminds all who can hear him that the Huns will soon be back. Meanwhile, they must get rid of all the bodies (seven thousand in all). Hagen taunts the Huns that Etzel should be leading such a pack of cowards. Kriemhild promises a shield-full of gold to whoever can bring her Hagen's head. Volker replies that with all this gold offered, the Huns should be doing better than they are.

Chapter 35: There is a good, hard fight between Hagen and Iring of Thuringia. He bounces off Hagen and then off Volker and then off Gunther but is finally killed by Giselher. Or so it seems, but he is only stunned and manages to escape, for which he is congratulated by Kriemhild. But when he attacks for a second time, he is slain by Hagen, and the other 1,004 Thuringians are slaughtered to a man, so that the blood flows out of the hall through the gutters.

Chapter 36: After repelling an attack by twenty thousand Huns, the Nibelungs ask for a truce. Etzel refuses them. Gernot, badly wounded, asks that he be let out of the hall to die in a respectable manner, but Kriemhild hears this and refuses them even this mercy, saying that, as a sister, she will relent only when they hand over Hagen. She then orders the hall to be set afire at all four corners. The Nibelungs suffer from the consequent heat, and Hagen orders them to drink the blood of the corpses to cool off. By morning six hundred Nibelungs are still alive against twelve hundred Huns, and the situation is virtually a stalemate.

Chapter 37: Rüdiger is taunted for not fighting, until he turns on and kills his taunter. (But, having escorted the Nibelungs to Hungary, he is in honor bound not to fight them.) He is finally persuaded, however, and summons his men. The Nibelungs are reluctant to meet him, for they understand his dilemma, but Rüdiger attacks them anyway. Finally, Rüdiger and Gernot kill each other simultaneously. Rüdiger is mourned by both sides. Etzel roars like a lion.

Chapter 38: A vassal, Helpfrich, is sent by Dietrich to find out what has caused this great lamentation. He discovers that Rüdiger has been slain. Hildebrand goes to claim the body, but is turned away. They therefore attack, "old" Hildebrand leading the way, and eventually kill Volker the Minstrel. Hagen, of course, vows immediate vengeance. Hildebrand exceeds his orders by having Rüdiger's body taken from the hall. Helpfrich kills Dancwart, but Giselher avenges this by killing Wolfhart, though Wolfhart's last blow is fatal to Giselher. Hagen drives Hildebrand out of the hall, at the same time wounding him.

Chapter 39: Dietrich of Bern, at long last, decides to fight Gunther and Hagen, the only two Nibelungs left. He is accompanied by Hildebrand, who appears to have recovered. Dietrich offers the two Nibelungs safety if they will turn themselves in. They refuse. In the ensuring fierce fight, Dietrich overcomes Hagen and has him bound. He is turned over to Kriemhild, who orders him to be thrown into a dungeon. Gunther is then captured by Dietrich in the same way and borne to Kriemhild. After a bitter exchange, Kriemhild beheads her brother Gunther and carries his head in to Hagen. Nevertheless Hagen taunts her that she still will not know where the Nibelung Treasure is. To Etzel's great grief, Kriemhild then strikes off Hagen's head. This is too much for old Hildebrand, that such a great warrior as Hagen should be beheaded by a woman, and snatching up his sword, he runs Kriemhild through. "There lay the bodies of all that were doomed to die"—and that means just about everybody on either side except Etzel, Dietrich, and Hildebrand.

"I cannot tell you what happened after that."

Two Views of the *Nibelungenlied*

Andreas Heusler and the *Nibelungenlied*

The view of the *Nibelungenlied* most generally accepted now, though there are still dissidents, was first put forward by Andreas Heusler, the great Swiss Germanicist, in his *Nibelungensage und Niebelungenlied*, 3d ed. (Dortmund, 1929). This is an invaluable work, not only covering in scholarly depth the whole *southern* portion of the story, but also embodying his theories as to the origins of the many new characters who appear in the poem, as well as the obvious cross-pollination from other legends in the Germanic languages. This is all the more remarkable when we consider that so much of this has to be hypothesized, for almost no written records remain except for the prose *Völsungasaga*, the *Hildebrand Lay, Beowulf*, the appropriate Eddic poems, and the *Thidrekssaga*. He is wise, I believe, in his insistence that the materials are Germanic, without reference to French, classical, or Russian elements. Any study of Propp or Thompson indicates that it is extremely difficult to label a folktale, for example, as peculiar to any one ethnic group.

He divides the *Nibelungenlied* into its customary parts. The first portion, Abenteuer (or chapters) 1-19 inclusive, is derived ultimately from what he calls a *Brunhildsage* (I should prefer the term *Siegfriedsage*). Abenteuer 20-39 inclusive are based upon an earlier *Burgundensage*. These two hypothetical sagas were formed probably in the twelfth century, and each was based on lays that started to be composed not long after the historical facts of the fifth century already commented upon (see introduction above), and growing through the next centuries, with various innovations by various bards. Heusler suggests at least five different authors at work on these sagas, with the fifth giving us the poem in its present form. Presumably the lost earlier poem, *Diu Not*, which preceded the *Nibelungenlied* by about a generation, was one of these. Heusler, however, reminds the reader constantly that the finished poem that we have is the product of an artist who exercised the artist's prerogative to change and to invent what he chose, so that it is, after all, rather futile to grub around after "sources." New times make for new ways of life, and the *Nibelungenlied* reflects an age of chivalry, where love (either familial or sexual) is preeminent, and duty to one's sovereign and one's personal code is paramount. And combined with these is the overriding Germanic instinct for revenge.

For example, in considering the revenge of Kriemhild for the murder of her husband, Siegfried (Kriemhild corresponds to Gudrun in our Saga), he calls attention to the death of Attila in 453 of a stroke while in bed with his wife, (H)ildeco, and derives Kriemhild's name from Hildeco. Ildeco is not, however, a Burgundian princess, and it seems insufficient evidence to convict her, as rumor had it, of the murder of Attila. At any rate, Heusler calls attention to the fact that the bards could not read (which is probably true of many), and all kinds of variation, embellishment, contamination, and additional increments could gradually accrue.

He wisely makes no attempt to identify Siegfried as a historical person, but he envisages a part played by him in the Brunhild saga, observing that many little hints, as they bob up in the *written* literature, may go back to the oral *märchen* traditions—the naked sword between Siegfried and Brunhild; the innocent, unsuspecting drinking from a brook, and so on. In short, he senses the presence at an early date of various short pieces about Siegfried. The importance of the Norse at this point is obvious. Heusler puts great emphasis on the two Eddic poems about Atli, which he thinks (like the rest of the Saga) come to Scandinavia by way of Germany. He also points out that all the pieces presenting Attila (Etzel, Atli) are derived from Ostrogothic sources, where the character of this figure has been changed from a bloody tyrant to a mild gentleman whose only besetting sin is greed. This, of course, applies to all surviving pieces in the story except for our

Saga, and even there it seems enough to describe him as "swart and grim."

At the same time, Heusler places emphasis on the "lost" materials. How many lays like the famous *Hildebrandslied* of the eighth century, which has survived, are to be assumed? Although he does not say it, he is thinking of a *Sigmundarsaga*. He calls attention to the fifteenth-century poem *Horned Siegfried*, as an example of the persistence of popular treatment of the hero here as well as in the Faroese and Danish balladry.

A few more considerations: Theodoric (Thydrek, Dietrich), an undoubted historical person, having become a hero in German legendry, must be included; so, too, must Hildebrand. The Nibelung treasure Heusler identifies, of course, with the legend of Fafnir, and takes a closer look at the origins of all the "new" characters who appear in the *Nibelungenlied*. Niflungland he places in northern Norway, and suggests that the unknown inhabitant of Bergen is responsible for the *Thidrekssaga* (of which more in a moment). Although he refers almost not at all to our Saga, he admits that the *northern* version makes more use of Brunhild, who tends to fade out in the *southern*. In speaking of "die nordische Prosa" he almost always means the *Thidrekssaga*.

Heusler's account of the progress from the lay to the epic (*Lied* to *Epos*), which constitutes pp. 228–45, is excellent, as full of insight as his master Ker or Munro Chadwick. And remember, he points out, that events might sound different in Passau from the way they would in Soest, for the milieu of the two places might demand completely different outlooks on love, duty, and honor, and the twentieth century is very unlike the thirteenth.

Friedrich Panzer on the *Nibelungenlied*

A somewhat different view of the *Nibelungenlied* is offered by Friedrich Panzer in his *Das Nibelungenlied* (Stuttgart, 1953). He is skeptical about Heusler's theory of preceding sagas, none of which can be produced, and revives the old theory of epic *lays*, which were finally wrought into place by an individual poet (though he does not rule out the earlier *Diu Not*). But he sees a strong influence from French poets in general and *The Song of Roland* in particular, and is willing to admit influences from the Celtic, the Norse, the Latin—as *Beowulf* shows some Virgilian influence, so too does the author of the *Nibelungenlied*. He sees the experience of the early Crusades as influencing the author in his concept of the Huns. He has a very thorough survey of the history of scholarship on the poem, and comes to his conclusions by a very incisive analysis of the poem as regards meter, language, style, conceptions of love (in which he rejects the influence of the Minnesinger), etymologies, historical bases for the characters, and the like. He even suggests that the author was a cleric. The difficulty, of course, lies in the fact that the story-combinations are arbitrary, and that we have here a conflation of more than one of them at an early date. In effect, he virtually concedes that the matter does not admit of any convincing kind of solution, although he finds enough differences between the end of Aventiure 19 and the rest of the poem to warrant the guess that there may have been two different authors.

In comparison, I should suggest that Heusler represents, from the German point of view, a more nationalistic, not to say, patriotic fervor; Panzer is the more cosmopolitan. However, I believe that the Icelandic saga represents an earlier form of the story, and, interestingly enough, a more allegorized form than either of the two important *southern* versions.

Synopsis of the *Thidrekssaga*

This is a huge and rather sprawling combination of sagas and other forms of storytelling. Jan de Vries, in his *Altnordische Literaturgeschichte* (see bibliography, no. 144),2:513–20, dates it about 1230, in any case in the first half of the thirteenth century. Thus it would appear to be perhaps a generation older than the *Völsungasaga*, and yet the whole question is very much touch and go. In any event, however, it comes after the *Nibelungenlied*. It is aptly described as ''an important mass of paraphrases in prose of German stories,'' and yet some scholars have suggested not only German but Finnish, and even Russian, elements in it. But as with the *Nibelungenlied*, the reader should be warned away from any narrowly national origins of any given folktale. There is a Norwegian ''membrane'' manuscript, somewhat deteriorated, and a few paper-manuscripts, one of which is Swedish. There is good evidence that there has been much interpolation of various stories, but the figure of Theodoric (Thidrek, Dietrich) is central. It has been noted that most of these ''interpolations'' are distinctly German in origin. All in all, there are nearly 450 chapters, and at least five different handwritings have been noted.

Although writing in Old Norse and presumably a Norseman, this author must have been a Germanophile. There has long been a persistent rumor that he was a trader in Bergen, Norway, and that he got much of his narrative material from Hanseatic traders coming north. But if so, he was continually looking southward. One series of chapters describes the birth and bringing up—if that is the term—of Sigurd, and there are a few chapters, rendering some confusion, involving an ''old'' Sigurd in the Saga of Detlev the Dane. Of one thing we can be sure—the sources are much less courtly than those pertaining to the *Nibelungenlied*, yet the influences of that older poem are clear enough, as we shall see in a moment. As to the relationship to our Saga, not too much time is given to the feats of young Sigurd, but what little we have is interesting. To take but one example, in the three accounts of Sigurd's birth in the three accounts of our Saga, the *Thidrekssaga*, and the *Nibelungenlied*, which cover not much less than a century among them, he has the same father, Si(e)gmund, but three different mothers—Hjördis, Sisibe, and Sieglind. What we get from an examination of this lengthy work is a true idea of the vast amount of *märchen*, folktale, and inventive legend floating about in oral tradition, and what applies to this saga may be taken in much less degree for the genesis of the *Völsungasaga*, for after all the latter had Eddic poems to follow. There is a difference in the concept of the boy Sigurd: in the *Nibelungenlied* he appears first as a rather arrogant young knight (but well brought up); in the *Thidrekssaga*, he is a *Wunderkind* brought up close to nature; in our Saga he is born after his father's death and reared by his stepfather and the untrustworthy Regin.

A synopsis of the appropriate chapters follows. I have made no attempt to give the chapter numbers as they appear in the standard edition, that by Bertelsen (Copenhagen, 1905-11). For one who can read German, the translation by Finne Erichsen (Jena, 1924) is recommended.

King Sigmund of Tarlungland marries Princess Sisibe of Spain. After he has returned home, he gets a message from his brother-in-law, King Drasolf, that he is going off to fight in Poland and earnestly desires Sigmund's help. Sigmund therefore leaves, entrusting the queen and his kingdom to the care of two warriors, Hartwin and Hermann. Hartwin conceives a lust for Sisibe; Hermann is good and loyal, but weak. Sisibe refuses Hartwin's advances, though he importunes her. When he hears that King Sigmund is on his way home, he goes out to meet him, telling him that in his absence Sisibe has been unfaithful to him. Sigmund orders that she be taken out into the forest and killed. But Hermann, though hitherto ineffective, is guilt-stricken, and in the forest turns on Hartwin and kills him. Unfortunately Sisibe, who has been pregnant, delivers a son and then falls dead.

The infant is placed in a glass vessel, described in the text only as a *gler pott*, of indeterminate size and shape. As Hartwin falls, mortally wounded, he kicks the glass container, with the baby in it, into a running brook, and it floats downstream. The babe comes ashore where a doe is nursing her fawns; she rescues the child and suckles him along with her own young. He is a large child at birth, and his growth is amazingly rapid. In the forest he is discovered by an old and childless dwarf, Mimi, who brings up the boy as his own. Mimi names him Sigurd: only by accident does he get the *Sig-* in his name over which Höfler has labored for so long! The boy is unruly and difficult and keeps on growing fast, and is so strong that Mimi becomes afraid of him, and conspires with his brother Regin, a dragon, to do away with him. One day Sigurd is out in the woods making charcoal, when the dragon bursts upon him, but Sigurd merely picks up a tree-trunk lying nearby and beats Regin to death. He is hungry, and so he eats some of the dragon's flesh, having first bathed himself after his efforts in a pool of the dragon's blood, which makes his skin horny, except for one spot in his back.

Having eaten this flesh, he is now familiar with the language of birds, and hears from them that Mimi is trying to get rid of him. He wastes no time in killing Mimi, using the sword Gram, which Mimi had just given him.

Soon Brynhild, sitting in her castle, is disturbed by an uproar in her courtyard. Sigurd has come and broken down her gate. She greets him courteously, tells him his name and lineage (about which he professes complete ignorance), and, hearing that he desires a steed, gives him Grani. Their relations are friendly enough but quite distant. Thanking her for her hospitality—she had put him up for the night while her servants were trying to capture Grani—he rides away to join other heroes. At this point comes the description of him as in chapter 22 of our Saga. This particular part of the *Thidrekssaga* is given over to similar descriptions of the appearance, armor, and physical attributes of the other heroes, which makes it unlikely that chapter 22 of the *Völsungasaga* is anything more than a borrowing from the

Thidrekssaga, and the relative dates of the two sagas indicate an interpolation in our Saga from the *Thidrekssaga*.

*   *   *   *   *   *

We now move southward into Niflungland, which appears to be somewhere in northern Germany or the northern Netherlands. The king of Niflungland is Aldrian—the name sounds suspiciously like that of a character in a medieval romance—who is away from his country for a time. In his absence an elf, an incubus or succubus, impregnates his wife in her sleep: the issue of this union is Högni, who grows up tall and homely, but an excellent warrior, though grim and forbidding of character. He is thus the half-brother of Gunnar. (Meanwhile Sigurd has attached himself to the retinue of King Thidrek.) Gunnar's sister is named Grimhild.

After Aldrian's death, Gunnar becomes King of the Niflungs. Sigurd, the vassal of King Thidrek, marries Grimhild, who brings him as her dowry half of her brother Gunnar's kingdom. Sigurd then proposes that Gunnar should marry Brynhild; he will help, for he knows all the ways to get to her. Gunnar consents. When they come to Brynhild, she receives Gunnar well but Sigurd very coldly, accusing him of not keeping his word to marry only her (despite the fact that the reader has not been told of any such agreement). Sigurd replies on behalf of Gunnar, excusing himself rather callously on the ground that Grimhild, having brothers, was a better match for him. Then Thidrek helps Sigurd to arrange the wedding of Gunnar and Brynhild, which is duly solemnized. That night Brynhild rejects Gunnar and hangs him on the wall, releasing him only at daybreak. Thus three nights go by. Gunnar ultimately realizes that he and Sigurd have become sworn brothers, and therefore requests Sigurd's aid. Sigurd tells him that Brynhild's great strength depends upon her virginity; Gunnar therefore gives him permission to rape her. Sigurd promptly performs the act, and in the morning takes a ring from her finger and substitutes another. Gunnar and Sigurd change back to their own clothes and go their way, nobody the wiser.

Gunnar appoints a regent and returns with Sigurd to

Niflungland, where he rules in peace with his brother Gernoz and half-brother Högni. (One may now leave them for a while, for the saga now deals with Attila, Eormanric, and Walter of Spain.)

Meantime Nibelungland flourishes through the harmonious relations of Gunnar, Sigurd, and the others at Wormiza (Worms). One day Brynhild enters her hall and finds Grimhild there, already seated. "Why don't you rise for your Queen?" asks Brynhild. "Because you are sitting in my mother's high seat, which is my sole privilege," answers Grimhild. "Go run away to the woods." "Who took your maidenhead and was your first man?" asks Grimhild. Brynhild gives what she thinks is the right answer. Grimhild, however, says she is lying and shows her the ring that Sigurd had taken from her as evidence that Sigurd was Brynhild's "first man."

Brynhild is both outraged and at the same time sorry that others have been listening to their quarrel. Blushing, she flees the city and runs into Gunnar, Högni, and Gernoz, who are coming home from the hunt. She tells them that Sigurd has broken his oath and told Grimhild all, that Grimhild has exposed her to all, and demands that her shame be avenged.

Högni suggests that she forget the matter, but Gunnar promises vengeance. They ride back to Worms, but Sigurd is still out hunting, not returning for several days, when he is treated as usual. Another hunt is prepared. This time Högni goes to the cook and orders him to make the food more salty than usual and to be slow to serve the drinks. Sigurd joins them at breakfast. Then they start off on the hunt, all but Högni, who secretly goes to Brynhild, who begs him to kill Sigurd, with his spear or sword or whatever. Högni then joins the hunt and downs a great boar. All go to a brook to drink, for the salted food has made them very thirsty. Högni seizes the opportunity to kill Sigurd with his spear while he is drinking. Sigurd eventually dies, saying bitterly that if he had expected this, it would have gone hard with all present. Högni arrogantly retorts that they had had their hands full killing one boar, whereas with his one spear-thrust he has brought down a great bison or bear. (Note the simularity of this to Sigurd's last words in the Saga, ch. 30.) While they are carrying away Sigurd's body, they are seen by Brynhild, who congratulates them, ordering them to put the corpse in bed with Grimhild. They do just that. Grimhild is naturally appalled. "You lie murdered!" she screams to the corpse, and looks at Högni. Högni denies the deed, saying that a great wild boar had killed Sigurd. "You are that boar!" she shrieks. Then she and her attendants bury Sigurd.

A few irrelevant chapters intervene. Now Attila, King of Susat (Soest), sends his nephew (Prince Osid) to woo Grimhild for himself, Attila. Osid consults with Gunnar, and Gernoz; all, especially Högni, are enthusiastic about the honor paid them by Attila, and Grimhild herself says that she would never dare refuse the offer. Attila and Thidrek are fetched and escorted into Worms, and there is great affection shown between Högni and Thidrek. As presents, Gunnar gives Gram to Thidrek and the steed Grani to the Margrave Rodingeir. Yet in Niflungland, Grimhild weeps constantly for Sigurd.

After seven years have gone by, Grimhild asks Attila to invite her brothers, who have been keeping Sigurd's treasure. She is willing to share this wealth with Attila if he will help her to get it back. Attila here is very greedy, as in the northern version. He knows about Sigurd's wealth that he gained from the dragon—we have not been told much about that ourselves—his own harrying, and that which he inherited from Sigmund, all of it denied Grimhild and him. And so the invitation is sent by two minstrels to Niflungland; they are very formally and elegantly attired. There is a message accompanying the invitation: Attila is now too old to rule, and he is therefore inviting Gunnar and Högni to share the rule of his kingdom until his little son, young Aldrian, is old enough to rule.

Högni advises against accepting this invitation because he suspects a trap laid by Grimhild. Gunnar rejects his advice, saying nastily that it is as bad as the advice that Högni's father gave his mother (a slap at Högni's illegitimacy), and he need not come if he is afraid. Högni prophesies the total destruction of them all, but orders all his liegemen to get themselves ready for the journey, including his sworn friend, Folkher. Queen Oda (Uote in the *Nibelungenlied*) tells them that she saw in a dream so many dead birds in Hunland that none was left alive in Niflungland, and foresees a calamity if they go. Högni pokes fun at her dream. She cannot prevail; even young Giselher wishes to go, and so they leave for Hunland.

When they get to the junction of the Rhine and the Danube (?), they can find neither ferryman nor ferry. Högni goes looking for one or the other in the nighttime and, coming upon a lake, sees two nixies. He hides their clothes and will not return them until they tell him whether he and his companions will (1) ever cross the river, and (2) ever return. They tell him that the Niflungs will cross the river but never come back, and so Högni kills them both. Going farther, he sees a man in a boat and hails him, saying that he is to fetch a man of Elsung's. The ferryman demands pay, because, he says, he has just been married and loves his bride very much. He accepts in payment a ring from Högni.

Meanwhile Gunnar and his men find a small boat and get into it, but it capsizes, and they all get drenched. They get aboard Högni's newly rented boat and row so hard that they break the oarlocks and the oars as well. Högni curses and in a rage cuts off the ferryman's head because, he says, that will prevent news spreading concerning the arrival of the Niflungs into Hunland. Gunnar is not satisfied, but Högni is defiant: "Why not do wrong? For I know now that none of us is coming back!"

Gunnar steers, but the rudder breaks in his hands. It is repaired, but just before they reach shore the boat capsizes again. They salvage it, however, by pushing it to shore and fix it up so well that the entire army gets across (!). The troops struggle on until nightfall, and they stop to rest while Högni keeps watch.

During the night he finds an armed man asleep, throws this man's sword away, and then wakens him. The man complains that his lord will find his land has been left unguarded, that Rodingeir's land will now be invaded because of his sloth. Högni is pleased with this answer and gives the man back his sword, as well as a gold ring. This man's name is Ekkeward; he warns Högni (when he has learned his name) to be continually on guard when they come to Hunland. He shows the way to Rodingeir's stronghold, and Högni leads the Niflungs there, where they spend a festive night.

There they dry themselves at the fire, eat, and drink.

Rodingeir's wife, Gudelinde, comments on their bright swords and armor and tells how Grimhild is mourning Sigurd. Rodingeir and she consider offering their daughter as wife to young Giselher, who is pleased to accept her in troth. Asked what he would like as a parting gift, Högni requests a shield that had belonged to Naudung, brother of Gudelinde, while young Giselher receives from his prospective father-in-law the sword Gram. Gunnar leads them away that same day.

Finally the Niflungs arrive in Soest, soaked by a heavy rain. Thidrek greets them at the gate. Grimhild sees them arriving and admires their appearance but continues to weep for Sigurd. Attila has fires laid to dry out the guests. Grimhild asks if Högni has brought her the Niflung treasure. "I have brought you the Devil and all my weapons," Högni answers, insisting that she forget about Sigurd and think instead of Attila. What is past is past. Grimhild turns away in anger. Thidrek and Högni go arm in arm to Attila's lavish feast.

Next morning Thidrek warns Högni of Grimhild's continuing weeping. The Niflungs wander about town, watched by Attila with his aide Bloedelin by his side. Attila is reminded of that former day when he and Erke, his first wife, knighted Högni. As Högni and Folkher pass through the town, Högni takes off his helmet and shows himself to be sallow and one-eyed (from an encounter with Walter of Spain), but nevertheless a handsome, tough individual. Attila orders a feast to be held *al fresco* in a convenient orchard.

Meanwhile Grimhild begs Thidrek to avenge her, saying she will help him to avenge himself upon Ermanric and Sifka (for events described in the *Thidrekssaga* but not germane here). He naturally refuses, under the circumstances. She turns next to Bloedelin, who also refuses because he is afraid of Attila. Nor is Attila himself in the least responsive. Obviously, then, she must accomplish this revenge by herself. In the orchard, she orders her guests (the Niflungs) to lay down their swords, but Högni asserts that he has never been brought up to hand his sword over to a woman, and laces his helmet even more tightly.

And so they sit down to the feast, still wearing their armor, although their weapons have been parked at the door—a common enough practice in Germanic legendry (cf. *Beowulf*, ll. 325 ff.). Högni has posted squires around the hall as sentinels. Grimhild bribes Iring by promising to fill his shield with gold if he will only start something. She then returns to her seat, where she is joined by her young son, Aldrian, whose father is Attila. She dares the boy to give Högni a buffet, which he does. Högni retaliates by beheading the boy and throwing the head into Grimhild's lap. He then turns and beheads Aldrian's tutor, "as he deserves."

Attila thereupon rises and orders the destruction of all the Niflungs. Meanwhile Grimhild has stretched ox-hides at the exits from the orchard, so that many of the Niflungs slip and fall. Seeing their exits blocked, they turn and kill almost everyone in the orchard.

Thidrek withdraws with his retainers, but Grimhild urges on the Hunnish warriors. (The garden in Soest is still called the Homgarten.) The Niflungs are badly outnumbered, but Högni breaches the wall, and they are able to get out. But Bloedelin and his men meet them in the street and punish them badly.

None the less, Högni leaps into a nearby hall and, with his back to the wall, defends himself successfully against everyone who comes at him. He is joined by Gernoz, Giselher, and Folkher. They call for Thidrek, but he is determined to stay out of the fight. All day long the combat goes on. Finally, at twilight, Gunnar is taken prisoner by Osid, who takes him to Attila. Grimhild persuades Attila to throw him into a snake pit in a nearby tower, where he dies. (You can still see that snake-tower in the center of Soest.) The Niflungs go berserk, killing everybody in the streets until it grows dark.

During the night, reinforcing Huns pour into the city. Högni takes charge of the Niflungs and sets fire to all the buildings in the neighborhood, so that they can have light by which to fight.

At daybreak, large-scale fighting continues, with the reinforced Huns pressing forward. Gernoz kills Bloedelin. Rodingeir is roused to action. Högni forges ahead; he is bloodied on both arms up to the very shoulders. He pauses in a hall for a while to rest himself. Rodingeir attacks the Niflungs, relieving some of the pressure on Högni. Grimhild sees her opportunity and sets the hall on fire, at the same time urging on Iring, who wounds Högni in the thigh. Grimhild urges him on some more, but this time Högni kills him. (There is still an Iring's Way in Soest.) Soon thereafter Giselher kills Rodingeir with the sword Rodingeir had given him, none other than Sigurd's old sword Gram. Folkher cuts his way through to Högni and thanks him for making his sword sing so well on the skulls of his foes. But when Thidrek hears that his great friend Rodingeir is dead, he makes his sword sing on Niflung helmets. Högni is gradually driven back, along with Gernoz and Giselher. Thidrek beheads Folkher, and his old master-at-arms, Hildebrand, kills Gernoz with his sword Lagulf.

Now Högni and Thidrek are fighting, then Giselher and Hildebrand. When Attila is seen coming down from his tower, where he has apparently been watching the course of events, Högni asks mercy for the "boy" Giselher, at the same time admitting that he, Högni, had been the murderer of Sigurd. Giselher points out that he had been only five years old when that crime took place. He runs at Hildebrand and is killed.

Högni, observing sardonically that their friendship seems to be breaking up, challenges Thidrek to single combat. Thidrek is enraged to have been so frustrated for so long by the son of a fairy. Högni retorts that Thidrek is a devil, and this enrages Thidrek so much that he begins to breathe fire. Högni is obliged to surrender.

Grimhild now brings a flaming brand, which she thrusts into the mouth of Gernoz, to see if he is dead. He is dead. She does the same to Giselher and kills him. This savage act is witnessed by Thidrek, who reports it to Attila. Attila, overcome by his wife's barbarous conduct, gives permission for someone to kill her.

Thidrek takes Högni to his quarters, where his wounds are bound, and although it is clear that he has been mortally wounded, a woman is supplied at Högni's request to spend the night with him. In one of the greatest feats of the Middle Ages he, near death as he is, begets on this unnamed woman a son, who will be called Aldrian. He gives this woman also the key to the Niflung treasure, for her to bestow upon the future Aldrian. Then he dies.

Total casualties: all the Niflungs and the noblest warriors of the

Huns, except for Attila himself, King Thidrek, and Master Hildebrand.

There never has been such a battle in the past, and one can still see traces of this grim combat in Soest.

Postscript

It is ironic that of the three specimens of medieval literature dealing with Völsungs and Gjukings (Burgundians, Nibelungs, Niflungs), all Germanic, the oldest, the *Nibelungenlied*, would appear to be the most finished in form and the most advanced in sophistication. The latest, our *Völsungasaga*, appears to be in many ways the most archaic, but perhaps the logical explanation for this would be the difference between the Continental valley of the Upper Danube and either the treeless stretches of Iceland or the rugged mountains of Norway. The *southern* form of the story is a study in revenge, but revenge carried out in a ''chivalric'' milieu, with medieval Christianity appearing at least in outward form, and courtly ideas of love and duty.

In contrast, our Saga has for its background the non-Christian character of the Eddic poems, and the wholly northern element of the hypothetical *Sigmundarsaga*. In the main, I believe we are justified in considering it, the youngest of the three pieces, as the most primitive. For we have here not only a real dragon and a real dragon-fight, much more spectacular than the casual braining of the dragon in the *Thidrekssaga*; a treasure actually recovered; a *vafrloga* or ''flickering fire''; changing of shapes (not just changing of clothes) wrought by witchcraft; a fairy-tale love story (though it goes sour); magical drinks of forgetfulness; actual quotations from the *Sigrdrifumál* and the *Reginsmál*, to say nothing of scraps of unidentified verse, some of them of indeterminate meter; and an Author who knows just what he is doing with these northern materials.

As for the *Thidrekssaga*, it is in comparison an overambitious work: on the one hand it follows the *Nibelungenlied* quite faithfully yet more crudely, but on the other hand it contains some starkly primitive details in the birth and bringing up of

young Sigurd (not found in the other two versions), at the same
time subordinating the material of the *Völsungasaga* to sagas of
other Germanic heroes, and introducing a large number of
strange characters.

If the reader observes carefully, however, he or she will see
many elements common to the three narratives, despite the
manifest variations. Compare, for example, the last words of
Sigurd in the *Völsungasaga* to the reply of Högni's taunt—"a(ny)
bison or wild boar." Or we have the quarrel of the two
queens—while bathing in the River (Rhine), before the cathedral
in Worms, or in Grimhild's hall, but a quarrel all the same, and
over the same subject of royal precedence. In Atli we have the
relatively mild figure whose besetting sin is avarice, for even
when Gudrun kills him in the *Völsungasaga*, having murdered
their two sons and served them up to their father in Thyestean style,
he cannot react with fury. Especially to be noticed in the two
works, the *Nibelungenlied* and the *Thidrekssaga*, is the way
Högni or Hagen takes the lead as the opponent of Kriemhild
(Grimhild); yet even this preeminence is hinted at in the
Völsungasaga. And as Högni or Hagen rises in importance, so
Brünhild or Brynhild tends to fade out of the picture, with no
spectacular suicide—indeed, we are never told that she is dead.

And so one could go on at great length. Further resemblances
will no doubt be unearthed—and further differences, too—by a
close reading of all three works. But that, of course, is beyond the
scope of the present work.

Glossary of Minor Characters

(excluding those named in the Genealogical Tables)

1. AGNAR, brother of Audi, given victory over Hjálmgunnar despite Odin's command. As a result, Brynhild is put to sleep. (Chap. 20)
2. ÁLF, prince of Denmark, stepfather of Sigurd and second husband of Hjördis. (Chap. 12)
3. ÁLF HUNDINGSSON, son of Hunding, enemy of Helgi. (Chap. 9)
4. ANDVARI, a dwarf in the waterfall of Andvarafors, seized by Loki in quest of wergild for Otr. (Chap. 14; also in *Skaldskaparmál*, chap. 39)
5. BERA, wife of Högni (Kostbera).
6. BIKKI, the evil counselor of Jörmunrek who betrays both Randver and Svanhild. (Chap. 40)
7. BJORN JÁRNSÍDA or Bjorn Ironside, son of Ragnar Lodbrók. (Chap. 8 of *Nornageststháttr*)
8. BRAGI, god of poetry. He may be a euhemeristic product of Bragi inn Gamli, famous Norwegian skald. See *Skaldskaparmál*, chap. 42.
9. BREDI, thrall of Skadi; King Sigi was so incensed that his thrall had had a better bag at the hunt than he that he leaped upon him, killed him, and buried him in a snowdrift. As a result, Sigi is outlawed, but with the help of Odin, escapes the land. (Chap. 1)
10. DVALIN, king of the dwarves. (Chap. 18)
11. EYLIMI, father of Hjördis and therefore father-in-law of Sigmund; his death in battle is avenged by Sigurd. (Chap. 11)

12. EYJOLF, son of Hunding and brother of Alf Hundingsson. (Chap. 9)
13. EYMOD, a Danish warrior. (Chap. 32)
14. FAFNIR, son of Hreidmar, who turns himself into a gigantic dragon guarding the Accursed Treasure; slain by Sigurd. (Chap. 18 and *Skaldskaparmál*, chaps. 39 and 40)
15. FENG, another name for Odin (chap. 17). Both this item and no. 16 are found in *Nornageststháttr*, chap. 3.
16. FJOLNIR, another name for Odin (chap. 17)
17. GANDALF, a Norwegian chieftain of the ninth century, in constant conflict with King Harold Fairhair of Norway. (*Nornageststháttr*, chap. 7)
18. GEST, the marvelous protagonist of the *Nornageststháttr*.
19. GOLNIR, a giant. (Chap. 9)
20. GOTI, steed of Gunnar. (Chap. 27)
21. GRAM, sword placed in tree-trunk by Odin (chap. 3). It is pulled out by Sigmund and is broken against Odin's spear in the final battle between Sigmund and Eylimi. The broken parts are rescued by Hjördis and given to young Sigurd on his request, whereupon it becomes his invincible sword, even killing Sigurd's slayer, Gutthorm.
22. GRANMAR, ally of Hunding in the battle with Helgi. (Chap. 9)
23. GRIPIR, brother of Hjördis, hence uncle of Sigurd, who had the power of foretelling the future. Sigurd consulted him and found out his future, just as it came to pass. (Chap. 16)
24. GUNGNIR, the spear of Odin. (Chap. 20)
25. GUDMUND, son of Granmar. (Chap. 9)
26. HAGBARD, one of the sons of Hunding. (Chap. 9)
27. HAKI(?), son of Hámund. (Chap. 25)
28. HAKON, retainer of King Hálf of Denmark, and father of Thóra, whom Gudrun visited in her widowhood. (Chap. 32)
29. HÁLF, king of Denmark during Gudrun's sojourn there. (Chap. 32)
30. HARALD FAIRHAIR, King of Norway in ninth century, and a powerful patron of skalds. Mentioned in *Nornageststháttr*, chap. 10.

31. HEMING, brother of Lyngvi. (*Nornageststháttr*, chap. 5)
32. HERVARD, son of Hunding. (Chap. 9)
33. HLODVI, King Louis I of France. (*Nornageststháttr*, chap. 10)
34. HJALLI, thrall and swineherd of Atli. (Chap. 37)
35. HJÁLPREK, King of Denmark, father of Prince Alf and father-in-law of Hjördis. (Chap. 13)
36. HJÁLMGUNNAR, king appointed by Odin to be victorious, but slain by Brynhild; her disobedience caused Odin to put her to sleep (chap. 20). He is referred to also in the *Nornageststháttr*, chap. 9.
37. HNIKAR, another name for Odin. (Chap. 17; also cited in *Nornageststháttr*, chap. 6)
38. HODDBRODD, son of Granmar, to whom Sigrun has been promised. (Chap. 9)
39. HŒNIR, a god in Asgard, companion of Odin and Loki in their various escapades. He is mentioned in the Eddic poem *Völuspá* as surviving *Ragnarök*, the cataclysm of the gods, and helping to found a new world. (Chap. 14; also in *Skaldskaparmál*, chap. 39)
40. HÖGNI, a king, father of Sigrún, not to be confused with the Gjuking prince by the same name. (Chap. 9)
41. HÖLKVI, steed of Högni the Gjuking. (Chap. 27)
42. HREIDMAR, father of Regin, Fafnir, and Otr, who with his sons exacted wergild from Loki, Hœnir, and Odin for their slaying of Otr. (Chap. 14; also in *Skaldskaparmál*, chap. 39)
43. HRIMNIR, a giant, father of Hljód, and father-in-law of Völsung. (Chap. 2)
44. HROPTR, another name for Odin. (Chap. 20)
45. HUNDING, a king attacked by Helgi. (Chap. 9; also in the *Nornageststháttr*, chap. 6). When Helgi killed him in battle, he earned the name Hundingsbane. He was father of Eyjolf, Hervard, and Hjörvard.
46. JARISLEIF, a warrior accompanying the Gjukings to visit Gudrun while she was in Denmark. His name suggests a Slavic origin. (Chap. 32)
47. LEIF, helmsman of Helgi. (Chap. 9)
48. LOKI, a god in Asgard; a trouble-maker representing

the spirit of evil in the universe. (Chap. 14)

49. LYNGVI, a king and unsuccessful suitor of Hjördis, who chose Sigmund instead and became the mother of Sigurd. Lyngvi found a pretext and attacked Sigmund; it was in this battle that Odin intervened and brought about the death of Sigmund. Later Sigurd avenged the death (chaps. 11 and 17) and, according to the *Nornageststháttr* (chap. 6), inflicted on Lyngvi the ''marking-of-the-eagle'' punishment deserved by the killer of one's father.

50. ÓINN, father of the dwarf Andvari, otherwise unknown. (Chap. 14)

51. OLAF (TRYGGVASSON), king of the Danes, introducer of Christianity to the Norse world, host and benefactor of Gest in the *Nornageststháttr*.

52. OLO (ALI), King of Denmark, reputedly murdered by Starkath. (Chap. 8 of *Nornageststháttr*)

53. ORKNING, a warrior of the Gjukings. (Chap. 35)

54. RAN (RON), wife of the sea-god Aegir, whose great net pulls down drowning men. (Chap. 14)

55. RANDVER, son of King Jörmunrek, hanged because he was accused by the evil counselor Bikki of seducing Svanhild. (Chap. 40)

56. REGIN, son of Hreidmar, foster father of Sigurd, who forged the sword Gram from its fragments, persuaded Sigurd to kill the dragon Fafnir, and was himself killed by Sigurd for suspected treachery. (Chap. 13)

57. RIDILL, sword of Regin. (Chap. 19)

58. SIGGEIR, husband of Sigmund's twin sister Signy, who kills Völsung in battle, and is ultimately killed by Sigmund and his son of incestuous union with Signy, Sinfjötli, in revenge for the killing of Sigmund's father. (Chaps. 3-9)

59. SIGAR, alluded to by Gudrun in her conversation with Brynhild on the subject of great heroes. (Chap. 25)

60. SIGRÚN, a Valkyrie, daughter of an otherwise unknown King Högni, who falls in love with and ultimately marries Helgi. (Chap. 9)

61. SIGURD HRING, a prince who ultimately broke apart Denmark and Sweden, becoming king of Sweden after the Battle of Bravell (ca.750). (*Nornageststháttr*, chap. 7)

62. SKADI, a thrall of King Sigi, but an "important man in his own right," who suspects King Sigi's tale about the disappearance of Bredi and ultimately finds his body, bringing about Sigi's exile. (Chap. 1)

63. SLEIPNIR, the famous eight-legged steed of Odin. His origins are explained in note 46 above. Sigurd's steed Grani was descended from him (chap. 13). The story was told originally in Snorri Sturluson's *Gylfaginning*, chap. 42.

64. STARKATH, son of Stórverk, originally an important Norse hero. But by the time we hear of him in the *Nornagestsþáttr* (chaps. 7 and 8), he has suffered epic degeneration into a bully and, what is worse, a murderer. In an encounter with Sigurd, the latter knocks out two of his molars, one of which was picked up by Gest and was made into the handle of a bell-rope at Lund.

65. SVEGGJUD, steed of Hoddbrodd in his battle against Helgi. (Chap. 9)

66. SVEIPUD, steed of Gudmund in the same battle. (Chap. 9)

67. THÓRA, daughter of King Hakon of Denmark, visited by the widow Gudrun after the death of Sigurd. (Chap. 32)

68. VALDEMAR, a Danish warrior. (Chap. 32)

69. VINGI, the treacherous henchman of Atli, who brings to the Gjukings the invitation to visit him, so that he may kill them and gain the Accursed Treasure. Later he is the first casualty of the battle. (Chaps. 33 and 34)

Bibliography

This is not intended as a complete bibliography of the saga-literature of Old Norse; rather, the list is confined to works in English or works bearing upon the Saga and its cycle in ways too important to ignore. When they are in French or German, I have attempted to give the essential gist of the works. My comments are directed to the particular point of view shown in the work, with my general estimate of its value.

Important Background Items

Before proceeding to the fuller list, I should like to call attention to six works of international scope that lay the foundations for the others:

1. Bowra, Cecil M. *Heroic Poetry*. London, 1952; rev. ed., 1966. A vastly erudite but thoroughly readable study of the origins, techniques, and traditions of development in European as well as Oriental epic literature. The entire book should be read, but the following are especially recommended: chapter 3, "The Hero," pp 91–131; chapter 5, "Mechanics of Narrative," pp. 179-214; chapter 6, "Techniques of Composition," pp. 215-53; chapter 9, "Scale and Development," pp. 330-65; chapter 10, "Tradition and Transmission," pp. 368-403; chapter 11, "The Bard," pp. 404–42; chapter 15, "The Decline of Heroic Poetry," pp. 537-67.

2. Chadwick, H. Munro. *The Heroic Age*. Cambridge, 1912. This is an old book, but a very valuable one. To many it is "outmoded," but a work, no matter how old, is "outmoded" only insofar as its author's mind is outmoded, and Chadwick's certainly is not. It is narrowed chiefly to a comparative study of Classical and Germanic literatures, pointing out, especially in its last chapter, the details common to both. It states for the first time Chadwick's concept of the development of the epic: (1) the occasional bardic lay; (2) a concatenation of more than one bardic lay; (3) a popularization of the resulting heroic epic material; (4) the medieval romance (in terms of either poetry or prose in the later stage). In the

subsequent work that Chadwick and his wife wrote, this explanation is somewhat modified and refined. It is one of the first important works, however, to lay stress upon the *oral* origins of heroic literature. I call attention particularly to this statement: "There can be no doubt that a story of some kind—in which the adventures of Siegfried were already combined with those of the historical Burgundian princes—was in existence long before the earliest extant records, and that from this story, whether it was embodied in a single poem or consisted only of a mass of lays and legends, both the Norse and German versions are derived" (p. 144). The last chapter, the first such comparative study—the entire work is comparative literature in the true sense of the word—might well be read first.

3. Chadwick, Munro, and Chadwick, and Nora Kershaw. *The Growth of Literature*. 3 vols. Cambridge, 1932–45. A massive work that elaborates much of the material of *The Heroic Age*, but extends many of its points to make it virtually a survey of all the epic literatures of the world. Volume 2, indeed, is devoted to Oriental epic literatures only. To illustrate a point: There is the same explanation of the genesis of epic heroic literature as in *The Heroic Age*, but this time the four stages are defined thus: (1) occasional bardic lay; (2) combination of more than one bardic lay to make a heroic epic; (3) popularization of this material; (4) what came after—in the case of the Celtic (or at least the Irish), the saga; in the case of the Norse, the saga; in the case of the English, the metrical romance (which, under the prevailing French influence, produces the German *minnesinger* and such "chivalric" romances or epics as the *Nibelungenlied*, a curious hodge-podge of the epic and the pseudo-chivalric, etc.). The reader will probably prefer volumes 1 and 3. I call particular attention to vol. 1, chapter 3 and 3:617 ff. In 1:56 ff. there is an important discussion of the Celtic saga, "with adventure and the emotional situations arising therefrom" to provide entertainment. Emphasis is laid from the start on the oral origins. Indeed, the authors insist that an unwritten literary tradition is a more developed, stronger force than had hitherto been recognized, and that it possessed a longer life than most scholars have allowed. Among backward and unlettered people, the spoken word had more force than a manuscript, unlike today, when the printing press (or better still, although the Chadwicks do not say so, the radio and television) is more definitive than the circulated rumor. In short, the work is a potent stimulus to those who believe in the oral genesis of literature and sets in place the train that leads to Bowra (no. 1 above).

4. Ker, W. P. *Epic and Romance*. London, 1908; 1931; 1957. An excellent survey of medieval European epic literature as it affects also the Celtic and Norse sagas. Again, the work should be read in its entirety,

but in particular chapters 3, 4 and 5 (pp. 100–157). It is not so extensive a study as the others mentioned above, but it is written with charm and insight and is another example of how a work, no matter when it was first published, can outlive many another more recent effort.

5. Propp, Vladimir I. *Morfologia skazki*. Translated by Reredos as *La Morphologie de conte* (Paris, 1970) and by Laurence Scott as *The Morphology of the Folktale* (Bloomington, Ind.: 1966). Published originally at Leningrad in 1928—the nearly half-century span from original to translation no doubt tells us something. The work discusses in detail, and with the rather doubtful aid of charts and formulas, the evolution of a folktale, its possibilities for variants, and contamination by other folktales. It shows how much a so-called epic work owes to these common features of a folktale, and in this respect it is a most valuable work, although I cannot say much for its expository tact.

6. Thompson, Stith, *Motif-Index of Folk-Literature*. 6 vols. Bloomington, Ind.: 1955; rev. ed., 1958. This is an extremely thorough listing of the motifs of the folktale in a worldwide coverage, tracing the influence of animals, plants and vegetation, human and domestic situations, and the effects of human behavior. As its title indicates, however, it remains primarily an index. Thus, if one is interested in eternal punishment of the "tedious" variety—the so-called Wandering Jew motif—one will find that there are over a hundred cases of such wandering, with the common ground of a single offense—blasphemy. As a whole the work is more valuable for the folklore analyst or the anthropologist than for the student of literature.

General Pertinent Works, with Comment on Devices

The following long list is intended to acquaint the reader with the salient works on both the Saga and, more generally, the whole progress of the Norse saga tradition. For those unfamiliar with German, Danish, or French, I have offered what I consider to be the chief points made, for most of these are not to be found in English translation. Those in English, however, I have marked with one asterisk; two asterisks indicate that the work is important; three, that the work is outstanding and should be read by every reader of the Saga in particular and of Old Norse literature in general. At the same time, I have tried to furnish some general information about each, although the reader should make his own judgment of material written in his own language.

7. *** Andersson, Theodore M. *The Problem of Icelandic Saga-Origins*. London and New Haven, Conn., 1964. The Saga-Man undoubtedly could and did on occasion use written sources, but his *art* and

presumably his *framework* were given him by tradition. The *inspiration* of the sagas is ultimately oral. The oral is then transferred to writing (the free-prose theory), or an unwritten tradition comes to written versions and then to the Saga (the book-prose theory). This is a most important work of fairly recent date, but one should remember that each saga presents its own particular problem.

8. * * d'Ardenne, Stephen. "Does the Right Side of the Franks Casket Represent the Burial of Sigurd?" *Etudes germaniques* 21(1966): 235-42. The author shows that it is instead a portrayal of the burial of Horsa.

9. Baetke, Walter. *Über die Entstehung der Isländersagas*. Berlin, 1956. For the German-reading reader and student, this is a most useful survey of the various views, but inclined to be dogmatic with too many *either/or* alternatives. I much prefer Andersson (no. 7). Baetke is absolutely right, however, in insisting that the sagas are works of art based on history, and not just cracker-barrel tales (although he does not, of course, use this term) to be told around a hot stove on a winter night.

10. * * Bellows, Henry A., trans. *The Poetic Edda*. New York and Oxford, 1926. An adequate though not brilliant translation in verse; the footnotes are good, but there is no bibliography. It has not aged well; I much prefer Mrs. Dronke's or Hollander's translation, mentioned below, although the former gives us only four Eddic poems. Bellows's notes, however, are helpful.

11. Benary, Walter. *Die germanische Ermanrichssage in die französischen Heldendichtung*. Halle, 1912. A somewhat schoolmasterish version of something much better handled by Caroline Brady (no. 20 below).

12. * * Blácam, Aodh de. *Gaelic Literature Surveyed*. New York, 1974. A fresh and well-written survey that has supplanted, I believe, the rather ponderous treatment in Douglas Hyde's *A History of Ireland*; it seems to me especially good in pointing out the resemblances in medieval literature between the Celtic and the Germanic.

13. Boer, Helmut de. "Hat Siegfried gelebt?" *Zeitschrift für deutsche Sprache und Literatur* 63(1939):250-71. This represents in general the common view, apart from the Vigfusson-Höfler axis to be discussed below (no. 58). For him there is really no satisfactory historical answer for Sigurd, just as there is no satisfactory one for Högni. Probably neither warrior is Burgundian; at least no Burgundian bard was responsible for them, but rather, Frankish ones. In fact, he tends to insist on a Frankish-Merovingian origin for both Sigurd and Brynhild. It is altogether a most useful article.

14. ———. *Das Attilabild in Geschichte, Legende, und heroischer Bil-*

dung. Bern, 1932. An excellent monograph. The author sees three aspects of the subject: (1) the churchly view of Attila as the Scourge of God; (2) the German baronial concept, as in both the Saga and the southern version of the story; and (3) Atli as brother of Brynhild and opponent of the Gjukings (Burgundians). He finds that some of these distinctive aspects are traceable to Jordanes and his account, in his *De Origine Actibusque Getarum* of the sixth century (Holder's ed., chap. 49), of Attila's funeral.

15. Boer, Richard G. "Ueber die rechte Seite des angelsächsischen Runenkästchen." *Arkiv för Norsk Filologie* 27(1910–11):215–58. Note d'Ardenne's study (no. 8 above). This so-called Franks Casket was the subject of much speculation during the first quarter of the present century, but it seems now that the carving and inscriptions on it represent either Anglo-Saxon or classical or scriptural story, and Boer's answer, like d'Ardenne's, is that it has probably no reference to the Sigurd story.

16. ———. "Ueber die Quellen von k.26-29 der Volsungasaga." *Zeitschrift für deutsche Philologie* 35(1903):28-329. Concerned with the Eddic poem *Sigrdrifumál* and its famous gap. Boer raises some unanswerable questions: how many stanzas or poems are missing? Are there two poems or more? He finds metrical variations, but that is no great surprise, since the *Sigrdrifumál*, as we have it, is something of a structural ruin. Did the Author of the Saga have instead an earlier prose version of the Saga? What of the likelihood of an *Igdurmál*, or Song of the Nuthatches? Did Sigurd visit Brynhild's foster father, Heimir, *before* going on to Hindarfell to release Brynhild? In effect, Boer has raised here most of the questions that have plagued scholars ever since the Saga was discovered. Yet he does not consider the theory of the *Meiri* or of the *Forna* as such.

17. ———. "Finnsage und Nibelungensage." *Zeitschrift für deutsches Altertum* 47(1903):125-160. The author sees here parallels between the Anglo-Saxon *Fight at Finnsburgh* and the supplementary episode in *Beowulf* (ll. 1068–1159a) and compares the leading narrative in the *Nibelungenlied*, with Hengest and Etzel as the respective protagonists. To me it is a very forced parallel.

18. ** Bouman, Arie C. *Patterns in Old English and Old Icelandic Literature.* Leiden, 1962. Associates the two little Old English poems, *The Husband's Message* and *The Wife's Lament*, with Sigurd and Gudrun in the Eddic poems and, of course, in the Saga. But since Gudrun knows only too well that Sigurd is dead (and they had never, as far as we are told, been separated), it appears that Bouman has somehow missed the point.

19. ** Brady, Caroline A. "Odin and the Old Norse Jörmunrekr Legend." *Publications of the Modern Language Association* 55(1940): 910–31. The author tries to show that in the Eddic poem *Hamdismal*, stanza 11, the term *Hroðrgloð*, "fame-glad one," which had usually been interpreted as a proper name, that of Jörmunrek's mother or mistress, is actually a term for Odin, the one who gives the order to stone Hamdir and Sörli. But if so, this is the only Eddic poem to speak of the intervention of Odin; all other references to the god involve the first portion of the Saga. Brady's argument is ingenious but not particularly persuasive.

20. *** ———. *The Legends of Ermanric*. Berkeley, Calif., 1943. See particularly pp. 1-121. This is in every way an excellent performance.

21. Brandl, Alois. "Zur Entstehung der germanischen Heldensage, gesehen vom angelsächsischen Standpunkt." *Arkiv für deutsches Altertum* 162(1932): pp. 191-202. Only tangential, for the fundamental reason that Old English does not have a surviving "heroic" saga that is native to England in content.

22. ** Brodeur, Arthur C. " 'Beowulf': One Poem or Three?" *Medieval Literature and Folklore Studies: Essays in honor of Francis Lee Utley*. Edited by Jerome Mandel and Bruce A. Rosenberg. New Brunswick, N.J., 1970, pp. 3-26. On the basis of characterization alone: one author but two scribes. This was a reply to Francis Magoun's articles listed below (nos. 91 and 93), which presumed as many as three poems.

22. *** ———. *The Prose Edda*. New York, 1923. A fine translation and a staple of the Anglo-Norse library.

23. Bugge, Sophus. "Die Heimat der altnordischen Lieder von den Wolsungen und den Nibelungen." *Zeitschrift für deutsche Sprache und Literatur* 35(1909): 240-71, 465-93. This title is confusing, for Bugge wrote no fewer than three articles of the same name and yet with widely divergent treatments. It is one of the latest and most eccentric works of this distinguished early scholar, and yet it still commands respect, although none of his conclusions seems sound today. It is first of all largely a discussion of nomenclature having to do chiefly with the *southern* branch of the story, including the *Thidrekssaga*. Sigmund, he believes, is of Ostrogothic origin, for he finds the *mundo*-suffix in the writings of both Procopius and Jordanes. Among other things, however, he suggests that Sigurd derives from Belisarius(!), pointing out that in chapter 13 of the Saga, when Reginn refers to Sigurd as a *hestasvein* ("stable-boy"), he is really making an oblique reference to "marshall" (O.H.G. *marah* + *scalc*), which is the very highest of military ranks.

Thus the expedition of Sigurd Fafnisbane against the sons of Hunding represents the expedition of Belisarius against the Vandals in Northern Africa (p. 481). Then the appearance of "Greekland Sea" for the Mediterranean and of "Norvasund" (the Straits of Gibraltar) (see n. 30 below) may not be so wild after all. But the "Greekland Sea" comes in that chapter of the Saga (22) which is in all probability borrowed directly from the *Thidrekssaga*, and I have already expressed my belief (n. 30 below) that Norvasund is a probable mistake for Orvasund. It is a very eccentric performance, but the author was so scholarly that it should not be dismissed as a senile vagary. In the first installment he deals thus with Sigurd (pp. 240–71), while in the second he equates Sinfjötli with Hercules.

24.————."Die Heimat der altnordischen Lieder von den Wolsungen und den Nibelungen." *Zeitschrift zur Geschichte der deutschen Sprache und Literatur* 22(1897): pp. 115-34. The title is the same as that in no. 23 preceding, but this is now an appropriate title, while it was not in the case of the other. I theorize that Bugge had composed three different articles, and that this was written first, the other two being published twelve years later. Here his theory is that the Norwegians first heard of Sigurd and the Nibelungs while they were in Britain, and that most of the Eddic poems were written down in Britain by Norwegian poets of the ninth and tenth centuries. This is possible, if we consider the northern two-thirds of the island of Britain; but if so—to take the most famous example of a Norse poem written in that area, the *Eiríksmál* of 954 which makes no mention of the Nibelungs—it places Sigmund and Sinfjötli in Valhalla and does not name Sigurd and the Nibelungs in any way.

25.————."Entstehung und Glaubwürdigkeit der isländischen Sagas." *Zeitschrift für deutsches Altertum und deutsche Sprache* 51(1909): 23-38. More or less a repetition of this same point of view found in the preceding no. 24. According to Bugge, the oral saga-telling arose between 950 and 1000, coming from the Viking occupation of Britain, whence it was carried to Norway and to Iceland. As an Anglo-Saxonist, I am most skeptical of his theory, for I see no evidence that the Icelanders had to wait until 950-1000 to begin their telling of stories.

26. * Ciklamini, Marlene. "The Problem of Starkathr." *Scandinavian Studies* 43(1971): 169–88. Studies this once-heroic figure through his debasement or epic degeneration, but does not refer to his loutish appearance in the *Nornageststháttr* (n. 24 above).

27. *** Dronke, Ursula B. "The Saga of Hrómund Grípsson and Þorgilssaga." *Saga-Book for Viking Research (Saga-Book)* 13 (1946–53): 51-77. Useful for the suggestion that certain events could have had an immediate *poetic* response.

28. *** Dronke, Ursula B., ed. and trans. *The Poetic Edda*. vol. 1. Oxford, 1969. An excellent edition, with copious introduction and notes, of the last four poems of *The Older Edda*; it is to be hoped that this series will be resumed. One of its great virtues is a fine synoptic translation into English.

29. Dumézil, Georges. *La Saga de Hadingus*. Paris, 1953. The best treatment of this particular visit to the Otherworld; see note 138 of the Saga.

30. Eckhardt, Karl A. *Der Wanenkrieg*. Bonn, 1940. As good an account as I know of the conflict between the Aesir and the Vanir; unfortunately I know of no English translation. This conflict was the inevitable result of differing standards of culture, producing different concepts of gods, a conflict that ended in a general compromise as the two cultures blended. See note 4 of the Saga.

31. Edzardi, Anton, trans. *Die Saga von den Völsungen und Nibelungen*. Stuttgart, 1881. A translation of the Saga into German, interesting only as a kind of museum piece that takes the attitude that the Saga is only the introduction to the *Saga of Ragnar Lodbrók*.

32. * Einarsson, Stefán. "Report on Rímur." *Journal of English and Germanic Philology* 54(1955): 255-61.

33.**———. " 'Hvat magi fótr faeti veita?' " *Scandinavian Studies and Notes* 20 (1948): 113-28. An interesting article that discusses a parallel between that line in the Eddic poem *Hamdismál*, stanza 15 (actually probably in stanza 13 originally, but the text is imperfect) which underlies Erp's cryptic "as much as foot helps foot" in chapter 42 of the Saga, and a passage in William of Malmesbury's *Chronicle of the Kings of England* (early 12th century). But it must be remembered that William of Malmesbury was living only a century after the Danish dynasty on the throne of England, which could be a time for Norse influences in the southern part of England, for the dynasty ended with the accession of Edward the Confessor in 1042. The article discusses also the incident of the plucked falcon in a work on Athelstan, the tenth-century English king who won the Battle of Brunanburh in 937. It shows furthermore that the author of the *Hamdismál* is familiar with the tradition of Randver in that Eddic poem (stanza 19), as told in chapter 40 of the Saga. It thus lends some credence to Bugge's theory, as outlined in his three articles mentioned above (nos. 23, 24, 25), that the Norse learned some Eddic material while in contact with England. The matter remains, however, highly doubtful.

34. ***———. *A History of Icelandic Literature*. New York, 1957. An excellent general introduction to the literature as a whole, somewhat popularized, perhaps, and biased in favor of the Icelandic over the Norwegian and Danish, but in view of its title this would be only natural.

35. Eis, Gerhard. "Das eddische Traumlied." *Arkiv för Norsk Filologie* 79(1963): 177-86. It opposes the idea that chapter 25 of the Saga is borrowed from the *Nibelungenlied*, yet pays relatively little attention to the likelihood that it is derived from the *Thidrekssaga*, or vice versa, preferring to believe that this whole scene is from a lost Brünhildelied.

36. Ettmüller, Ludwig. "Beiträge zur Kritik des Eddalieds." *Germania* 18(1873):160-74. An older study that shows the confusion among early students of the Saga caused by the gap in the Regius MS of *The Poetic Edda*. Ettmüller is hinting here at the existence of the *Meiri*, although he does not use that word; nevertheless, he postulates a third *Sigurdarkvida* as part of the *Sigrdrifumál*. Otherwise the study is hardly germane to our Saga, merely another view suggested by the notorious gap in the *Sigrdrifumál*.

37. ***Finch, Ronald G. "The Treatment by the Compiler of Sources in the *Völsungasaga*." *Saga-Book of the Viking Society* 16(62-65) pp. 315-53. There are some very useful remarks by this the last editor of the Saga (1965). In fact, I wish the author had placed some of these in his synoptic text-*cum*-edition. In general his comments are: "the compiler [Author] had a negative attitude toward poetic vocabulary and diction, toward unnecessary and superfluous detail, and toward repetition—all of which is abundantly clear. Kennings are rejected wherever they occur [?] . . . he is more of a pragmatist than a poet." The author points out that many details are either overlooked or ignored—in any event omitted—such as Brynhild's killing of Sigurd's little son, Sigmund. "The compiler is transforming, and with surprising thoroughness, his sources into a plain prose narrative." The mythological references cannot well be omitted, yet he is notably antisentimental, as in the account of Gunnar's death. With most of these pronouncements I am in only partial agreement. The Brynhild problem, Finch believes, is aggravated by the Compiler's omission of many stanzas of the *Sigrdrifumál*, but I think he has too little to say about either the *Meiri* or the *Forna* theories, and I certainly believe that he is much too hard on the Author.

38. **Fleet, Mary. "The Recent Study of the *Nibelungenlied*." *Journal of English and Germanic Philology* 52(1953):32-49. What was true in 1953 is not necessarily true today, a quarter of a century later. Yet this is a useful study, even though it discounts the pro-German and Heuslerian interpretations, with which I tend to agree. In any event, this study is only tangential to our Saga.

39. Fuss, Klaus. "Brynhild." *Zeitschrift für deutsche Philologie* 72(1953-54):110-18. This studies the development from the heroic

Valkyrie to the later embittered woman. This change is in large measure reconciled by her continuing courage. "Out of the sleeping shield-maiden comes the earthly woman, who learns from experience with the hero, how her life can indeed be altered." In general the author is sympathetic toward Brynhild, but in my opinion does not pay sufficient attention to her *märchen* or fairy-tale qualities.

40. Genzmer, Felix. *Das Nibelungenlied*. Stuttgart, 1967. A good translation into Modern German, with an excellent brief introduction, unfortunately not in English. For the English reader, see A. T. Hatto (no. 55 below).

41. Giesebrecht, Anton. "Ueber den Ursprung der Siegfriedssage." *Neues Jahrbuch der deutschen Sprache* 2(1837):203-34. Although very old, and oriented toward *The Nibelungenlied*, the article is among the first to try to identify Siegfried with a historical figure—in this case, King Sigebert of Metz (d.575), first husband of the Visigothic princess Brunihildis. I might accept Brunihildis, not as a Hunnish princess but as a Frankish queen, but Sigebert's name is not Siegfried's, and the man himself does not, in my opinion, deserve translation into a super-hero. The study is highly significant, however, as the beginning of an interpretation of the character that has culminated in the recent work of Höfler (see below, items 59 and 61). As I have pointed out earlier, I regard the origins of Brynhild, Sigmund, and Sigurd as ultimately mythological.

42. Giesebrecht, Wilhelm, and Buchner, Rudolf, eds. Gregory von Tours's *Historia Francorum*. Berlin, 1955. The standard German edition.

43. Goebel, Julius. "On the Original Form of the Legend of Siegfried." *Publications of the Modern Language Association* 12(1897):461-73. An intelligent and reasonable study, but one directed more closely to the southern branch of the story, in particular *The Nibelungenlied*; besides, it is often quite arbitrary in its flat-footed statements.

44. **———. "The Evolution of *The Nibelungenlied*." *Journal of English and Germanic Philology* 17(1918):1-20. The article rather impatiently identifies Sigmund's slaying of a dragon, as told in *Beowulf*, with Siegfried's killing of Fafnir, saying that this is a case of "epic transference," although such transference is usually from father to son rather than from son back to father. Besides, countless tales of the slaying of dragons (which are symbolic of mortal enemies) go back into prehistory, when primitive man slew primitive monsters, through the Oriental, the Babylonian, and on into the Middle Ages. These cannot all be Siegfried, and the case of St. George immediately comes to mind. And

then why not Perseus? In brief, Sigurd is not Sigmund, and I object to the article.

45. Grimm, Wilhelm. "Die mythische Bedeutung des Wolfes." *Zeitschrift für deutsches Altertum* 12(1860)203-28. Points out the universality of the wolf as a symbol of ferocity and outlawry, but notes that in Old Norse *vargr* is a more sinister term than the ordinary *úlfr*. For its time this is a definitive study, as might be expected.

46. Grönbech, Vilhelm. *Vor volkeset i oldtiden*. Copenhagen, 1909-12. Translated by ***William Worster as *The Culture of the Teutons* (Copenhagen, 1932) and into German by Ellen Hofmeyer, *Kultur und Religion der Germanen* (Hamburg, 1937). A very important basic work, more for its psychological insight than for its philosophy. The main divisions can be altered in different ways, but in any case it presents us with a finished building without analyzing that building brick by brick. I find it a very good survey of Germanic culture and its earlier religious approaches.

47. Grönbech, Vilhelm. *Nordiske Myter ok Saga*. Copenhagen, 1927. An excellent treatment, but unfortunately there is no English translation of which I am aware. Apart from the wealth of information, the most useful comment is that the author, in discussing certain complex matters, combines his resources, as he says, in the same way that the Author of our Saga combined his various traditions relating to Sigurd and the Gjukings.

48. Gutenbrünner, Siegfried. *Die jüngere Edda*. Düsseldorf, 1966. The most recent German treatment of the *Poetic Edda*. I find no startling new discoveries, but it is a thorough job.

49. Hallberg, Peter. *De isländske Sagaer*. Copenhagen, 1965. Another very good comparatively recent discussion. In Hallberg's view, the sagas are deliberate works of art created by the fusion of a popular and a national story-telling style on the one hand and a foreign literary style on the other. The second half of this statement indicates that it makes a great deal of difference which particular saga one is studying, as is obviously true, but it also raises in our minds the still unsolved though very appropriate question of Irish literary influences.

50. ———. *Den fornisländsk poesien*. Stockholm, 1964. Translated by ***Paul Schach and Sonja Lindgrenson (Lincoln, Neb., 1975) as *Old Icelandic Poetry*. The work, both in the original and in translation, is a splendid performance. It begins with an examination of Snorri Sturluson's poetics as demonstrated in the *Prose Edda* and moves from there to a consideration of both skaldic and Eddic verse, with some translation of a few of the more difficult and obscure of the skaldic verses. The reader might well study this before any other treatment of the subject.

51. Hanna, Helen I. "Siegfried-Arminius." *Journal of English and Germanic Philology* 19(1920):439-85. An important midpoint in the controversy over the origins of Siegfried, which began with the musings of Giesebrecht in 1837 (see item 41 above) and which culminates in the works of Höfler (nos. 60, 61, and 62 below). It is a very good survey of the controversy to date (1920), but now has only historical interest, because Höfler's discussions, though highly debatable, have superseded those in Hanna's survey.

52. ***Hanneson, Johann S. *The Age of the Sturlungs*. Vol. 36 of *Islandica*. Translated by Eirikr O. Sveinsson. Ithaca, N.Y., 1953. An almost indispensable account of the period in Iceland of Snorri Sturluson and later.

53. Harris, Joseph G. "Genre and Narrative Structure in some Icelandic *þaettir*," *Scandinavian Studies* 44(1972):1-27. This does not, however, consider the *Nornageststsháttr*, and if it did the author would find that it did not conform well to his thesis. He nevertheless reminds us, and quite properly, that with a very few exceptions the heroes are all Icelanders and the sovereigns Dano-Norwegian kings.

54. **Harris, Richard L. "Odin's Old Age." *Southern Folklore Quarterly* 33(1969):24-38. With the coming of Christianity, Odin is gradually reduced to a minor figure even in Scandinavia: "The possibility of the Old Man is seen to be more likely," and so on. I have already commented on this article above.

55. ***Hatto, A. T. *The Nibelungenlied*. Baltimore, Md., 1965. In my opinion, this is the best English prose translation of the epic, and its comments are clear, incisive, and thorough. Not for him are there any Höflerian fantasies, whether based on facts or not. He includes also a summary in several pages of the *Thidrekssaga*, which is very helpful. This material is at the end of the book (pp. 293-353). All in all, it is a solid performance. If I should quarrel with the translation, it is the kind of objection usually raised against a prose translation of an original poem. There is also in the first dozen "Aventiuren" a kind of coyness, especially in the treatment of the female participants. In short, this rather simpering influence lies in the original, for which a possible influence from the French romances and the Minnesinger must be to blame. There a few howlers, as when, in Aventiure 33, Ortlieb is beheaded by Hagen, and then his tutor; "such pitiful wages did he mete out to that pedagogue." The work, however, remains highly recommended.

56. Heller, Richard. *Die literarische Darstellung der Frau in den Isländersagas*. Halle, 1958. A study showing how the women, young or old, are strong, determined, brave, forceful, and wise.

57. Heusler, Andreas. "Götterdichtung und Sprachdichtung." *Edda*. Jena, 1920. The introduction and notes only are by Heusler. How old

these myths were, which are native, and which either Christian or non-Christian we do not know any more certainly than before. All that we can be sure of is that most religious pieces appeared *after* heathendom had passed.

58. ———. *Die Anfänge der isländischen Saga*. Berlin, 1914. "With many sagas one thinks first of them as dictated (by an oral poet, of course); the parchment then takes down the language of the Saga-Man with all the fidelity of a phonograph." I find this statement much too rigid; besides, I do not believe it necessary to follow the implication here that some of these sagas had a necessarily prose origin: witness the Eddic poems. I gather that Heusler is referring to the *Ur*-sagas, now lost.

59. ———. *Nibelungensage und Nibelungenlied*. See Part Two, "Two Views of the *Nibelungenlied*."

60. ———. "Das nordische Altertum in seiner Beziehung zum westgermanischen." *Archiv für das Studium der neueren Sprachen und Literatur* 142(1921):161-73. The mythology of the Eddic poems is in the main the work of Norwegian and Icelandic poets of the Viking Age. Heusler calls particular attention (p. 168) to the pervasive nature in the Norse of ethical ideas apart from chivalric formulas. The Norse sagas stand on the first steps of the development of Germanic sagas.

61. Höfler, Otto. *Siegfried, Arminius, und die Symbolik*. Heidelberg, 1961. This is an important study and a highly controversial one, to which I have already referred. The book identifies Siegfried *symbolically* with Arminius or Hermann, leader of the Chersoni, a Germanic tribe, against the Romans under Varus, in the historic Battle of the Teutoburger Forest of Westphalia in the year 9. The name of the tribe, the Chersoni, Höfler identifies plausibly with the word *hart*; the dragon that Siegfried killed, Fafnir, symbolizes the dragon on the battle-standard of a Roman legion involved in the battle. Hermann was murdered by his in-laws in 21. Höfler overlooks the fact that the Romans under Germanicus avenged the defeat in 9. Höfler observes that there are still traces of this—Siegfried killed the dragon on the Gnitaheath, which corresponds to the locale of the first battle in 9(?); he meets Brynhild on Hindarfell, or Hind (Hart) Mountain, and so on; but he has a little more success with his parallels when he moves to the southern branch of the story. He fails to take account of the *märchen* elements in the case of Sigurd—sleeping beauties, magic spells, unapproachable females, magic fires—though Höfler responds enthusiastically to the opinion that Siegfried was the greatest of all epic heroes. So were Arthur, Roland, El Cid, and a host of Homeric warriors.

Höfler then lists all the scholars preceding him who have argued for the historicity of Siegfried; see Helen Hanna's article (item 51 above), but one will not find her name listed, because only her name is Continental Germanic.

My personal objection is that Höfler's theory is just a little too apt, too mechanistic, and at the same time somewhat forced, not to say distorted, which is pretty much Kuhn's objection (item 78 below). If Sigurd killed a dragon, so did Sigmund, so did Beowulf, so did Ragnar Lodbrók, so did Frotho, and there is no use in saying that these are all the same event performed by the same hero. As *symbolism*, of course, it is acceptable enough; if Siegfried represents Hermann, who liberated the Germanic tribes from the legend of Roman invincibility, *if only for a time*, well and good.

62. ———. *Kultische Geheimbünde der Germanen*. Frankfurt-am-Main, 1934, pp. 188-206. This is another most interesting study, subject to the same kind of criticism as the preceding item 61. Höfler believes Sigmund and Sinfjötli, as wolves in the forest (chapter 7 of the Saga), to be representing confederated warriors masked as beasts who conducted guerrilla warfare against Romans and other interlopers. They were, in other words, "Odin-heroes." If this can be accepted, it could explain the very prominent part that Odin plays in the first dozen chapters of the Saga. These confederates would then linger in the folk memory of all patriotic Germanics. In both this work and the preceding, Höfler sees the Odin-warriors as Chersoni, protecting the Germanic frontiers, such as they were, particularly against Romans. In my opinion, however, *Beowulf* establishes Sig(e)mund as much more than a guerrilla Odin-warrior.

63. ———. *Siegfried, Arminius und Nibelungenhort*. Vienna, 1978. The author summarizes his previous theories, then turns to the site of the battle of the Teutoburger Wald, which he describes as covering an area of about six hundred square miles south of Minden along the upper reaches of the Weser River. The result is that we remain ignorant of the exact spot, and since the battle was not over in one day, there is a large area to be covered. At any rate, the general locale has been pretty well determined. He then spends a lot of time trying to locate the Gnitaheath, with some success. His most interesting innovation is to discuss the finding of a buried Roman treasure near Hildesheim, Germany, mostly of silver and crystal, which, says Höfler, could be transmuted by the passing of time and the making of legends, into a rich gold treasure. This he declares, must have belonged to a Roman officer of high rank—none other than Varus, the defeated Roman general. How Varus happened to be transporting such a treasure into the wilds of Germania is not made clear. All the way through, Höfler is laying about him, trying to put

down those who were opposed to his original identification of Siegfried with Arminius. One of his opponents, Hans Kuhn, comes in for refined academic abuse, what with Höfler's *sic*'s, question-marks, and exclamation-points in brackets nearly every time he quotes Kuhn, whom he usually refers to by his full name as "Hans Kuhn," whereas the others are Heusler, Panzer, Delbrück, and so on. It is obvious that the two scholars are not fond of each other, but such open quarreling in an academic monograph, though it may add heat, certainly adds little light. I speak of Kuhn below (no. 79). Even when he speaks of de Boor (no. 13 above), who can find no historical counterpart, Höfler is sympathetic to the thought de Boor expresses that there *might have been* one.

Höfler now admits the universality of the dragon theme in all parts of the world—it would seem that the critics have driven him to study up his draconology. Yet I still find traces of the idea that Siegfried is the greatest, that the battle of the Teutoburger forest decided that the Germanic tribes would never be assimilated into the Roman Empire as were the Gauls and others. But they were, of course. Has Höfler never heard of the Huns, and after them of Charlemagne and the fatal division of the Frankish Empire, whence sprang so much of the later friction between France and Germany? Finally, in the matter of the Accursed Treasure, he should have consulted Thompson, who in his index shows some fifty examples of the same, not just the treasure trove that the unfortunate Varus left behind in a mountainside. Now, however, we know why in the northern version represented by our Saga, the treasure was sunk in the Rhine, whereas in the *Nibelungenlied* it is taken out of a mountainside. *Alii idem fecerunt!*

64. ＊＊＊Hollander, Lee M. *The Poetic Edda.* Austin, Tex., 1962. A splendid performance, a most valuable contribution by one of the finest of American Old Norse scholars. Its introduction, notes, and general observations are as important as the translation. In my opinion, it completely supersedes the translation by Bellows, mentioned above (no. 10).

65. ＊＊———. "Is the Lay of Eric (*Eiríksmál*) a Fragment?" *Acta Philologica Scandinavica* 7(1932-33):248-57. The answer seems to be: Probably not.

66. ＊＊———. *The Skalds.* Princeton, N.J., 1947. A good survey of the field, though necessarily brief, with translations from a few of the better-known skalds, such as Bragi Boddason, Thuodolf of Hvin, Egil Skallagrimsson, Einar Helgason, Kormak Ogmundarson, and others. Should be read along with Hallberg (item 50 above).

67. ＊＊Holtsmark, Anne. *Heroic Poetry and Legendary Sagas* (Copenhagen, 1966), especially pp. 9-21. A readable and gracious discussion by one of the most agreeable present-day writers on the subject.

68. ***Jackson, William H. P. *The Literature of the Middle Ages.* New York, 1961. An excellent brief comparative study of the literatures of Western Europe during the Middle Ages.

69. **Jones, Gwyn. "History and Fiction in the Sagas of the Icelanders." *Saga Book of the Viking Society* 13(1946-50):285-306. A thoroughly useful and entertaining article, highly recommended.

70. ***———. *A History of the Vikings.* Oxford, 1968. Strongly recommended for its comprehensive view of the whole period of the Norse invasions; often brilliant.

71. Joseph, Herbert B. "The þáttr and the Theory of Saga-Origins." *Arkiv för Nordisk Filologie* 87(1972):89-96. This should be read after reading the *Nornageststháttr.*

72. Kelchner, Georgia D. *Dreams in Old Norse Literature and Their Affinities in Folklore.* Cambridge, 1935. A stimulating study pointing out how frequently dreams are experienced by women and are usually premonitory of some disaster, private or otherwise. The book should be read in connection with chapter 25 of the Saga (Gudrun and Brynhild) and chapters 31-35 (the Gjukings).

73. **Koht, Halfdan. *The Icelandic Sagas.* New York, 1931. It contains a very good discussion, although it now sounds rather dated.

74. Krappé, Alexander H. *Etudes de mythologie et de folklore germaniques.* Paris, 1929. A set of essays by this distinguished folklorist in his characteristically rambling style, but stimulating.

75. ———. "Völsungasaga XII." *Zeitschrift für deutschen Altertum* 56(1931):163-67. The author takes the question raised by Prince Alf in chapter 12 of the Saga about ascertaining the approach of day as belonging to the riddle-literature of the *märchen*, having an Oriental origin but common in Indo-European folklore.

76. ***———. "The Valkyries." *Modern Language Review* 21(1926):55-73. A most interesting general consideration of those who serve the gods in any way, militarily or domestically.

77. ———. "Les dieux Jumeaux dans la réligion germanique." *Acta Philologica Scandinavica* 6 (1931-32):1-25. An engrossing study of the Heavenly Twins and their tradition in Germanic myth and other folkloristic aspects—the preference in the Saga for *two* sons, as with Signy and Gudrun, or the mythological association with Castor and Pollux in the Greek tradition, Hengest and Horsa in the Anglo-Saxon, and Harold and Barold in the Middle English.

78. Kroes, H. W. J. "Die Sage vom Nibelungshort und ihr mythischer Hintergrund." *Festgabe Frings.* Berlin, 1956, pp. 323-37. An acute study of the Accursed Treasure as it appears in folklore and in the Völsung story, unfortunately not in English and, even more unfortunately, buried in a *Festschrift*. It should be compared with Höfler's

study in item 61 above.

79. Kuhn, Hans. *Das alte Island*. Düsseldorf, 1971. A very able account of Iceland and its history, unfortunately not in English translation, to the best of my knowledge.

In reference to the Kuhn-Höfler controversies, I may say that the controversy is mostly on Höfler's part. There is nothing to be gained by taking any notice of a review or of hostile comments from critics, because one may expose himself further. Kuhn is far too secure a figure to be bothered by such matters; in addition to this work just mentioned, I should call attention to his *Nationalismus in Germanistik und Dichtung* (Munich, 1966), particularly pp. 113-25, and to a very useful article, "Das Römische Kriegswesen im germanischen Wortschatz," *Zeitschrift für deutsches Altertum* 101(1972):13-53.

80. Kummer, Bernhard. *Die Dichtung von Helgi und der Walküre*. Vol. 1, part ii, of *Verlag der Forschungsgefragen unserer Zeit*, known as *Edda*. Oslo, 1959. A discussion of the intrusive Helgi material of chapter 9.

81. Landmann, Karl. "Die nordische Gestalt der Nibelungensage und die neuere Nibelungendichtung." *Program des Realgymnasiums zu Darmstadt* (Darmstadt, 1887). Again, this is very old, but it is interesting to see that it views these stories as a history of German youth, taking, of course, the German rather than the Norse side, as the German scholars of the time were accustomed to do. It is still a question whether some of them have changed, as Höfler's works have illustrated.

82. **Larsen, Henning. "Sigrdrifa-Brynhild." *Scandinavian Studies* 4(1917):65-73. As a counterbalance to the older students, this bright article, a kind of pioneer study in this country, urges the separation of personages merged, let us say, in Friedrich Panzer's *Studien zur germanischen Sagengeschichte* (Munich, 1912), especially the separation of Sig(e)mund from Sigurd/Siegfried and of Brynhild from Kriemhild in the general lore.

83. ***Latouche, Robert. *From Caesar to Charlemagne*. Translated by Jennifer Nicholson, London, 1968. A rapid and popular survey of the Frankish and Burgundian kingdoms, following closely the scheme of its title; highly recommended as introductory reading in the field.

84. *Leake, Jane A. *The Geats of "Beowulf."* Madison, Wis., 1967. This rejects the usual identification of the Geats with the Gautar of Sweden; the author prefers the Getae of the northern Balkan peninsula. I cannot agree.

85. Lehngrüber, Wilhelm. *Die Erweckung der Walküre*. Halle, 1936. Points out the connection between the awakening of Brynhild and the rousing of the Sleeping Beauty, thereby emphasizing the fairy-tale origins of the lady.

86. ***Lehmann, Winfred P. *"Lin* and *Laukr* in the Edda." *Germanic Review* 30(1955):131-47. Shows that both flax and the leek are symbols of fertility, and that the latter has often a clearly phallic significance. Reference is made to Hanna Bächtold-Stäuble's *Handwörterbuch des deutschen Aberglaube* ("Dictionary of German Superstitions"). Berlin and Leipzig, 1927-1941, vol. 1 (under (*Knob*) *lauch*, pp. 1-6, and *Lein*, pp. 1176-1200).

87. ***Lewis, Archibald R. *The Northern Seas: Shipping and Commerce in Northern Europe, A.D. 300-1100.* Princeton, N.J., 1958. An extremely valuable book; it should in reality be required preliminary reading before one essays the literature of any western European country in the period specified. Thus the opinion that these eight centuries were all years of conflict is exploded, and we learn that even the Huns (whose name is a symbol of destruction and death), were anxious for trade and commerce and solicited them.

88. *Liestøl, Knut. *The Origin of the Icelandic Family Sagas.* Oslo, 1930. A useful survey of the type of saga in which our Saga is not usually included; it has now, I should say, been supplanted by Theodore Andersson (item 7 above).

89. Lukmann, Niels. *Ermanric hos Jordanes og Saxo.* Copenhagen, 1949. I know of no English translation and in any case find Caroline Brady's a more comprehensive book (see no. 20 above).

90. **MacCulloch, John A. *Eddic Mythology.* Boston, 1930. A competent study, but now somewhat outdated.

91. **MacKenzie, Donald A. *Teutonic Myth and Legend.* New York, 1934. My comment about this is much the same as about the preceding (no. 90).

92. ***Magnusson, Eirikr. "Edda." *Saga-Book of the Viking Society* 1(1882-96):219-39. An important article, although its findings have not been accepted by everyone. "(The Book of) Oddi = Edda," by palatal mutation of *o* to *e*, but this, the author warns us, is unquestionably of late date (not before the thirteenth century). Nevertheless, the author says, "the solution of the vexed and long discussed question: who was the probable collector of the songs of the *Poetic Edda?* need not wait much longer for a satisfactory answer." Unfortunately, many are still waiting.

93. **Magoun, Francis P., Jr. "Beowulf A'." *Arv: Journal of Scandinavian Folklore* 14(1958):95-101.

94. ———. "Beowulf B." *Early English and Norse Studies*. Arthur Brown and Peter Foote. London, 1963. Pp. 127-40. These two studies by Magoun are not cited because they are particularly relevant to the Saga, for they are not. They illustrate, however, the cyclical nature of criticism: here we are back in the days of the mid-nineteenth century,

with Ettmüller, Müllenhoff, Lachmann, Wolf, and other exponents of multiple authorship. But whereas Magoun proposes only three separate poems (with or without separate authorship)—*Beowulf A, Beowulf A '*, and *Beowulf B*—the nineteenth-century critics were willing to go as high as six different authors. Now in *Beowulf* we have a rather sophisticated example of the second stage of epic composition, as proposed by Chadwick (items 2 and 3 above), and there is no question that *Beowulf* is also a mélange of narrative, gnomic verse, lyric, and reflective writing. Yet we still come down to the fact that some one person set up these disparate elements in sequence, and to take but one factor, characterization, we can still argue for a single author, as did Brodeur (item 22 above).

95. Müllenhoff, Karl. "Die alte Dichtung von den Nibelungen." *Zeitschrift für deutsches Altertum* 23 (1878):113-73. Let us consider this salient work by one of the older critics cited in the preceding note (no. 94). Müllenhoff was noted for his allegoristic approach. Beowulf represents Man fighting against the sea (for Grendel is an *eoton*, a sea monster). Next Beowulf fights Grendel's dam. Who is she? The sea-bottom bears the sea; the dam bore Grendel; therefore Beowulf is now Man fighting the dangers of the sea-bottom. Müllenhoff's approach—for the time and for his country only moderately arrogant—indicates that only professional scholars can know; therefore let amateurs keep away! Yet this article is most useful in defending the masculinity of Skadi in chapter 1 of the Saga, and is one of the very first to do so. It is, of course, an erudite study, but one obsessed with the German material. In my opinion Müllenhoff tends to overstress the Helgi story. He sees a division in the Saga with the death of Sigmund and birth of Sigurd. He tries various etymological explanations of proper names, but they are not convincing. He continued his study in the next volume of *ZfdA* 24(1879):132-66, but concerns himself there with the *Nibelungenlied*.

96. Neckel, Gustav. "Zur Volsunga Saga und den Eddaliedern der Lücke." *Zeitschrift für deutsche Philologie* 37(1905):19-29. A useful contribution to the *Meiri* problem, discussing various ways in which the gap in the Regius MS could have been filled. There is not, however, anything startling.

97. **Paff, William J. *The Geographical and Ethnic Names in the Þiðrekssaga*. Harvard Germanic Studies, vol. 2. Cambridge, Mass., 1959. A highly useful compilation that should be considered in the reading of the Höfler items mentioned above (nos. 61-63).

98. ***Pálsson, H., and Edwards, P. *Legendary Fiction in Medieval Iceland*. New York, 1968. A highly readable and useful introduction by a prolific translator of Icelandic saga material.

99. Pestalozzi, Rudolf. "Siegmunds Schwert." *Zeitschrift für deutsches Altertum* 52(1910):259-69. The old Saga of Sigmund was a "Frauensaga" from the north. To the author, the incest with Signy is the basic factor. Yet in my opinion the author mistakenly declares that the passage in *Beowulf* dealing with Sigmund is merely a song. If he means by that a brief epic lay, it is possible, but a rereading of this passage (see introduction pp. 34-35 above), will show that the passage is not really a song, but lines *about* a song or songs delivered for the entertainment of Geatish warriors celebrating the hero's recent epic feat, since it is said to be unfamiliar to them. I do not see that this study gets us very far.

100. Petsch, Robert. "Gunnar im Schlangenturm." *Zeitschrift für deutsche Sprache und Literatur* 41 (1916):171-79. The author points to the "spielmännerischen" or entertainer's nature of this scene, which must therefore be a "southern" detail. But does he mean that the Norse had no entertainers of this variety? He also points out an analogous incident told by Lucian. The important thing, however, is his recognition of the *märchen* quality of the detail.

101.————. "Dornröschen und Brynhild." *Zeitschrift für deutsche Sprache und Literatur* 42(1917):80-97. This is an important article, for it calls attention to the familiar predicament of the Sleeping Beauty (Dornröschen), and cites also a parallel in Basile's *Pentameron* in which a hawk flies to a tower where the Sleeping Beauty is to be found. These are only traces of the familiar story, of course, but that hawk changes the story from folklore to the chivalric. I consider the author to be on solid ground here.

102. ***Philpotts, Bertha S. *Edda and Saga*. London, 1931. A sound and entertaining introduction to the subject, not so profound as the work of the Chadwicks (nos. 2 and 3 above), and considered by many to be outmoded long before its time. I cannot agree.

103. Ploss, Emil. *Siegfried/Sigurd der Drachenkämpfer* Köln/Graz, 1966. Vol. 17 of *Beihefte der Bonner Jahrbücher*. An interesting response to Höfler's first book on the subject (no. 61 above), especially in reference to the universal worldwide practice of dragon killing (Drakonologie), which he thinks Höfler and others should have examined to a greater extent. Actually, in his last book (no. 63), Höfler does this, although one gets the impression, for all that, that nobody did it so well as Siegfried.

104. Pritsak, Imeljan. "Der Titel Attila." *Festschrift für Max Vosmer*. Wiesbaden, 1954. Pp. 404-19. Despite the use of *atta* ("pater," "father"), in Ulfilas's version of the Lord's Prayer, the author shows that it is baby talk, for the Gothic knew the *fadr*-root, as in

Fadar (Galatians 4:6). Moreover, *atta* is Hunnish rather than Gothic baby talk, so that *Attila* is a not much more impressive name than *Daddykins.*

105. Rassmann, Adolf. "Woden und die Nibelungen." *Germania* 26(1881):279-315. Odin favors the Nibelungs (Burgundians) out of revenge for the insult done to him by Hreidmar and his sons; thus he makes Sigurd Fafnisbane the greatest of all heroes. Rassmann offers a very German opinion: that "no other people in the world has ever come to the idea that their highest god is to bestow honor on a chosen family and to protect it in every way." On the whole, a pretty naive business.

106. Reuschel, Helga. " 'Wie ein Fuss die anderen.' " *Zeitschrift für die deutschen Sprache* 63(1939):237-49. What would have happened if Odin had not intervened in the fight between Jörmunrek and the two sons of Gudrun? The author points out that the animus (as in many of the family sagas) is usually between half-brothers or step-brothers; their tragedy is the tragedy of an ethnic custom.

107. Schier, Kurt. *Sagaliteratur*. Stuttgart, 1970. Pp. 72-75. A very handy little manual to assist in the classification of the Norse sagas. I call particular attention to his classification of the *Völsungasaga* as a heroic saga (*Heldensage*).

108. ***Schlauch, Margaret. *Romance in Iceland*. Princeton, N.J., 1934. A thorough and charmingly written discourse on the later sagas, including our own, of which she once made a translation (1930), now unfortunately out of print.

109. Schmidt, Ludwig. "Ueber den Namen 'Arminius.' " *Germania* 28(1883):342-46. The most effective of the early objections to "Arminius" as referring to a German name, although it may once have been explained as such. It certainly does not, however, have to be the equivalent of Siegfried. In the same journal, 36(1891):314-16, he attacks Jellinghaus for supporting the idea—another skirmish in a long war.

110. Schmidt-Wiegand, Ruth. In a review of Otto Höfler's book (item 61 above), to which she gives the title *Sigurðr inn hunzki* ("Hunnish Sigurd"), written for *Zeitschrift für deutsche Philologie* 74(1963):109-13, the author discusses Höfler's views of Germanic proper names in *hún* translatable in terms of O. N. *húnn* ("bear-cub") and the O.H.G. prefix *hún-* ("dark, brown, black, swart") as referring not only to the Huns but also to Sigurd (as in chapter 22 of the Saga) and to Atli (chapter 25), who is called *svartr* ("dark," "swarthy"), which is applied by Höfler also to Högni. Obviously, then, we should never think of Sigurd/Siegfried as a Nordic blond.

111. Schneider, Hermann. *Eine Ur-Edda*. Halle, 1948. Discusses with great authority and learning the possibilities of material anterior to the surviving Eddic poems, with special attention to variations in meter that exist in those now extant, and postulates a lost poem on Odin from some ancestor to the *Hávamál* ("Speech of the High One"), distinguishing sharply between what he considers Christian and non-Christian influences. Academic as far as the Saga goes, but a fine performance.

112. ———. *Germanische Heldensage*. In *Grundriss der germanischen Philologie* 10, sec. 3. Berlin, 1945. Virtually a staple for the subject, even though he gives our Saga little more than a small section (2:157-210). Not available, however, in English translation.

113. ———. "Zur Sigmundsaga." *Zeitschrift für deutsches Altertum* 54(1909):330-54. Considers the welding of the Sigmund and Sigurd stories via the father-son relationship, with the good sword Gram to link them, as not taking place on the Continent before 900. We have already seen, to judge by the *Eiríksmál*, that it had not taken place universally by 954. Schneider considers the Eddic prose fragment *Frá dauða Sinfjötla* ("On the Death of Sinfjötli") rather than the Saga as the source, which is a reasonable assumption. But why is this prose fragment not considered a part of a lost *Sigmundarsaga?*

114. ———. "Verlorene Sigurddichtungen." *Arkiv för Nordisk Filologie* 45(1929):1-34. This is another excellent major study, with three important points: (1) the *Meiri* theory explains many gaps and eccentricities in the Saga, probably accounting for most of chapter 25. (2) Is Sigurd in this *Meiri* version killed in the forest or, as in the northern version, at home in bed (cf. the Saga)? Finally, (3) what happened to Budli: did the Gjukings kill him? The author shows that Brynhild is known as *Sigrdrifa* in the northern version only. All in all, a very important article, but like so many of the authoritarian studies in German, it seems hypnotized by what the Eddic poems may or may not say.

115. **Schofield, William H. "Signy's Lament." *Publications of the Modern Language Association* 17(1902):284-95. It speaks of parallels between the passing of Sinfjötli and the passing of Arthur and other resemblances to the Celtic. This is a very attractive pioneer article, but of course it is not to be considered in the same class as Bowra or the Chadwicks, to say nothing of de Vries (item 139 below).

116. Schuette, Gudmund. *Sigfrid und Brynhild, ein als Mythus verkannten historische Roman aus der Merowingerzeit*. Copenhagen and Jena, 1935. I have touched upon this study in the Introduction. As I think I have made clear, I have no great love for the identification of

either Sigmund with Sigismund of Burgundy or of Sigurd with Sigebert of Metz.

117. ———. ''En historisk Parallel til Nibelung-Sagnet.'' *Arkiv för nordisk Filologie* 24 (1907–8):1–41. This is a generally useful study, though some of the historical parallels that the author attempts seem to me extremely far-fetched and strained. Still, it is interesting to compare some of Schuette's findings with those of Paff (see item 97 above).

118. See, Klaus von. ''Freierprobe und Königinenzank in der Sigfridsage.'' *Zeitschrift für deutsches Altertum* 89(1958-59):163-72. Suggests that the riding through fire and the changing of shapes are younger, later details. The presence of these details in Celtic legendry, however, scarely seems to me to warrant his thesis except insofar as the Norse came into contact with the Celtic relatively late (past 850), as I believe it did.

119. ———. *Germanische Heldensagen*. Frankfurt-am-Main, 1971. A sound and judicious study without the usual Germanic *parti pris*. The author is inclined to attack the work of Höfler (see items 61 and 62 above) on the origins of the Siegfried figure. He shows to his satisfaction that the Norse materials, in terms of mythology, are of later date by comparing the Eddic poem *Hamdismál* with the parallel passages in the Saga; but this kind of thing can go on forever inconclusively.

120. ———. ''Die Werbung um Brünhild.'' *Zeitschrift für deutsches Altertum* 88(1957-58):1-20. This is a very good article, but in my opinion it is based too firmly on the Eddic poems extant and only on those, and is constantly yielding at the same time to the *Thidrekssaga*. It takes the quarrel between the two queens as its central point, though admittedly not in the old tradition. Certain of von See's assumptions seem hard to maintain: for instance, which does he *assume* to be the latest of the three poems about Sigurd in the Regius MS of *The Poetic Edda?* He also examines, without too much eventual success, the folk theme of the proxy wooer and the naked sword. The account of the genesis of the Saga also seems somewhat overblown.

121. Seip. Didrik A. ''Om et skriftlig grunnlag för Eddadiktningen eller deler av den.'' *Maal og Minne*, vol. 51. Oslo, 1958. This should be considered along with the following item 122.

122. **———. ''On the Original of the Codex Regius of the Older Edda.'' *Sturtevant Studies*. Lawrence, Kan., 1952, 103-06. These two articles, (including no. 121 above) aim to show that the Eddic poems were originally written down in Norway, and that a Norwegian MS was brought to Iceland, probably before 1200. Moreover, many of these Eddic poems may have been given their present forms by Icelandic skalds in Iceland.

Bibliography 251

123. Sijmons (Symons), Barend. "Zur Helgisage." *Zeitschrift für deutsche Sprache* 4(1877):166-203. This excellent early study by a distinguished Dutch scholar does not regard the impingement of the Helgi story (chapter 9 of the Saga) as essential; he also refuses to identify the Helgi of the Eddic poems with the Helga mentioned in *Beowulf* 1. 61, and does not believe that the Ylfings and the Völsungs are the same. He sees the Eddic *Helgakvida Hundingsbana I* as a series of fragments, not one poem, and admits the Danish origins of the story. The Norwegian Helgi Hjörvarthsson has blended with the Danish Helgi Hundingsbane.

In spite of its age, this should still be considered a definitive study, for Sijmons had an uncanny ability to prove right in the long run. As to the relation of the Helgisaga to our Saga, note that what he calls the Helgi incident is "quite superfluous and a case of loose attachment"; he observes at the end that "the whole development of the Helgisaga . . . in all its stages . . . [has] the same features as a single saga, which gradually assumes details from other sagas, until finally the original saga has become virtually unrecognizable."

124. ***———. "Untersuchungen über die sogenannte Völsunga Saga." *Beiträge zur Geschichte der deutschen Sprache und Literatur* 3(1876):199-304. This superb study, already past its centennial, has stood the test of time, and very little of abiding significance has done anything to refute its main lines of exposition; moreover, it is, in contrast to most of the earlier studies, beautifully written and is altogether the greatest possible monument to the tradition of the German scholarship of its age, although written by a Dutchman. Its major points may be listed as follows (and its title should be especially noted, considering the "sogenannte" ["so-called"], for scholars were still a bit uncertain what to call the Saga): (1) Codex Regius 1824 b4° should be dated near the end of the fourteenth century; (2) the Saga should end with chapter 42, because what follows—the *Saga of Ragnar Lodbrók*—is an entirely different saga ("we have here two completely different monuments to study"); (3) there is an excellent discussion of the parts that short tales, fairy tales, ballads, *rímur*, and the like may have played in the composition of the Saga; (4) although he does not refer to the *Meiri* by name, Sijmons obviously is thinking along those lines, but (5) he postulates in addition an earlier saga, which did not know Aslaug, and hence removes any possible connection with the ensuing Ragnar Lodbrók story; (6) as for Aslaug, he believes her to be imported from a Norwegian folktale akin to that of Cinderella; (7) he faces the problem of Sigrdrifa-Brynhild and concludes that they are one woman and not two women; (8) he realizes that the Author knew the extant Eddic poems, but his treatment of them in

the Saga "is, however, handled in a free, independent manner"—in fact, he believes that this very independence led the Author to include Aslaug and all that she entails; (9) he believes that the Helgi-Sigrún and Sigurd-Brynhild relationships are elements of medieval romance that the Author did not fully comprehend—in short, he scents the *märchen* theory; (10) chapter 22 of the Saga could be a borrowing from the *Thidrekssaga*, or the *Thidrekssaga* could have taken the passage from the Saga, and in either case, whichever saga is the earlier, such borrowing is in the nature of the *Riddarsögur*, which both sagas tend to represent (apparently he rejects the "Heldensage" classification for each saga); (11) these "knightly" sagas tended to derive in Norway from the reign of King Haakon IV ("the Old"), that is, from 1250 on to the death of the king in 1263; (12) there may be a separate lost poem or poems (what we have come to refer to as the Meiri or the Forna), which may have been as long as five or six of the extant Eddic poems. All in all, it is a magnificent seminal study.

125. Singer, Samuel. "Brünhild." *Zeitschrift für deutschen Sprache und Literatur* 42(1915):538-44. This is yet another study of the Sigbert-Brunhildis marriage of the sixth century, already referred to. Now, however, this once attractive theory has fallen down before the more recent identifications, or attempts thereat, like those of Höfler. The study is still valid, however.

126. **Smith, Kirby F. "The Werwolf." *Publications of the Modern Language Association* 9(1894):22-28k. A good list for a beginning, but long since superseded by the indices of Propp and Thompson.

127. Sprenger, Ulrike. *Praesens Historicum und Praeteritum in den altisländischen Sagaen*. Basel, 1951. A discussion of the rather peculiar habit of the Saga-Men to alternate between the present and past tenses in their narrative, even within the same sentence—"So he comes in and said," and the like. The author establishes, from the study of some eight or ten sagas, that the use of the preterite is traceable to the influence of the Eddic poems, which is reasonable, but is not so successful in accounting for the historical present, which tends to lend a homely, "winter-stove" effect to the narrative. There is the wise observation that this difference should best be disregarded by the apt translator. It is, of course, notable that this peculiarity seems to be a thirteenth-century trick of style, so that the Saga would be subject to it at that particular time, as any translator would know.

128. ***Steblin-Kamensky, M.I. "On the Nature of Fiction in the Sagas of Icelanders." *Scandinavica* 6, no. 2(1967):77-84. "Even if we succeed in discovering what the ideas of a thirteenth-century Icelander were, we are forced to express them in a modern language, and this tends

inevitably to modernize them. What unified the saga-literature . . . is
. . . this: that it all treated of the past. They were all regarded
as truthful.''
129. ———. "Tidrforestillingene i islendingasagae." *Edda*
55(1968):357-61. "The greatest difference between the psychology in
these sagas and the psychology of modern people lies in the conception of
the past and the future in relation to contemporary time.''
130. Strömbäck, Dag A. "Sejd." *Nordiska texter och indersökeningar utgivna i Uppsala av Bengt Hesselman*. Stockholm and
Copenhagen, 1935. The observation is made here that shape-changing,
divination, and so on in Norse story are strongly influenced by Lapps and
other Finno-Ugrian tribes. Here Thompson's *Motif-Index* is always
most helpful.
131. Strom, Folke. *Nordisk hedendom*. Göteborg, 1961. An excellent account of the pre-Christian beliefs of Scandinavia, but I know of
no English translation; consult the works of Turville-Petre named below.
132. Sydow, Carl von. "Brynhildsepisoden i tysk tradition." *Arkiv
för nordisk Filologie* 44(1928):164-88. Definitely directed toward the
southern form, represented by *The Nibelungenlied* and the
Thidrekssaga.
133. ***Thorp, Mary. "The Archetype of the Nibelungen
Legend." *Journal of English and Germanic Philology* 37(1938):5-17. A
sound review, but somewhat overmechanized and overdiagramed.
134. ***Turville-Petre, E. O. Gabriel. *The Origins of Icelandic
Literature*. Oxford, 1953. This, as is usual with this author, is a splendid
performance; indeed, along with Gwyn Jones, I should regard him as the
leading British expert on Old Norse matters. His four works named here
are indispensable; their titles speak for themselves.
135. ***———. *Myth and Religion of the North*. London, 1964.
136. ***———. *The Heroic Age of Scandinavia*. London and New
York, 1951.
137. ***———. *Scaldic Poetry*. Oxford, 1976.
138. Uhland, Ludwig. "Zur deutschen Heldensage: I. Sigemund und
Siegfried." *Germania* 2(1857):344-62. As with so many of these early
studies, the author goes straight back to the Frankish-Burgundian
Sigeferth. Moreover, the study interprets the Geats of *Beowulf* as the
Jutes.
139. Vries, Jan de. *Kelten und Germanen*, vol. 9 of *Bibliotheca Germanica*. Berlin and Munich, 1960. Gives a fine general comparative
study, distinguishing sharply between Graeco-Roman on the one hand
and Celto-Germanic on the other, commenting particularly on the
clearly perceptible differences in the development of human and divine

practices between the two peoples, and yet fully aware of their obvious commonalities. He stops just short of acknowledging a common ground, but since he is discussing two neighboring ethnic groups within the Indo-European family, he is just being the careful scholar.

140. ———. "Die Helgilieder." *Arkiv för nordisk Filologie* 72(1957):123-54. Traces the Eddic poems on the subject before they were written down in Norway or Iceland.

141. ———. "Heimdallr, dieu énigmatique." *Etudes germaniques* 10(1955):257-68. An interesting study of this perhaps the least known of the Norse gods.

142. ———. "Keltische-germanische Beziehungen auf dem Gebiete der Heldensage." *Zeitschrift für deutsche Sprache* 75(1953):229-47. This is a kind of early draft for the important work named in item 138 above. The author cites, for example, the parallel of the sword in the tree trunk and the test of a sword's sharpness in water, and is one of the first European scholars to call attention to Thompson's Motif-Index (item 5 above), to show the universality of such clear parallels. It is also an important article because it points out such parallels as far back as the Greek and Latin.

143. ———. "Das zweite Gudrunslied." *Zeitschrift für destsche Philologie* 77(1966):176-99. The author considers this poem, the Eddic *Gudrúnarkvida II,* as composed toward the end of the twelfth century by skalds at the Norwegian court, inspired by a now–lost Germanic poem, which was in turn inspired by still another Germanic poem, now also lost. Might this not be a good thesis for the composition of our Saga?

144. ———. *Altnordische Literaturgeschichte,* rev. ed. Berlin, 1967. This massive work gives comparatively little space to the Saga, but the author suggests an earlier *Ur*-Saga; it was probably in prose, not in verse. He finds that Celtic motifs are particularly noticeable in the Sigmund chapters of the Saga (through chapter 10), which must represent a later working of a much older concept.

145. ***Ward, Donald. *The Divine Twins.* Berkeley, Calif., 1968. A valuable contribution to the concept of the Divine or Heavenly twins, reflected in the Saga by the recurrence of *two* sons in the family throughout the Saga (if Signy has two sons to send to Sigmund for testing, and they are both killed, she has two more to be killed in Siggeir's hall). This does not include Sinfjötli. Gudrun has two sons by Atli, both killed in revenge. She has three sons by Jonak, but according to the Eddic poem *Hamdismál,* the third, Erp, is only a stepson.

146. Wessén, Elias. *Studier til Sveriges hedna mytologi och fornhistoria.* Stockholm, 1924. An excellent treatment of Swedish heathendom, but I know of no English translation.

147. Wieselgren, Per. "Völsungasaga und Liederlücke." *Arkiv för nordisk Filologie* 50(1934):70-89. Discusses the effect of the gap in MS Codex Regius of *The Poetic Edda* in terms of the Saga; a very careful and well-reasoned article.

148. "Quellenstudien zur Völsungasaga." *Acta et Commentationes Universitatis Tartunensis.* Tartu, 1935. A very important analytical study, chiefly of language, between the Saga and the Eddic poems that served as source material. Wieselgren gives the Author some deserved credit. The conclusion of his introduction should be read if possible (for it is in German) by every reader of the Saga: "It may well be said that the Author is not so bad as his calling. He has little understanding of poetry, it is true," but he then goes on to say that the Author was a sober recorder with no flights of imagination, who pieced together the various contents as well as he was able, that he had no central idea apart from a vaguely biographical or historical one. The doubtful chapters 22-25 were probably added later, whether by the Author himself or by somebody else is not clear. In short, the Author was dealing not only with the Eddic poems but also with a lost *Sigurdarsaga* and, I should add, with a probable *Sigmundarsaga* as well. The work is invaluable for its findings in the matter of the Author's use of his known sources.

149. **Williams, Gwyn. *An Introduction to Welsh Poetry.* Philadelphia, 1952. A very readable and sympathetic survey, useful for collateral reading for the Welsh as Blácam's is for the Irish (see item 12 above).

150. Wolf, Alois. *Gestaltungskerne und Gestaltungswesen in der altgermanischen Heldendichtung.* Munich, 1969. For attention to the Saga, see the scattered references in the index. This is mainly a discussion of the Eddic poems, with the Saga as a kind of end-product; it is therefore in a way a reversal of Wieselgren's study (no. 147 above). It discusses in particular the final chapter of the Saga in relation to the Eddic poem *Hamdismál* and considers the final battle between Atli and the Gjuki brothers in terms of the *Atlamál* and the *Atlakvida*, as well as the quarrel between the two queens, which cannot be referred to any Eddic poem except one from the lost *Meiri* material. In all versions, needless to say, the Eddic poems are accorded the greater praise.

151. ***Wood, Cecil. "*Sigurðarkviða en skamma*, stanza 69." *Scandinavian Studies* 35(1963):29-36. This article calls attention to the fact of Brynhild's observation, "the doors of Hel shall not slam shut on Sigurd's heels" and her cremation with Sigurd as pointing to a conventional, formal conclusion, more Christian than otherwise.

152. ***Wood, Frederic T. "The Age of the *Völuspá*." *Germanic Review* 36(1961):94-107. This is a most useful article; the author

agrees with a date near 1000, on eschatological grounds, and points to the resemblance of this Eddic poem to the Sybilline Book, which represents an oral diffusion from Goths (both Eastern and Western) near the Black Sea through the Balkans, Austria, Germany, Jutland, Sweden (even into western Russia), on to Norway and Iceland, where the surviving written Eddic poem was put into writing some time between 950 and 1000. His conclusion tends to support my theory of the route traveled by the Burgundian-Frankish legends into Scandinavia and thence into collision with the Celtic, rather than across the English Channel.

153. Zeller, Rose. *Die Gudrunlieder der Edda*. Stuttgart, 1939. Considers the four Eddic Gudrun poems: *Gudrúnarhvöt* ("Of the Great Grief"), from shortly before 1100; *Gudrúnarkvida II*, from a text near 950, now lost in the original; *Gudrúnarkvida I*, a late offshoot from near 1200; and *Gudrúnarkvida III*, by a later (post-1300) Christian poet. The article is useful as an example of the variation in dates proposed for the various surviving Eddic poems.

154. Zink, Georges. "Réflexions sur la littérature germanique." *Etudes germaniques* 13(1958):193-207. This is an excellent critical survey of the older critics and historiographers of the Saga, especially Heusler, Panzer, and Schroeder. Zink points to the Christianization of Siegfried, a chosen one of God, who is recalled after slaying evil (Fafnir), thus resembling Beowulf as a Christ-image (as some see it). I should call it a good, but typical product of the 1950s.

155. ———. "Les Légendes héroiques de Dietrich et d'Ermanric dans les littératures germaniques." *Bibliothèque de la société des études germaniques*. Lyon, 1950. Good, but as far as Ermanric is concerned, I much prefer Brady (no. 20 above).

Index

(excluding persons named in the Glossary of
Minor Characters, henceforth "GL.")

Æsir, 87, 92; in relation to Accursed
Treasure, 80–81, 161–62. *See also*
Vanir

Alberich (dwarf), 195–96, 200

Aldrian (father of Hagen/Högni), 203,
214

Aldrian (son of Attila), 216, 219

Aldrian (son of Högni), 220

Alsvid (son of Bekkhild), 95–97

Andvarafors (waterfall), 80

Andvaranaut (ring), 81, 104, 106, 108,
162, 165–66. *See also* Ring, as de-
vice of recognition

Apple, fructifying, 56–57

Aristocratic skills and endowments: beauty,
90, 95, 98–99, 122, 127, 174; bra-
very, 71, 78–79, 87–88, 95, 98, 107,
128–29, 174; bright (keen) eyes, 78,
87–88, 94, 114, 132, 134; chess skill,
78, 109; craft skills, 78; good breed-
ing (manners), 94–95, 99; harp-playing
talent, 24, 129; hunting prowess, 55,
96, 198–99; intelligence, 55, 92, 127,
163; knowledge of foreign tongues, 78;
leadership, 85; martial prowess, 85,
91, 95, 98, 104, 126, 127; noble
bearing, 94, 101; popularity, 83; pre-
cocity in martial arts, 57, 66, 69, 100;
riding ability, 95, 103, 165; rowing
ability, 125, 217; runic knowledge, 78,
91–93, 121–23; sailing ability, 70,

84, 91; speaking ability, 91, 95; sta-
ture, 57, 64, 78, 95, 98, 101, 118,
174: strength, 57, 95, 174; tapestry-
making skill, 96, 109, 110, 118, 120,
182; wealth, 68, 79, 88, 101, 105,
122; weaponsmithing and weapons main-
tenance skills, 81–82, 96–97, 135,
145 n. 52; wisdom, 68, 91, 93–95,
99, 127, 146 n. 70

Aslaug (daughter of Sigurd and Brynhild),
45–46, 105, 136–37, 149 n. 106,
161, 168, 169 n. 10. See also *Saga
of Ragnar Lodbrók; and* Genealogical
Table (p. 11)

Atlakvida, 24–25, 155 n. 161, 208

Atlamál, 24–25, 154 n. 152, 155 nn.
158–59, 208

Atli, 46, 105, 120–21, 126–32, 164,
192; appearance and character, 98,
222; as historical person, 31. Orders
death of Gunnar and Högni, 127–29,
166; killed by Gudrun and son of Högni,
131, 166. See also *Atlakvida; Atlamál;*
Attila; Dreams, prophetic; Etzel; Huns;
and Genealogical Table (p. 11)

Attila, 218–21; appearance and character
of, 208–9, 216; differing treatment of
by different authors, 51 n. 11, 192;
as historical person, 30–31, 51 n. 11.
Demands that Niflungs be killed, 219;
assents to killing of his wife, 220. *See*

257

also Atli; Etzel; Huns
Author: as Christian, 138 n. 2, 142 n. 28;
geographical knowledge of, 138 n. 3,
139 n. 11, 142 n. 30; skill of, 25,
27, 43–49, 156 n. 167, 221; use of
sources by, 23–27, 38, 42–43, 148 n.
98, 150 n. 113, 154 n. 152. *See also*
Codex

Balmung (Siegfried's sword), 194, 202–3
Barnstock, 58, 139 n. 10; Celtic analogue
to, 41
Beasts of Battle. *See* Eagles; Ravens; Wolves
Bekkhild (Brynhild's sister), 95, 148 n.
95. *See also* Alsvid
Beowulf, 29, 33–36, 149 n. 99
Beowulf, 32–38, 190 n. 27, 171, 204,
207, 219; quoted, 34–36
Birds, talking, 89, 163–64, 213; Celtic
analogue to, 41
Borghild (wife of Sigmund), 68, 72–73,
175
Brunhild, 195–99; athletic prowess of,
195; deceived by Siegfried and Gunther,
196; quarrels with Kriemhild, 198;
role of, in comparison with Brynhild,
209, 222. *See also* Brunihildis; *Brun-
hildsage* (hypothetical); Brynhild; Ring,
as device of recognition; Quarrel of the
queens
Brunhildsage (hypothetical), 207–8
Brunihildis, 31, 38
Brynhild, 89–100, 103–18, 164–66, 179,
213–15; differing portrayal of by dif-
ferent authors, 192, 222; as fairy-tale
character, 32, 41; as historical person,
30–31, 51 n. 12; inconsistencies in
Author's portrayal of, 44, 149 n. 106,
150 (nn. 109, 113), 151 n. 114;
relation of to Sigrdrifa, 146 n. 70. Meets
Sigurd for first time, 90, 164, 179,
213; deceived by Sigurd and Gunnar,
104, 165, 214; quarrels with Gudrun/
Grimhild, 105–8, 184, 215; com-
mits suicide, 117, 166, 182, 222. *See
also* Brunhild; Foreknowledge; *Hel-*

reid Brynhildar; Quarrel of the queens;
Ring, as device of recognition; *Sigrdri-
fumál*; *and* Genealogical Table (p. 11)
Budli (father of Brynhild), 98, 103, 105,
164
Burgundensage (hypothetical), 193, 207
Burgundians: in history, 30–32, 154 n.
146; as originators of Völsung legend,
38–39. *See also* Gjukings
Burning of enemy in hall, 68, 94, 108,
127, 132, 148 n. 92, 166, 205, 219
Busiltjörn (river), 79

Celtic culture: and Germanic culture, 28–
29, 151 n. 118; and Germanic liter-
ature, 33–34, 39–40, 52 n. 18, 136–
37; influence of on Saga, 23, 40–41
Chivalric milieu, 25, 193, 195, 208, 221
Cloak of invisibility, 195–97
Codex: date of, 25–26; history of, 21,
49–50 n. 1; illegible portions of, 22,
141 n. 20, 154 n. 154; as later version
of Saga, 27, 193; in relation to chapter
divisions, 89, 100, 123; in relation to
Saga of Ragnar Lodbrók, 136–37
Compensation, with gold or goods, for per-
sonal injuries: for deception of Bryn-
hild, 110–11; for killing of Borghild's
brother, 72; for killing of Brynhild's
uncle, 111, 151 n. 114; for killing
of Fafnir, 163; for killing of Otr, 81,
161–63; for Signy's humiliations, 68,
141 n. 25; for treacherous killing of
Gunnar and Högni, 129; for treach-
erous killing of Sigurd, 114, 119–20
Cremation, 48, 117–18, 182
Crow's mantle, 56, 139 n. 5. *See also*
Shape shifting
Cuchulain, 29, 40, 151 n. 115

Dancwart (father of Gunther and Kriem-
hild), 194, 202
Dancwart (brother of Hagen), 194, 196,
204
Dietrich of Bern, 202–6. *See also* Theo-
doric; Thidrek

Diu Not der Nibelungen (lost), 193, 208–9
Dragons, 35–36, 213, 221. *See also* Fafnir
(GL); Shape shifting
Dreams, prophetic: of Atli, 121; of Bryn-
hild, 116; of Glaumvör, 124; of Gudrun,
98–100; of Kostbera, 123; of Kriemhild,
194, 198, 201; of Uote, 201
Dwarfs, 145 n. 64. *See also* Alberich;
Andvari (GL.); Mimi; Regin (GL.)

Eagles: as beasts of battle, 92, 126, 154 n.
148; "blood eagle," 179, 189 n. 14,
191 n. 34; in dreams, prefiguring death,
124, 194
Edda, Older (or *Poetic*), 142–56 passim;
manuscript of, 50 n. 1; relation to
Nornageststháttr, 190 nn. 24, 30; use
of, by Author, 22–25, 42–45, 193,
221; use of, by Snorri, 160, 169 n. 5.
See also Atlakvida; Atlamál; Fáfnismál;
Forna theory; *Gudrúnarhvöt; Gudrúnar-*
kvida II; Hamdismál; Helgi (Hundings-
bane); *Meiri* theory; Oddrun; *Reginsmál;*
Sigrdrifumál
Edda, Prose, 22, 52 n. 25, 139 n. 4,
189 n. 10; authorship and date of,
159–60; form of Völsung story in,
160–61: *Gylfaginning,* 138 n. 1, 140
n. 13; *Háttatál,* 160; *Skaldskaparmál,*
145 n. 56, 151 n. 119, 153 n. 133,
159–70
Eiriksmál, 37, 39
Eitil (son of Atli and Gudrun), 130 (not
named). *See also* Genealogical Table
(p. 11)
Erke (wife of Attila), 218. *See also* Helche
Ermanric (Hermanric, Eormanric), 29–
30, 44, 50–51 nn. 8–9, 169 n. 7,
218. *See also* Jörmunrek
Erp (son of Atli and Gudrun), 130 (not
named), 155 n. 161
Erp (son of Jonak and Gudrun), 132,
135, 155 n. 161, 156 nn. 164–65,
167–68, 169 n. 5
Etzel, 31, 192, 200–201, 203–6. *See*
also Atli, Attila

Fáfnismál, 23, 142 n. 27, 145 n. 61,
160; quoted, 163–64
Fairy tales. *See* Folkloristic elements
Fates. *See* Norns
Ferryman, 202, 217
Fitela, 35, 37. *See also* Sinfjötli
Fjörnir (member of Gunnar's household),
124
Flateyjarbók, 50 n. 1, 171, 190 n. 31
Flickering flame, 103–7, 164–65, 184,
221; called "great light," 90; Celtic
analogue to, 41
Flyting, 70–71, 142 nn. 32–33. *See also*
Quarrel of the queens
Folkher, 217–20. *See also* Volker
Folkloristic elements: Celto-Germanic,
40–42, 136–37; of Heroic Age, 28–
32; Norse, 189 n. 11; universality of,
42, 207, 211–12. Motif of Bear's Son,
33; of burning brand or taper, 172;
of third child, 156 n. 164, 169 n. 5;
of two sons, 140 n. 16; of Unapproach-
able Female, 150 n. 113, 195. *See*
also "Lay" theory; Oral composition
Foreknowledge: of Brynhild, 94, 99–100,
106, 108, 115, 117, 149 n. 106;
of Gripir, 83, 111, 112, 115; of Gud-
run, 120, 133; of Odin, 140 n. 13;
of nixies, 201, 217; of Norns or "spae-
wives," 69, 186–87; of Sigmund, 76,
100; of Signy, 59. *See also* Dreams,
prophetic; Norns
Forna theory, 23–24, 42, 148 n. 91
Frankland, 39, 90, 146 n. 68, 173–76,
188 n. 2
Franks, 31, 38–39, 193. *See also* Burgun-
dians
Fredegund (killer of Sigibert), 31
Frekastein (battle site), 72
Frigg (wife of Odin), 56, 139 n. 4

Gard, realm of, 104, 149 n. 105
Gautland, 58, 60, 139 n. 11. *See also*
Geats
Geats (Gautar, Ḡeatas), 33, 51 n. 17,
139 n. 11

Gernot (brother of Gunther), 194, 199, 200, 204–5

Gernoz (brother of Gunnar), 215–16, 219–20

Giants, 37, 56–57, 71, 138 n. 1, 139 (nn. 6, 9), 182–85, 190 n. 31

Gibica, 30, 189 n. 18. *See also* Gjuki

Giselher, 194, 199, 202, 204–5, 217–20. *See also* Gislhari

Gislhari, 30

Gjuki, 98, 101–2, 164. *See also* Gibica; Gjukings; *and* Genealogical Table (p. 11)

Gjukings, 192, 221; description of, 98; historical antecedents of, 30. *See also* Burgundians; Niflungs; *and* Genealogical Table (p. 11)

Glaumvör (wife of Gunnar), 122, 124–25

Gnitaheath (lair of Fafnir), 79, 122, 163, 165, 175

Gondomar (Burgundian nobleman), 30

Gotelinde (wife of Rüdiger), 202. *See also* Gudelinde

Goths. *See* Burgundians

Goti (Gunnar's horse), 103, 164–65; referred to as "famous steed," 125

Gram (reforged sword), 76, 85, 87–90, 146 n. 69, 178, 180, 213, 216, 218, 220; as barrier between bedfellows, 104, 116–17, 149 n. 106; as folktale motif, 40, 45; as killer of Gutthorm, 114, 166; length of, 95; reforging and testing of, 40, 82, 163, 175. *See also* Barnstock

Grani (Sigurd's horse): anachronistic reference to, 71, 143 n. 34; as carrier of Accursed Treasure, 90, 101, 164, 184; choosing of, by Odin, 45, 79; choosing of, by Brynhild, 213; color of, 48 (black), 79 (gray); as gift to Rodingeir from Gunnar, 216; response of to flickering flame, 103–4, 107, 165; saddle-buckle of, 181; sympathy of for his master, 96, 118

Greekland Sea, 94, 148 n. 94

Grimhild (sister of Gunnar), 214–16, 218–20, 222; as historical person, 30–

31. Marries Sigurd, 214; in bed with Sigurd's corpse, 216; marries Atli, 216; killed with Atli's permission, 220. *See also* Gudrun; Kriemhild; Quarrel of the queens

Grimhild (wife of Gjuki), 98, 101–3, 105, 119–20, 151 n. 119, 164. *See also* Witchcraft

Guardian spirit, guardian women. *See* Norns

Gudelinde (wife of Rodingeir), 218. *See also* Gotelinde

Gudrun, 98–100, 105–10, 115–16, 118, 120–21, 129–35, 164–67; differing portrayal of, by different authors, 24–25, 155 n. 158, 192, 222; as historical person, 30–31, 208. Marries Sigurd, 102, 164, 179; quarrels with Brynhild, 105–8; in bed with Sigurd's corpse, 115; marries Atli, 120, 166; fights as shield-maiden, 126; slays her sons, 46–47, 130, 166; slays Atli, 131, 166; floats to land of Jonak, 47, 132, 167; magical assistance of to Hamdir, Sörli, and Erp, 135. *See also* Aristocratic skills and endowments; Dreams, prophetic; Grimhild (sister of Gunnar); *Gudrúnarhvöt*; *Gudrúnarkvida II*; *Gudrúnarrœdu*; Kriemhild; Marriage, opposition to, by bride; Quarrel of the queens; *and* Genealogical Table (p. 11)

Gudrúnarhvöt, 24, 46–49, 155 n. 162; quoted, 46–48

Gudrúnarkvida II, 23, 37, 153 (nn. 134, 136, 139), 190, n. 30; quoted, 119

Gudrúnarrœdu, 182; 190 n. 30

Guiding spirit. *See* Norns

Gundahari, king of Burgundians, 30

Gundram, king of Franks, 31, 37

Gunnar, 101–3, 105, 108–10, 112–17, 119, 121–22, 124–29, 164–67, 179–80, 214–19; appearance of, 98, 167; differing portrayal of, by different authors, 24; as historical person, 30. Changes places with Sigurd, 103, 164–65, 214; humiliated by Brynhild, 214; agrees to visit Atli, 122, 166, 216; in snake pit, 24, 48, 129, 166, 219. *See also* Aristocratic skills and endowments; Burgundians; Gunther of Worms; Oath of brotherhood; *and* Genealogical Table (p. 11)

Gunther of Worms, 194–201, 204–6. Changes places with Sigurd, 196–97; humiliated by Brunhild, 197; agrees to visit Etzel, 201; beheaded by Kriemhild, 206. *See also* Burgundians; Gunnar; Gundahari

Gunther (son of Siegfried and Kriemhild), 197

Gutthorm, 98, 113–14, 118, 151 n. 119, 156 n. 165, 164–66, 169 n. 5, 181

Gylfaginning. See *Edda, Prose*

Hagen, 194–206; differing treatment of, by different authors, 222; as historical person, 32. Kills Sigurd, 199; opposes visit to Atli, 201; beheaded by Kriemhild, 206. *See also* Högni

Hamdir, 132, 134–36, 156 n. 165, 167–68; as historical person, 30; stoning of, 45, 136, 168. See also *Hamdismál*; *and* Genealogical Table (p. 11)

Hamdismál, 24, 156 nn. 165–67, 169 n. 5; quoted, 136

Hamnius, 30, 50 n. 9. *See also* Hamdir

Hámund (son of Sigmund), 69, 174–75, 178

Hart, golden, 100

Hawks, 96, 117, 167, 169 n. 7; in dreams, emblematic of aristocratic warrior, 99, 121, 194; emblematic of honor, 133

Heimir (foster-father of Brynhild), 95–96, 103, 105, 136, 168

Hel (the goddess or her underworld realm), 81, 117, 121, 127, 130, 135–36, 144 n. 50, 152 n. 128, 153 n. 140, 154 n. 152, 182–83

Helche (wife of Etzel), 200. *See also* Erke

Helgi (Hundingsbane), 69–72, 142 (nn. 30, 32), 149 n. 98, 169 n. 10, 188 n. 3; Author's treatment of, 45. Kills Hunding and three sons, 69, 174–75; kills Hoddbrod at Frekastein, 72. *See also* Aristocratic skills and endowments

Helkvi (Högni's horse), 103; referred to as "famous steed," 125

Helmet of terror, 87, 90, 145 (nn. 60, 62), 163

Helreid Brynhildar, quoted, 182–85

Hermann (Arminius), leader of the Chersoni, 38–39

Heroic Age, 28–29, 32

Hildebrand, 202, 204–6, 209, 220–21

Hildebrand lay, Hildebrandslied, 207, 209

Hildico (Ildico), wife of Attila, 30–31, 208

Hindarfell, 41, 89, 164. *See also* Flickering flame, Hindarheath

Hindarheath, 179, 189 n. 16. *See also* Hindarfell

Hjördis, 73–78, 82, 163, 174, 212

Hlymdale (home of Heimir), 103, 105, 168

Hniflung. *See* Niflung (son of Högni)

Hnitud (ring), 173

Högni, 98, 101, 103, 109–10, 113–17, 122–28, 164–67, 179, 214–20; appearance of, 167, 169 n. 6; differing treatment of, by different authors, 222; as historical person, 32. Plays role in betrayal of Sigurd, 113–14, 165, 215–16; opposes visit to Atli, 122, 216; dies at Atli's court, 128, 166, 220; *See also* Aristocratic skills and endowments; Hagen

Hrotti (sword), 90

Hunland (Hungary), 56–57, 74, 138 n. 3, 151 n. 117; in *Nibelungenlied*, 201–6; in *Thidrekssaga*, 216–21

Huns, 29–32, 154 n. 146, 169 n. 6, 192. *See also* Genealogical Table (p. 11)

Incest, 37, 41, 64, 68, 140–41 n. 19

Járnamóda (battle site), 180

Jonak, 132–33, 167

Jörmunrek, 132–36, 167–68, 169 n. 7;

as historical person, 30; reputation of, for cruelty, 152 n. 126, 155 n. 162. Has son Randver hanged, 133, 167; has Svanhild trampled to death by horses, 134, 167; maimed by Hamdir and Sörli, 136, 168. *See also* Ermanric (Hermanric, Eormanric)

Kennings: for battle, 146 n 71; for gold, 144 n. 51, 160–62, 164, 166; for serpent, 151 n. 121, 153 n. 137; for ship, 145 n. 54, 146 n. 73, 188 n. 7; for sword (?), 151 n. 123; for toes, 24; for warrior, 147 n. 90. *See also* Skalds

Kostbera (Bera), wife of Högni, 122–25, 153 n. 143

Kriemhild, 192–206, 222; as historical person, 30–31, 208. Marries Siegfried, 197; finds Siegfried's body, 199; marries Atli, 200; killed by Hildebrand, 206. *See also* Dreams, prophetic; Grimhild (sister of Gunnar); Marriage, opposition to, by bride, Quarrel of the queens

Lagulf (Hildebrand's sword), 220

"Lay" theory, 34, 193, 209. *See also* Oral composition

Leek (magical and medicinal herb), 69, 92, 118, 142 n. 27

Maravech (husband of Brunihildis), 31

Märchen. See Folkloristic elements

Market, 74, 143 n. 38

Marriage, opposition to, by bride: by Brynhild, 104, 108; by Gudrun, 120, 131; by Kriemhild, 194, 200; by Signy, 58–59, 68

Meiri theory, 23–24, 27, 42, 149 n. 104

Mimi (dwarf), 213

Mirkwood, 154 n. 146; called "dark forest," 125

Murder (concealed killing), 55, 81, 138 n. 2

Naudung (brother of Gudelinde), 218. *See also* Nuoding

Nibelungenlied: date of, 193; sources of, 193–94, 207–10; as a southern version of the story, 32, 42, 53 n. 28, 155 n. 159, 190 n. 29, 192, 207, 210–12, 221. *See also* Nibelung, Prince; Niflungs; *Thidrekssaga*

Nibelung, Prince (guardian of Accursed Treasure), 194

Nibelungs, 194, 196, 202, 221. *See also* Niflungs, Niflungland

Niblungs, 47, 164. *See also* Niflungs

Niflung (son of Högni), 131, 155 n. 159

Niflungland, 209, 214–16. *See also* Nibelungs

Niflungs: in *Skaldskaparmál*, 166–67, 169 n. 6; in *Thidrekssaga*, 214. *See also* Gjukings; Nibelungs; Niblungs; Niflung (son of Högni); Niflungland

Nixies, 201, 217

Nobility, early Germanic concept of. *See* Aristocratic skills and endowments

Nornagest, 39, 175, 186, 188 n. 4, 191 n. 41. *See also* Gest (GL.)

Nornageststháttr, 22, 50 n. 1, 172–92, relation of to Saga, 43, 171–72. *See also Tháttr* (pl. *Thaettir*)

Norns, 92, 141–42 n. 27; as Fates or Weird Sisters, 47, 81, 87; called "goddesses," 124, 153 n. 144; called "guardian women," 75, 143 n. 40; Norn called "guardian spirit," 111; Norn called "guiding spirit," 59; as prophetesses, 69, 186–87

Norvasund (place name), 70, 142 n. 30

Oath of brotherhood, 102, 114, 116, 151 n. 119, 164, 214

Oda (mother of Gunnar), 216. *See also* Uote

Oddrun, 117, 152 n. 125, 155 n. 160

Odin, 53 n. 28, 139 n. 4, 140 n. 13; beasts of battle as pets of, 145 n. 57, 151 n. 122, 177; bynames of, 145 n. 59, 146 n. 78, 147 n. 81, 188 n. 8; Celtic analogues to, 41; as lord of Valkyries, 139 n. 5, 148

n. 97; in relation to Accursed Treasure, 161–62; as unifying device of Author, 45–46. Founds Völsung line, 55; rescues Sigi, 56; places sword in Barnstock, 58; cures Sinfjötli in disguise of weasel and raven, 66; takes Sinfjötli's body, 73, 143 n. 37; causes Sigmund's death, 75, 143 n. 41; helps Sigurd choose Grani, 79, 143–44 n. 46; accompanies Sigurd to battle, quieting a storm on the way, 84, 145 n. 58, 176–79; helps Sigurd kill Fafnir, 86, cf. 168 n. 2; identified as cause of Brynhild's magic sleep, 91, 184; causes death of Hamdir and Sörli, 136, 156 n. 167

Olaf Tryggvasson, 171–73, 181, 185–88

Oral Composition: in Saga and storytelling generally, 40–43, 172–73, 181; in poetry, 32–36, 40–42, 52 (nn. 18, 22), 208. *See also* Folkloristic elements; "Lay" theory; *Rímur*; Skalds

Ortlieb (son of Etzel), 200, 204

Place names, used heavily as rhetorical embellishment, 69–72

Punishments, cruel and unusual: Author's attitude toward, 44; confinement in snake pit, 48, 129, 166, 191 n. 34; exposure in stocks, 61; heart removed from living person, 127–29, 166; living persons entombed, 67, 141 n. 23; lungs removed from living person ("blood eagle"), 179, 189 n. 14, 191 n. 34; trampling to death by horses, 47, 135, 155 n. 162, 167

Quarrel of the queens, 105–8, 165, 184, 192, 198, 215, 222

Rampart of shields, 90, 184

Ravens: as beasts of battle, 145 n. 57, 154 n. 148, 177, 179; with particular regard to Odin, 41, 66, 145 n. 57. *See also* Eagles; Wolves

Regin (dragon), 213 (not identical to dwarf

Regin [GL.])

Reginsmál, 144 n. 49; 160; 188 (nn. 3, 8), 221; quoted, 81, 84, 174–79

Rerir, 56–57, 139 n. 4. *See also* Genealogical Table (p. 11)

Revenge, duty of, for injuries to kinsmen, 138 n. 2, 208; for betrayal of Oddrun, 127; for kidnapping and killing of Hámund's daughters, 99; for killing of Borghild's brother, 72–73; of Eylimi, 76, 100, 175, 179; of Fafnir, 89; of Gunnar and Högni, 129–31, 166; of Hunding, 69; of Sigmund, 83, 85, 100, 175, 179; of Sigurd, 115, 126; of Svanhild, 134, 167; of Völsung, 63, 65, 68. *See also* Compensation, with gold or goods, for personal injuries

Rhine River, 129, 146 n. 68, 166, 175, 200, 203, 217

Rhinegold. *See* Treasure, Accursed

Rímur, 26, 43, 141 n. 24

Rímur fra Völsungi hinum óborna, 27, 43, 138 n. 1

Ring, as device of recognition, 197–98, 214–15. *See also* Andvaranaut (ring)

Rodingeir, Margrave, 216–20 (corresponds to following)

Rüdiger, Margrave, 200–202, 205 (corresponds to preceding)

Runes, 40, 78, 91–93, 121–23, 143 n. 44, 145 n. 64; referred to as "reddened staves," 119

Saga of Ragnar Lodbrók, 21–22, 136–37, 149–50 n. 106, 191 n. 34

Sarus, 30, 50 n. 9. *See also* Sörli

Schielbung, Prince (guardian of Accursed Treasure), 194

Sea-drake (Sigurd's ship), 83, 145 n. 54

Shape shifting: into form of crow or raven, 56, 66; of another person, 63–64, 103, 105; of dragon, 81, 163; of fish, 80–81, 162; of otter, 81, 161; of serpent, 155 n. 157; of swan, 139 n. 5; of weasel, 66; of wolf, 62, 65, 155 n. 160. *See also* Odin; Witchcraft

Siegfried: Celtic analogue to, 41; legend of, 38, 208–9; role of, as compared with Sigurd, 32, 192–94; as slayer of dragon, 194–95. Changes places with Gunther (twice), 196–97; marries Kriemhild, 197; killed by treachery, 198–99. *See also* Sigurd; Skin, unnaturally toughened

Siegfried (son of Gunther), 197

Siegfriedsage (hypothetical), 207–8

Sieglind (mother of Siegfried), 194, 212

Sieglind (nixie), 201

Siegmund, 194, 197, 199, 201, 212. *See also* Sigemund, Sigmund

Sigemund, 35–38. *See also* Siegmund, Sigmund

Sigi, 55–56, 139 n. 9. *See also* Genealogical Table (p. 11)

Sigibert, King of Metz, 31, 38

Sigismund, King of Burgundians, 31, 36, 38

Sigmund, 62–68, 72–76, 100, 149 n. 99; Celtic analogues to, 41; legend of, 27, 31–32, 36–39, 41–43, 45, 53 n. 28, 57, 168, 212. Kills she-wolf, 62; commits incest unknowingly with Signy, 64; lives as outlaw with Sinfjötli, 65–66; takes revenge on Siggeir, 66–68; drives away Borghild, 73, 175; marries Hjördis, 74, 175; falls in battle, 75, 174. *See also* Aristocratic skills and endowments; Incest; Siegmund; Sigemund; *Sigmundarsaga* (hypothetical); Skin, unnaturally toughened

Sigmund (son of Sigurd), 102, 115, 118, 151 n. 118, 165–66

Sigmundarkvida (hypothetical), 27

Sigmundarsaga (hypothetical), 27, 38, 42, 141 n. 24, 156 n. 167, 193, 209, 221

Signy, 57–62, 140 n. 16, 141 n. 19; Author's treatment of, 43; Celtic analogue to, 41. Commits incest with Sigmund, 64; aids Sigmund in destroying her family, 63, 67; commits suicide, 68. *See also* Incest; Marriage, opposition to, by bride; Sieglind

Sigrdrifumál, 23–24, 161, 190 n. 31, 221; quoted, 91–93

Sigurd, 41, 44–46, 78–118 passim, 145 n. 61, 149 n. 106, 163–86 passim, 188 n. 3, 192, 211–15; Celtic analogues to, 40–41; as fairy-tale character, 32, 39; as historical character, 38–39, 51 n. 12; legend of, 23–27, 37–39, 146 n. 68, 151 n. 117, 189 n. 19, 190 n. 28, 212, 222; preeminence in appearance and stature, 78, 94–95. Meets Odin, 84, 176–79; defeats sons of Hunding and their allies, 85, 178; kills dragon, 86, 163, 179, 213; meets Brynhild for first time, 90, 164, 213; marries, 102, 164, 179, 214; changes places with Gunnar, 103–5, 164–65, 214; killed by treachery, 114–15, 165–66, 181–82. *See also* Aristocratic skills and endowments; Gram; Grani; *Reginsmál*; Siegfried; Sigmund (son of Sigurd); *Sigurdarkvida* (fragment); *Sigurdarkvida in meira* (hypothetical); *Sigurdarkvida in skamma*; Skin, unnaturally toughened; *and* Genealogical Table (p. 11)

Sigurdarkvida (fragment), 112

Sigurdarkvida in meira (hypothetical), 23

Sigurdarkvida in skamma, 23, 151 nn. 114, 116

Sinfjötli, 64–73, 140–41 n. 19, 168, 174–75; Author's treatment of, 43; Celtic analogue to, 41; as Fitela in *Beowulf*, 35, 37. Saved by Odin (in guise of weasel and raven), 66; poisoned by Borghild, 31, 73, 175; body of removed by Odin, 73. *See also* Aristocratic skills and endowments; Flyting; Skin, unnaturally toughened; *and* Genealogical Table (p. 11)

Sisibe of Spain (wife of Sigmund), 212

Skalds, 33–34, 39–40, 144 n. 51, 159–168, 169 n. 11

Skaldskaparmál. See *Edda, Prose*

Skin, unnaturally toughened, 40–41, 168, 194–95, 213

Skulls, used as goblets, 130, 166
Snaevar (son of Högni), 125
Snorri Sturluson. See *Edda, Prose*
Solar (son of Högni), 125
Sörli, 132, 134–36, 156 n. 165, 167–
  68; as historical person, 30; stoning of,
  45, 136, 168. See also *Hamdismál*;
  and Genealogical Table (p. 11)
Southern version of story, 30, 50 n. 4,
  192–222. See also *Nibelungenlied*;
  Thidrekssaga
Spae-wives, 186. See also Foreknowledge;
  Norns
Suicide. See Brynhild; Signy
Sunilda, 29–31. See also Svanhild
Supernatural Powers. See Apple, fructi-
  fying; Cloak of invisibility; Foreknow-
  ledge; Runes; Shape shifting; Thorn of
  sleep; Witchcraft
Svaflod (lady of Brynhild's retinue), 109–10
Svanhild, 132–34, 165; as historical per-
  son, 29–31; execution of, 134, 167.
  See also Aristocratic skills and endow-
  ments

Tarlungland (home of Sigmund), 212
Tháttr (pl. *Thaettir*), 25–26, 171–72,
  191 n. 34; "*Helgatháttr*," 45. See
  also *Nornageststtháttr*
Theodoric, 32, 209, 211. See also Die-
  trich of Bern; Thidrek
Thidrek, 214, 216, 218–21. See also
  Dietrich of Bern; Theodoric; *Thidrekssaga*
Thidrekssaga, 212–21; authorship and date
  of, 209, 211–12; as Heroic Saga, 25;
  as source used in *Völsungasaga*, 24; as a
  southern version of the story, 32, 148
  n. 94, 207, 209, 221–22
Thing, the, 91, 138 n. 2, 146 nn. 71,
  73
Thorn of sleep, 91
Treasure, Accursed: in *Beowulf*, 35–36;
  as Grani's burden, 90, 164, 179, 184;
  coveted by Atli, 121, 126–28, 216;
  coveted by Gunnar, 113; coveted by
  Hagen, 199–200; curse laid on, 81,

87–88, 162; size of, 90, 95–96, 101,
  122, 200; history of, 79–81, 161–63;
  hiding of, in the Rhine, 129, 166,
  203; former owners of, 155 n. 159,
  194, 196. See also Andvaranaut
Trolldom, Trolls. See Shape shifting

Uote (mother of Gunther), 194, 197,
  201. See also Oda (mother of Gunnar)

Vaerings (Varangians), 94, 148 n. 93
Valkyries, 139 n. 5; as servants of Odin,
  56, 71, 148 n. 97, 150 n. 111; as
  shield-maidens, 72, 98, 148 n. 96, 164,
  183. See also Brunihildis; Gudrun
Vanir, 92, 139 n. 4, 147 n. 88. See
  also Æsir
Volker, 195, 202–5. See also Folkher
Völsung, 57–61, 139 n. 9; birth of, un-
  natural, 27, 45, 56–57; heroic speech
  of, 15 (in Norse), 60–61; name of,
  confusion about, 36. See also Aristo-
  cratic skills and endowments; *Rímur fra
  Völsungi hinum óborna*; Waels, Wael-
  sing
Völsungasaga: date of, 25; manuscript of
  (see Codex); narrative constituents of,
  as sub-sagas, 26; as northern version of
  story, 41–42, 46, 50 n. 4; origins of
  (see Atli; Brynhild; Folkloristic elements;
  Gudrun; Gunnar; "Lay" theory; Sig-
  mund; Sigurd); as political allegory, 31;
  publishing history of, 21–22; sources
  of (see Author; Codex)

Waels, Waelsing, 35–36, 52 n. 21
Wergild. See Compensation, with gold
  or goods, for personal injuries
Widsith, 33, 36, 172, 189 n. 18
Werewolves. See Shape shifting; Wolves
Witchcraft: causing storm, 176; as de-
  fining characteristic of Grimhild, 98,
  117; by Gudrun, 135; by Hreidmar,
  161; with magic wand that burns victim,
  182; by a Norn, 187; in prophecy, 92,
  147 n. 86; in relation to magic potions

or foods, 73, 101–2, 114, 119, 143 n. 36, 152 n. 124, 153 n. 135; in relation to shape shifting, 62–63, 65–66, 103, 221. *See also* Apple, fructifying; Cloak of invisibility; Foreknowledge; Shape shifting; Thorn of sleep

Wolves: as beasts of battle, 124, 126, 151 n. 122, 154 n. 148, 177, 183; emblematic of deadly hostility, 89, 94, 100, 113–14, 121–22, 174; emblematic of outcast condition, 71, 118, 138 n. 2; as shapes put on by men or women, 61–62, 65–66, 140 n. 19. *See also* Eagles; Ravens